FRAGMENTS OF INFINITY

ESSAYS IN RELIGION AND PHILOSOPHY

A FESTSCHRIFT IN HONOUR OF

PROFESSOR HUSTON SMITH

edited by
ARVIND SHARMA
McGill University

PRISM UNITY

Published in Great Britain 1991 by:
PRISM PRESS
2 South Street
Bridport
Dorset DT6 3NQ

and distributed in the USA by:
AVERY PUBLISHING GROUP INC.
120 Old Broadway
Garden City Park
New York 11040

Published in Australia 1991 by:
UNITY PRESS
61 Ortona Road
Lindfield
NSW 2070

ISBN 1 85327 066 0

Typeset by Spooner Typesetting & Graphics, London NW5
Printed and bound in the Channel Islands by the Guernsey Press Limited.

Contents

Contributors

Stafford Betty is Professor of Religious Studies at California State University, Bakersfield, and studied under Huston Smith at the 1987 NEH Summer Seminar in Berkeley. His latest book is *Sunlit Waters* (1990), a fable about the beaching of a sperm whale. He has just finished a novel, *The Imprisoned Splendor*, set partly in the afterlife. His speciality is India, his religious background Roman Catholic.

Marc Borg holds a D.Phil. from Oxford and is the Chair of Religious Studies at Oregon State University. He is currently Visiting Professor of New Testament at the Pacific School of Religion at Berkeley, and also chairs the section on Historical Jesus for the Society of Biblical Literature. He is the author of numerous articles and four books, including *Jesus: A New Vision* (Harper and Row, 1987).

M. Darrol Bryant is Chair of the Department of Religious Studies at the University of Waterloo and an Associate Professor of Religion and Culture, Renison College, Waterloo, Ontario, Canada. He is the author/editor of more than twelve books in the field of religion, including *A World Broken by Unshared Bread, God: The Contemporary Discussion*, and *Interreligious Dialogue: Voices from a New Frontier*. He has been a Visiting Professor at the Indian Institute of Islamic Studies in New Delhi, and at the Dr. Radhakrishnan Institute for Advanced Studies in Philosophy at the University of Madras.

James S. Cutsinger, who holds a Ph.D. from Harvard, is an Associate Professor of Religious Studies at the University of South Carolina, where he teaches Christian theology and spirituality. His intellectual interests include the Platonic tradition and contemporary exponents of the perennial philosophy, notably Frithjof Schuon. His publications include *The Form of Transformed Vision: Coleridge and the Knowledge of God*.

Victor Danner was born in 1926 in Mexico. Reared and educated in the U.S., he received his B.S. in Arabic Studies (*magna cum lauda*) from Georgetown University in 1957 and his Ph.D. in Near Eastern

Languages and Literatures from Harvard University in 1970. In the interim, Professor Danner served in Rabat, Morocco as the director of the American Language Center, which was affiliated with the U.S. Embassy.

For 23 years, Professor Danner taught Arabic, classical Arabic literature, Islam, Sufism, comparative religion, comparative mysticism and Koranic studies. He has authored several books including *Ibn 'Ata'illah: The Book of Wisdom* (New York: Paulist Press, 1978) and *The Islamic Tradition: An Introduction* (New York: Amity House, 1988), and numerous articles and book reviews in encyclopaedias and professional journals. Professor Danner also lectured extensively and was widely travelled. A noted expert in the field of Middle Eastern Studies, he was often interviewed for radio and television.

Mary Ann K. Danner

Marilyn J. Gustin is an independent scholar and writer. She holds a Ph.D. from the Graduate Theological Union at Berkeley and wrote her doctoral dissertation on René Guénon.

Ben Johnson is the Senior Pastor of Salem Lutheran Church in St. Cloud, Minnesota. Following the completion of his doctorate in Biblical Studies at Harvard University, he served for 15 years as Professor of New Testament at Hamma School of Theology (Trinity Lutheran Seminary) in Ohio. He has also studied at Gustavus Adolphus College, Lutheran School of Theology in Chicago, and Oxford University.

Franklin Littell is often referred to as the Father of Holocaust Studies in America. He is Emeritus Professor of Religion at Temple University and Adjunct Professor in the Institute of Contemporary Jewry, Hebrew University (Jerusalem). He is Chairman of the Board of Trustees of the William O. Douglas Institute, Seattle, an institute for the study of contemporary social issues; Chairman of the Board of the Hamlin Institute, Philadelphia, an institute for the study of religious liberty and persecution; and Chief Executive Officer of the Center for the Study of World Religions at Temple University. He was educated at Cornell College, Iowa, Union Theological Seminary, and received his Ph.D. from Yale University. He is a minister in the United Methodist Church.

Seyyed Hossein Nasr was born in Iran. He studied in America where he received his B.Sc. in physics from M.I.T., and his M.A. and Ph.D.

in the History of Science and Learning, with concentration in Islamic Science, from Harvard. From 1958-79 he was Professor of Philosophy at Tehran University. In 1979 he became Professor of Islamic Studies at Temple University and is now University Professor of Islamic Studies at George Washington University.

Jean-Louis Michon was born in France and holds a Ph.D. in Islamic Studies from the University of Sorbonne. He has been associated with the United Nations in various capacities over the past two decades. He has travelled extensively, especially in the Islamic world. His publications include: *The Autobiography (Fahrasa) of a Moroccan Sufi: Ahmed Ibn'Ajiba (1747-1809)*, translated from Arab mss. into French with introd. and notes — Leiden 1969; and *The Moroccan Sufi Ahmed Ibn'Ajiba and his Mi'raj, a glossary of the technical terms of Islamic mysticism* (in French; Paris, 1974).

Philip Novak received his Ph.D. under Huston Smith at Syracuse University. He is currently a Professor in the Department of Philosophy and Religion at Dominican College, San Rafael, California. Articles by him concerning the comparative philosophy of religion and the ecology of mind have appeared in *Buddhist-Christian Studies, The Encyclopedia of Religion, Listening, Parabola* and *ReVision.*

Kenneth Oldmeadow teaches in Australia. He is the author of *Frithjof Schuon and Perennial Philosophy: A Study of Traditionism* (forthcoming). He recently delivered a lecture on aboriginal religion from a traditionist perspective at the Institute of Traditional Studies in Colombo, Sri Lanka.

Kathleen Raine is a Blake scholar, internationally recognized as one of the outstanding living English poets. Her most recent publications include *Yeats the Initiate* (Dolmen Press, Dublin, George Allen and Unwin); a new edition of her critical essays, *Defending Ancient Springs* (Golgonooza Press in conjunction with Lindisfarne Press, U.S.A.); and the third volume of her autobiography, *The Lion's Mouth.*

James B. Robinson received his B.A. from Wabash College and his Ph.D. from the University of Wisconsin-Madison in the area of Buddhist Studies. While his particular area of scholarship has been the Buddhist Tantra, he became interested in the concept of a primordial tradition through reading the works of Huston Smith, and has done research in this area as well. In 1987, he received an NEH grant to study with Huston Smith. He is currently Associate Professor of Religion at the University of Northern Iowa in Cedar Falls.

Henry Rosemont, Jr., Ph.D. from University of Washington, has taught at Oakland University, Brooklyn College, Fudan University (Shanghai), and is currently Professor of Philosophy at St. Mary's College of Maryland. From 1972 to 1988 he was Book Review Editor of *Philosophy East & West*, and President of the Society for Asian & Comparative Philosophy 1976-78. His most recent book is *Chinese Texts & Philosophical Contexts* (Open Court, 1990).

Delwin Byron Schneider received his education both in the United States and Japan. Receiving a Ph.D. degree in 1961 in Tokyo from Rikkyo University, he became a post-doctoral Fellow at the Center for the Study of World Religions, Harvard University. He has taught at Gustavus Adolphus College, St. Peter, Minnesota, and since 1970 in the Department of Theological and Religious Studies in the University of San Diego.

Arvind Sharma is Professor of Comparative Religion in the Faculty of Religious Studies at McGill University, Montreal, Canada.

James B. Wiggins is the Chair of the Department of Religious Studies at Syracuse University in upstate New York, and has served as the Executive Director of the American Academy of Religion since 1983.

Biographical Sketch

Professor Huston Smith was born of missionary parents in Soochow, China on 31st May 1919. He lived in China until he was seventeen, his youth there providing an appropriate background for his subsequent interest in comparative philosophies and religions. He was to return to Asia no less than eight times for field-work.

After receiving his early education in China at the Shanghai American School (1932-6) Professor Smith attended Central College, Fayette, Missouri, and obtained his B.A. in 1940.The pursuit of higher studies led him to the University of California at Berkeley, and culminated in his obtaining a Ph.D. from the University of Chicago in 1945.

Professor Smith began his teaching career in the summer of 1944 as a Visiting Lecturer in Philosophy at the University of Colorado, where he was to teach again in the Spring of 1947 as an Assistant Professor of Philosophy. He taught at the University of Denver in the meantime as Assistant Professor of Philosophy and Religion. He then taught at Washington University as Associate Professor of Philosophy; and after serving as a Visiting Master Teacher at Stephens College in the Spring of 1956 he was appointed as the Professor of Philosophy at Washington University the same year. In 1958 Professor Huston Smith began teaching as Professor of Philosophy at the Massachusetts Institute of Technology, a position he held for fifteen years until 1973, spending the Autumn of 1966 as Visiting Professor of Philosophy at the University of California (Santa Barbara). It was also in 1958 that Professor Smith published the now famous work, *The Religions of Man*, which has sold over two million copies.

For the next ten years, from 1973 to 1983, Professor Huston Smith was the Thomas J. Watson Professor of Religion and Distinguished Adjunct Professor of Philosophy at Syracuse University. Thereafter he served as Hanna Professor of Philosophy at Hamline University from 1983 to 1985.

Professor Smith's teaching career has been devoted to bridging intellectual gulfs: between East and West, between science and the humanities, and between the formal education of the classroom and informal education via films and television. Interest in education beyond the classroom led Professor Smith to produce three series of filmed programs for National Educational Television: 'The Religions of Man', 'Science and Human Responsibility' (with Arthur Compton), and 'The Search for America'. His films on Hinduism, Tibetan Buddhism and Sufism have all won awards at international film festivals. His phonograph record, The Music of Tibet, which embodies his discovery of the capacity of certain Lamas to sing multi-tones simultaneously, was acclaimed by *The Journal of Ethnomusicology* as 'an important landmark in the study of extra-European musics, and in fact of music itself.'

Holder of seven honorary degrees, Professor Smith was one of six professors in 1964 to receive the national E. Harris Harbison Award of Distinguished Teaching, and was featured guest that year on the opening and closing programs of ABC's 'Meet the Professor' series. In 1961 he was invited as the first Charles Strong Lecturer on World Religions to the universities of Australia. Twice he has been appointed Distinguished Visiting Lecturer to the United Chapters of Phi Beta Kappa, and in 1964 he was Annual Lecturer to the John Dewey Society.

Professor Smith's publishing career provides a fitting foil to his teaching career. In addition to *The Religions of Man*, Professor Smith is the author of several books and over fifty articles in professional and popular journals. He now lives in Berkeley and is the father of three daughters. His wife, Dr E. Kendra Smith, is a psychotherapist.

Prologue

Every major religious tradition comprises a tradition of study within itself but the study of the religious tradition as a whole, and especially of religious traditions in the plural, which characterizes what we now call religious studies, is a relatively modern phenomenon.

Such study of religion or religions in modern times has almost self-consciously set out to be value-free. At first such freedom from value was enshrined in the claim that such a study of religion was 'objective', as distinguished from the subjective nature of value judgements. In staking out such a claim the study of religion was consciously trying to replicate the scientific model. It was soon realized, however, that religion did not really exist in any vital sense apart from its followers or human subjects who embodied it, and that to dissociate it from the subjective dimension was tantamount to studying an arid abstraction. The study of religion incorporated this insight by continuing to be still value-free but in a phenomenological rather than a scientific sense; in the sense that the students of religion bracketed their own value judgements while studying the religions followed by others.

This explicit rejection of value judgements regarding the various religious traditions, however, carries with it an implicit value judgement: that the various religious traditions are unique and therefore essentially different, and also by implication, exclusive. We may regard this as the *traditional* approach to the study of religion which currently dominates the field. In fact the traditional approach is exclusivist in a double-barrelled sense, inasmuch as the Western religious tradition, particularly as represented by Christianity and Islam, tends to adopt such an attitude towards other religions.

Another traditional approach is represented by religions such as Hinduism. The Hindu approach to the phenomenon of religious diversity has tended to emphasize the commonness among the traditions in terms of both the subject and the object. At the level of the subject it emphasizes the universality of the human capacity for religiosity, at the level of the object it emphasizes the commonality of the goal or destination even though the paths leading to it may differ. This inclusivism of the Hindu tradition has been welcomed in some quarters and criticized in others, but remains a valid if often unavailed option in religious studies.

There is, however, another option allied to the above, but distinguishable from it. This may be called the *traditionist* approach to the study of religion as distinguished from all of the others mentioned above, which may for convenience be collectively referred to as the *traditional* approaches to the study of religion. Thus some of the *traditional* approaches to the study of religion regard themselves as value-free, while others only evaluate one religion in terms of another. It is obvious, however, that to the followers of the various religions themselves, their religions are neither value-free nor are meant to be valued in terms of another religion. In fact they enshrine the supreme value — truth, a truth by which they strive to live and for which they are even willing to die. Thus viewed the truth-claims of the various religions comprise the heart of the matter. How then are the conflicting truth-claims to be assessed?

At this point the distinction between what have been called the *traditional* approaches, and the *traditionist* approach represented by the essays in this volume, becomes useful. The traditional approaches could also be characterized as neutral, exclusivist and inclusivist. The first, associated with the modern academic study of religion, claims to be neutral in theory but in practise is more prone to emphasizing differences, although it does recognize similarities as a heuristic convenience. The second, often associated with the religions of the West, especially with Christianity and Islam, regards its own truth-claim as ultimately the only true one. The third, often associated with the religions of the East, especially Hinduism, looks on all religions as equally valid.

By way of contrast to these *traditional* approaches — whether neutral, exclusive or inclusive — the *traditionist* approach, far from being anemically neutral, looks upon all the religious traditions of humanity as different manifestations of a single primordial tradition. It bypasses both the exclusivist claims of the religions of the West and inclusivist claims of the religions of the East, in favour of a transcendent and universal claim which, while scrupulously respecting the particularity of each tradition, sees it as a specific manifestation of an underlying and overarching primordial tradition.

The main representatives of this *traditionist* approach to the study of religion are, among others, René Guénon, Ananda Coomaraswamy, Frithjof Schuon, Seyyed Hossein Nasr and Huston Smith. The papers in this volume extend the horizon of this *traditionist* approach in the comparative study of religion.

SECTION I: TRIBUTES

CHAPTER 1

Pearls on a String

Arvind Sharma

It was so long ago that it is difficult to say exactly when with precision; but it was not so long ago that it is impossible to say approximately when. It must have been the late 1950s. We were then living in the city of Agra, famous for the Taj Mahal, and less famous for the mausoleum of Akbar not too far away. The world has always preferred romance to ecumenism!

It was a winter morning and the whole family lay basking in the sun, browsing through the newspapers; my father, however, perhaps as a mark of intellectual distinction, was reading a book. As we sat around, read and chatted, we also periodically partook of the Indian preparation called *pān*. It consists of betel-leaves with a touch of lime and a nut and, if properly blended, produces a glow in the body a minute or two after ingestion. I remember this obscure detail because although the leaves are green, the nut brown and the lime white, when they all mix with saliva which is colourless the spit turns red — an illustration of how the whole can be greater than the sum of the parts. Hindu materialists cite this as an example of how consciousness could emerge from a conglomeration of material elements.

But I digress. As we sat there whiling away the morning hours under a capacious awning on a large lawn, my father put down the book he had been reading and asked for a *pān*. While this was being prepared he said to us, 'This is indeed amazing.'

'What is?' we all asked, our curiosity piqued.

'It is indeed amazing that a westerner can write so perceptively about Hinduism.'

'But,' I said, 'I thought it was a Hindu's privilege to write perceptively about other religions.'

'Then you had better revise your views. It seems some of them

3

possess this virtue too.' By this time the *pān* had arrived. He took it with one hand and with the other put the book on the table. I glanced at the title: *The Religions of Man* by Huston Smith.

Huston Smith, M.I.T., Cambridge (is there one in the USA too?), *The Religions of Man* — it all seemed a muddle of names, subjects and places — all distant echoes from somewhere which at the time seemed nowhere.

II

Years passed. More years passed. I ended up in Cambridge (Massachusetts) myself. The talk had just finished and the speaker emerged, beating off the siege of questioners. I was standing at the door and suddenly I realized I was standing in the presence of Professor Huston Smith. It is as if the echoes had led to the sound — perhaps of one hand clapping (*pace* Hakuin); who knows. This then was the moment.

'May I ask a question?' I said, after we had shaken hands.

'Go ahead.'

'At the end of your book you recommended listening with an open mind to what the different religions had to say about truth. But in today's talk you were talking about the Absolute. Have you changed your position?'

'Absolutely,' he said.

None of us laughed. The situation was too grave for that — as the Prophet told Ā'isha when she wondered if men and women would not be staring at their biological differences as they stood naked awaiting Judgement.

III

I was meeting my sister after a decade. We met in Philadelphia, maybe because it is the city of brotherly love, but this may be carrying etymology too far. I had moved to Cambridge from Syracuse shortly after she had moved to Syracuse from Delhi. I thought I would begin at the beginning.

'How was Syracuse?'

'I got my degree and all that. But you remember the book our father used to carry all the time with him in Agra?' This was a poignant moment. Our father had passed away in the meantime.

'Which book was that?'

'Don't you remember? *The Religions of Man*. He virtually shredded it through constant use. Anyway, you know what? I met Professor Huston Smith, its author, in Syracuse.'

'You did?'

'Yes indeed. It was so exciting. And you know he offered the best defense of the caste system I have ever heard.'

'Didn't help defend our country against foreign invaders,' I said, somewhat testily.

'I mean the principle of it. It has to do with the relative size of the spheres of work. The worker has the smallest field of vision, especially in an agricultural society. He only knows about his work, his village, etc. But the merchant has a wider sphere — he travels, he deals with others, with other villages and towns. The warrior-administrator has an even larger sphere of vision — he has to deal with boundaries of kingdoms and large administrative units. The one with the larger field of vision occupies a higher place in the hierarchy.'

'And the priests, etc., are at the top because they deal with the whole of society, the universe, cosmos . . .' I extrapolated.

'Exactly,' she said. 'It is a case of the smaller box fitting into the larger, and so on.'

'Why didn't I think of this?' I asked her.

She took one long look at me and let it fly. 'Because you have lived in the West for too long!'

Perhaps I deserved it. But first my father, then I, then my sister — Professor Huston Smith was becoming a family affair!

IV

The passage is probably known to every sensitive Indian student of Indian history. It is the passage in which Lord Macaulay pours scorn on Indian learning, on its 'astronomy which would move laughter in girls at an English boarding-school' and 'geography made up of seas of treacle and seas of butter'.[1] He was alluding, of course, to the Purāṇic view of the cosmos. It is sketched in outline by A.L. Basham as follows.

In the Purāṇas Jambudvīpa is described as a ring around Meru, separated from the next continent, Plakṣadvīpa, by an ocean of salt. Plakṣadvīpa in turn forms a concentric circle round Jambudvīpa, and so on to make a total of seven continents, each circular and divided from its neighbour by an ocean of different compositions, starting with Jambudvīpa's salt ocean and moving outwards, of treacle, wine, ghee, milk, curds and fresh water respectively.[2]

One can easily see that the scheme corresponds to no known geography and it had puzzled me, and may have puzzled others as well, as to why it might have come to be formulated at all. Did the people who formulated it believe it because of its very absurdity (the scandal of the cross argument)? Macaulay would, of course, say that they were just idiots but this argument seemed too obvious to be true, if it was claimed of the other that it was too absurd to be false. A.L. Basham played his role of the 'friendly *mleccha*' by referring to it as a 'brilliantly imaginative picture of the world'[3], but this was being apologetic, not analytic.

Light came from an unexpected source. While leafing through a bound volume of the previous issues of *The Journal of the American Academy of Religion* my sight was arrested unexpectedly by the account Huston Smith provided of his first psychedelic experience, produced by his 'own first ingestion of mescaline':

> Another phrase came to me: 'empirical metaphysics'. The emanation theory and elaborately delineated layers of Indian cosmology and psychology had hitherto been concepts and inferences. Now they were objects of direct, immediate perception. I saw that theories such as these were required by the experience I was having. I found myself amused, thinking how duped historians of philosophy had been in crediting those who formulated such world views with being speculative geniuses. Had they had experiences such as mine they need have been no more than hack reporters.[4]

If the Vedas could, at least in part, contain accounts of the ecstatic adventures into another universe of experience (through *soma*), why not the Purāṇas?

V

Surely it is a magic moment in the study of religion, when the experience or insight of someone who does not belong to your own tradition enhances your own understanding of it. Huston Smith has done it for me; and I am sure for many more. The best guide points out the way back to your home, and the best guest helps one discover the unsuspected wonders of one's own house. But then is he a guest anymore?

Notes

1. Edward Thompson and G.T. Garratt, *Rise and Fulfilment of British Rule in India*, Central Book Depot, Allahabad 1962, p.661.
2. A.L. Basham, *The Wonder That Was India*, Grove Press Inc., New York 1954, p.489.
3. *Ibid.*
4. Huston Smith, 'Wasson's *Soma*' from *Journal of The American Academy of Religion* XL:4, p.481, note 2(9).

CHAPTER 2

The Chun-Tzu

Philip Novak

If you would know Huston Smith, start with China. Born there to American missionary parents, it was there he spent the greater part of his first seventeen years. Beholding him, one wonders whether fantastic tales about Chinese magic are not true after all. There is something distantly — and yet distinctly — Asian in his physiognomy. China paused on his skin, it seemed, before proceeding to his marrow. But proceed it did.

Open the pages of the *Analects* to Confucius' descriptions of the *chun-tzu* (ideal gentleman) and you touch Huston's fiber. *Chun-tzu* literally means 'son of a ruler', but the Confucian tradition reserves the term for one who possesses a truly human heart, who cherishes the arts of learning and teaching, and who is as concerned to teach by moral example as by intellectual knack. That, for starters, is Huston.

For those who had come to graduate school seeking Wisdom (and some of us *had*), Huston incarnated the spirit of the Quest. He embodied a graceful balance between academic objectivity and an abiding sense that we moderns had much to glean from wisdom traditions. He was one of the most senior professors in the Department of Religion, and he held the prestigious Watson Chair, yet all who knew him felt he was, at heart, but another wayfarer on the Way marked out by the saints and sages of the human past. Huston, the *chun-tzu*, became my mentor. I began to learn as much from how he was as from what he said.

The *chun-tzu*, says Confucius, is meticulous in the performance of reciprocal duties. I once asked Huston why, after I had completed my doctorate, he worked so hard to help me land a job in the tight

8

market. He explained that in China a teacher's duties are not complete until he helps his student get established.

The *chun-tzu* is also a social adept, as skilful in moderating intellectual conversation as he is in mollifying a surly neighbor. Deferential and courteous, he wields the marvellous, hidden power of formality — the *real* Chinese magic. From Huston I learned that formality opens lines of communication that a too-easy familiarity tends to clog. Huston is a reserved man, and one of such massive impartiality that those who approach him seeking signs of special favor often come away instead with a heightened awareness of their own dubious motives. And yet, for all that, he remains the eminently approachable 'Huston', as the many who have sought his counsel will attest.

Huston's Chinese grain contains Taoist squiggles as well. He once led thirty students, three professors, and their families on an academic year around the world. Logistical nightmares, outrageous proposals for exotic side-trips, and cross-cultural difficulties that would have made a lesser mortal tear out his hair were handled by Huston with the unruffled ease of a man on a Sunday stroll. The Taoists call this quality *wu-wei*, or creative quietude. As the *Tao Te Ching* has it:

> The Sage
> Puts himself in the background
> But is always to the fore
> Remains outside but is always there ...
> Through his actionless activity all things
> Are duly regulated.

For those who would come to know Huston only through his work, China bestowed a final gift: a profound appreciation for non-Western cultures that fated him to be a bridge builder. At 37 he published the book that was to make the whole world his lecture circuit. *The Religions of Man* has sold over two million copies in six languages and, amid a host of more recent world religions texts, is still going strong.

No single culture or tradition, however, can shape the soul of a bridge builder. His life has been an earnest, incessant pilgrimage. Certainly the Judaeo-Christian tradition, in which he was raised and in which he served for a time as a minister, has played an important role. But there were also tenacious explorations of the other traditions. In the 1950s weekly sessions with a Hindu swami led him deeply into the contours of the Vedanta and the practice of yoga. In the 1960s a full dose of Zen training in Japan and a friendship with the great Zen scholar D.T. Suzuki opened wide the Dharma-Gate of Buddhism. In the 1970s new intellectual allegiances provided entry into the House of Islam and the Sufi brotherhood. In all these adventures there were lessons for his students: if you want to know, you must taste.

I have travelled with Huston and watched him in the company of contemplatives hailing from various climes. The scene, often repeated, has etched itself in my memory. The scholar greets the robed figure and their eyes meet. Something nearly palpable flows between them. Rapport seems instant, mutual respect obvious.

What do those tranquil souls see in Huston's that makes him one of them? Perhaps the very thing seen by the master of ceremonies last year at a banquet attended by 800 representatives of religions the world over. Twenty honored guests, Huston among them, sat at a long table atop a stage. As the meal proceeded each was introduced; positions or academic pedigrees were duly noted. Eventually it came time for the closing remarks, Huston's task that evening. The master of ceremonies stepped to the podium, broke the routine, and in lieu of a list of credentials, introduced Huston in six words. 'He is,' said the MC, 'a man with a golden heart.'

There is much else to say, of course. But I remember that once, during a seminar that was being hobbled by the irrelevant expostulations of an over-talkative graduate student, Huston passed each of us a slip of paper bearing the following message: 'In a setting such as this, it is tempting to comment on many things. Unfortunately there is time only for the essential. Learn the art of omission.' It is a piece of advice with relevance far beyond the occasion that brought it into being. And so I close, esteemed teacher, omitting much.

Note

This tribute was originally published in the *Syracuse University Magazine* Vol.3, No.2 (February 1987), p.48, and permission to include it in this volume is gratefully acknowledged.

CHAPTER 3

Tribute to Huston Smith as a Teacher

Marilyn Gustin

Huston Smith was only a name to me when I began searching for dissertation committee members. His was a famous name, to be sure, even a little venerable. But well-known names, even when one is grateful for their writings, can seem unreachable. Still, he was one of the few professors who knew anything about my chosen topic, so when someone told me he had retired to the Bay Area (where I was at the Graduate Theological Union) I was elated. A letter, a phone call, an unexpected meeting at the American Academy of Religion, and he graciously consented to serve on my committee. It has been primarily in this capacity rather than in the classroom, that I have known him.

It is often assumed that scholarship makes a teacher. Surely without scholarship, teaching would not occur. A teacher, however, is much more than an articulate bundle of information pronounced from a particular angle. A teacher is a whole person in relationship to other whole persons. A good teacher makes him/herself available to students as the whole person and not merely in a role. At this, Huston Smith is a master.

Yet that can sound as if relating wholly, personably, to students is merely a skill. But Huston Smith is simply the man that he is, putting himself, his sensitivity, his knowledge, his kindness at the disposal of his student. If it has cost him anything to learn to do this, it no longer shows. He is a human being who happens to teach — and very well — but who does not become less human in the process.

In memories of conversations with him at the beginning of

11

dissertation work, two qualities shine out. One is his consistent gentleness. It is not only that he treats one well; many professors do that. Huston is saturated with kindness. It flows from him as naturally as his breath. At the same time, he was completely frank. He said straightforwardly that he was nervous about my project because he could not see my plan. 'You may well have a good one,' he hastened to add. This combination of plain-spokenness and kindness allowed me to know exactly where I stood with this gentleman who could have so much to say about my future. It was encouraging indeed.

Contacts with Huston were always surprising. Only now does the chief reason for the surprise become clear. This man does not manipulate people or situations, nor does he seem to have hidden agendas. Influence has indeed come to him, but he seems uninterested in competitive power games. That alone is refreshing. Here, too, his personal candidness reflects his ability to be himself in the teaching situation. By so doing, he must have warmed many hearts over the years.

In three incidents during the dissertation work, Huston demonstrated an alert sensitivity to me as a student. It can only be described as extraordinary. It is finally this lovely aspect of his character that makes Huston a great teacher and not merely a good one.

The first incident occurred when I mailed the committee members my outline and suggested that they need not reply unless something was amiss, and then would they please call. Huston called — but only to reassure me that the projections seemed to him right 'on target' and I could proceed confidently. Stronger than his words, however, was the call itself, an unnecessary thing, but so expressive of his sensitivity to student difficulties.

The second of his gracious phone calls came the evening before my oral examination. His purpose was to tell me that the dissertation was wonderful, I should sleep peacefully! Again, unnecessary, but it reflected his acute awareness that nights before orals can be long and miserable for students, and he wanted mine to be less so.

For the orals I travelled from our home in Tucson to Berkeley, and since it had been a while since my residency there, I was alone for the ordeal. Then it was over, successfully. I would call my husband, but celebrations were to be postponed until my return. So I was astounded when Huston quietly invited me home for supper with him and his wife. I felt so touched by such thoughtfulness — and the willingness to act on it. Stumbling, I managed to say something about

12

how unusually kind this was, especially since we were only a little more than acquaintances. He smiled and said simply, 'There are some times in life when a person should not be alone. This is one of them.'

It seems likely that Huston himself would find none of these events unusual or worthy of comment. Each is simple and none required great sacrifice. The rare one who does such things, though, is one who sees other hearts, who cares about their state of well-being. These deeds beyond duty's obligations, offered by an honored teacher to a student without any claim, witness brightly to his alertness of heart and generous sensitivity.

With Huston Smith, discussions were fun, questions and answers sharp and illuminating, information always fruitful. These qualities are rightfully expected from a fine professor. It is beyond them that one looks to find a great teacher. In Huston, greatness is honesty of person, penetrating sensitivity, but above all, his flowing kindness.

CHAPTER 4

Reflections on an Unforgettable Colleague: Huston Smith

James B. Wiggins

When Huston Smith comes to mind many associations accompany the image: determined seeker and defender of truth; gentle and sagacious quester; and generous and loyal friend. In his years as a colleague at Syracuse University from 1973 to 1984, during which time he served as Thomas J. Watson Professor of Religion, I experienced him in all those ways. His decision to move on to a semi-retired, emeritus status emphasized how significant his presence had been, and how challenging would be the task of creatively replacing him.

No philosophical realist was ever more vigorous in insisting upon the existence of truth, nor was any skeptic ever more cautious in citing the human difficulties in reaching truth, particularly any account of it for which he has little sympathy, than is Huston Smith. But neither realist nor skeptic could draw much comfort from his meticulous, detailed and sometimes devastating critiques of those positions when they began to slip into ideology. Further, that propensity and ability to critique other positions never prevents Huston Smith from strongly and firmly declaring his own position on any question at issue.

Huston is deeply familiar with the history of philosophy in both the West and the East, and he is no less familiar with the religions of humanity. His seeking the truth has made him a pilgrim in quest of the grail of truth, and no impediments have prevented him from pursuing that quest. He is a world traveller who has visited more religious shrines and become personally acquainted with more priests, gurus, rabbis, masters and ministers than most of us have heard of. Similarly, he is personally acquainted with many of modernity's greatest philosophers and theologians. For any one of them might impart an insight valuable to understanding truth.

But the vigilant quester has also doggedly adhered to the view that the multitudes, who continue to hold certain views in each of the world's great religious traditions (including that of the history of western philosophy), have kept in touch with essential insights that must be retained. Western modernity has, through its science, its philosophy and its pathos-filled theology gone sadly and badly astray. No merely rhetorical flourish on Smith's part leads him to implore us 'to rejoin the human race'. (Huston Smith is, however, one of the most mesmerizing and effective public speakers I have been privileged to know, and is a rhetorician of great skill.) By that admonition he apparently means to jar the confidence, which he regards as unwarranted, of contemporary *isms*, whether scientism, religious fundamentalism, or any other. All are anathema, in his view. Why?

Huston Smith's paradoxical perspective is that all angles of vision, and what they permit to be envisioned, are equally perspectival. He is deeply aware that humans repeatedly display a propensity to reify their own perspectival envisionments, and thereby to treat these views as if they were the whole of reality and truth. But even though humans do that (i.e. in religious terms they commit *idolatry*), for Smith it does not follow that the perspectival view entails or requires embracing relativism. For him that is but another *ism*. Rather, what is required is a careful exploration of the great traditions in a comparative fashion. This entails not only a familiarization with the written texts, the holy books, the ideas and concepts, but also, when possible, a familiarizing with living exemplars and adherents.

Face to face conversations with believers constitute a critical aspect of Huston Smith's approach to understanding. And what a remarkable, sensitive and engaging conversationalist he is! Rarely will one encounter anybody more present in a meeting than is this man. With a gaze even more penetrating than his gentle questions, he presents a formidable persona. Deep reflection and meditation upon what he garners from his encounters follows. During that process there may be questions of clarification, requests for references, or inquiries about the accuracy of his perceptions and memories. From the crucible of his imagination and mind eventually emerges his critical assessment of what he has explored. Then begins his effort to validate his assessment. Is he saying things recognizable and intelligible to the adherent from whom he sought to learn? If not, where did he miss? Is what he is representing acceptable, as well as recognizable and intelligible? If not, why not? Then, unrelenting, comes his critical judgement regarding how near or far the view is from the Truth.

When one becomes aware of the persons Huston most deeply reveres and of the ideas and systems of thinking to which he is most powerfully drawn, it is not surprising that names like Confucius, the Buddha, Jesus, Socrates, the Dalai Lama, Plotinus, Shuon, et al., are prominent among them. Nor will it surprise that the 'perennial philosophy' is so positively valued.

En route to affirming the truths that he believes to be self-evident, Smith puts himself squarely in the company of those in each generation who have shared the vision. Echoing William Blake, Huston Smith avers: 'The fully realized human being is one whose doors of perception have been cleansed.'[1]

And the life of one who experiences through cleansed doors of perception — what of that? Will such a one be beyond pain and sorrow, suffering and death? No! 'Not invariance but appropriateness is his [sic] hallmark, an appropriateness that has the whole repertoire of emotions at its command.'[2]

And yet the fundamental honesty of Smith requires from him an acknowledgement of the paradox of how infinitely far humans are from the infinitely near 'sacred unconscious'. Though they strive mightily, many humans experience only their striving. That, too, is a part of the human experience and it is a part that Huston Smith, it seems to me, only minimally attends. Suffering, corrigible conditions, cruelty, are indignities to the human spirit and to specific human beings that some among us are dedicated to attempting to relieve and reduce, even to eliminate. That is not in any direct way an obvious part of Huston Smith's project.

How crucial it is that determined seekers like Huston Smith continue in the quest upon which they have embarked. If it is not a path that most of us will, or even can, tread, it is nonetheless a journey for which the rest of us can be grateful. Even if we doubt that the relativism, thought by many to be a corollary of the perspectival affirmation that even Huston Smith recognizes, has been overcome by his arguments against it, many of us attempt in our own ways to overcome relativism. Formally, we are with him. Further, some of us for whom positivistic historiography has no more interest or sustaining power than it does for him, applaud his determined opposition to positivism.

Huston Smith has won his way into the most elevated philosophical circles of our day. His years on the faculty at Washington University, MIT and Syracuse University included unceasing conversations not only with scientists of the first order, but also with some pre-eminent contemporary philosophers. In the philosophical and the scientific world with which he is so intimately acquainted I have little sense of how Huston Smith is regarded. Perhaps others writing in this volume will help apprise us of that.

But I do have a sense of how Huston Smith is regarded in the field of the academic study of religion. On the one hand, the millions of copies of *The Religions of Man* that have been bought by, among others, students in courses in the study of religion, testify to how widely his work is known and how highly it is regarded. Few, if any, books of the type can remotely rival its influence. On the other hand, Huston Smith is regarded as an enigma in much of the sub-discipline of the philosophy of religion. Many are aware of him and of some of his work, but few seem to know how to assess what they know. Probably much of the reason for this peculiar situation owes to his championing a mode of thinking that seems to many to be quaint, even anachronistic. But that is further reason for appreciating his determined efforts to pursue a way that is not modish. Recent champions of philosophical pluralism must surely appreciate his alternative voices. Religious studies scholars, having never known anything other than a multiplicity of voices in most sub-disciplines, may not adequately appreciate or permit themselves to be challenged by the quiet persistence of the approach and practice of Huston Smith's thinking. That would be to miss a highly edifying and enlightening opportunity and experience.

As colleague and friend Huston Smith is one I deeply admire. His contributions to our fields of common interest, his loyalty to the institution in which we worked together for a decade, and his presence in a department where his sensitivity, experience and stability were so important are but some of the reasons he will always be on the short list of most unforgettable people I have known.

Notes

1. Quoted in 'The Sacred Unconscious' from *Beyond the Post-Modern Mind*, Crossroad, New York, 1981, p.181.
2. *Ibid*, p.183.

SECTION II: ARTICLES WRITTEN IN HONOUR OF HUSTON SMITH

CHAPTER 5

The Great Chain of Being in the Lives of the Faithful: The Status of Purgatory Today

L. Stafford Betty

It is one thing for professional philosophers to debate the Great Chain of Being, but quite another for professors to make it relevant to their not-so-philosophical undergraduates, or pastors of souls to their flocks. By lucky accident I recently came to see that the Great Chain of Being — with its layers of reality and value arranged hierarchically according to intensity, power, goodness, truth, realization of potential, divine presence or absence, and so forth — is of more than academic interest. The focus of this serendipitous discovery was, of all things, purgatory, which for Catholics (Roman, Anglican or Orthodox) is located midway (eschatologically speaking) between earth and heaven, and in the Great Chain of Being forms one of the links in the chain's middle range, which in recent years has grown rusty and untidy from neglect.

Not long ago my wife's grandmother died. Her life had been full and her devotion to the Roman Catholic Church apparent to everyone who knew her. But she, like most of us, was no saint. As family and friends chatted and drank at the wake, I suddenly felt tempted to ask a delicate question. 'Where do you think she is now?' I said between clinks of glasses.

After the initial shock, one of the woman's daughters said that of course she was in heaven. 'Do you agree?' I asked another of her daughters. This daughter thought that her mother would have to reincarnate and learn certain crucial lessons in the next life that she failed to learn in this one. Finally I asked the dead woman's son. 'Personally, I think she's in purgatory,' he said.

All three responses came from Catholics in their fifties. What explains this diversity of belief? What does it mean? And is it to be deplored or applauded?

Not long ago I had another occasion to think about what awaits us after death. Only this time there was no party. A man — another Roman Catholic — who had determined to commit suicide wanted to talk to a theologian to get a reading on the latest after-death teaching in the Church. He was under the impression that at the moment of death God would judge him, forgive him, and usher him into the eternal joy of heaven. He just wanted to be sure that he was right. I happened to answer the office telephone when he called.

What do you tell a man like this? What *is* the Catholic Church's teaching nowadays? The doctrine of purgatory is an article of faith for Catholics, but I have heard no mention of it from the pulpit for fifteen years. A popular retreat master and Jesuit priest, James McCown, confirmed my feelings when he told me that purgatory has 'definitely been put on the back burner' and is 'something of an embarrassment' to the Church. So what do you tell the would-be suicide? Do you tell him that according to a 1982 Gallup Poll 25 per cent of Catholics believe in reincarnation? Do you tell him that suicide is a mortal sin and that the penalty, as he should know from his catechism days, is eternal hell? Or do you tell him, 'Yes, you *can* expect to be with God, no matter how you have lived'?

That man is alive today, stays in frequent contact with me, and considers me his friend. He maintains, rightly or wrongly, that the answer I gave him saved his life. I told him that there was every reason to believe that he would carry his troubles with him into some kind of an intermediate world between earth and heaven, but with an additional burden: he would be unable to affect conditions back on earth, and he might desperately want to.

'Is this the Church's teaching?' he said, obviously disappointed.

What could I say? What would you have said? I said that it was 'not inconsistent' with the Church's teaching, and that I had excellent reasons for my views on the subject. I told him that I was something of an authority on afterlife beliefs and insisted that before he take his life he read one short book. He agreed to do this. Not surprisingly, that book[1] was not written by a Catholic and it was not particularly biblical. But it called the man to his senses.

I am convinced that the Church needs to get purgatory out of mothballs. Not the old version that I grew up with: the purifying fire with 300 days off for saying 'Jesus, Mary, and Joseph'; the sort of place you could avoid altogether by making the Nine First Fridays or a Perfect Act of Contrition. This spiritual sleight-of-hand is an embarrassment to the modern Church, as well it should be. But the idea behind purgatory is not only sound but spiritually invigorating. It was this idea that might have saved my friend's life.

Unfortunately, this is not the sort of answer that most Catholic authorities entertain today, at least in the United States. Many well-meaning priests imply, if they do not actually teach, that the average Catholic can look forward to heaven at the moment of death. This happy heaven-for-everybody mystique has infected not only the pulpit but the parochial schools. The robust, strenuous, honestly hopeful life that a proper understanding of eschatology would encourage — an understanding based on a proper estimate of our place on the Great Chain of Being — is largely missing in contemporary Catholicism. The effect has been spiritually and morally debilitating, especially on the young. I believe that purgatory needs to be reinterpreted, renamed and then preached forcefully from the pulpit.

You might expect that Catholic theologians would be of help in this matter. Most are not. Typically they decline to talk about purgatory at all. In *The Catholic Periodical and Literature Index* there was only one entry under Purgatory for all of 1984, and again only one in 1985.

Many Catholics regard the late Karl Rahner and Hans Küng as the Church's leading modern theologians. What do these two say? Writing in 1976, Rahner called purgatory 'a process of maturation "after" death for the whole person.'[2] (Note the inverted commas around "after".) In 1981 he was clearer: 'The idea of the intermediate state contains a little harmless mythology.'[3] Rahner did not believe in purgatory as an after-death state of temporal duration, or of anything analogous to temporal duration.

What about Küng, author of *Eternal Life*? Like Rahner, Küng denies that purgatory is an 'interim phase' between death and the fullness of heaven. For Küng, *'Purgatory is God himself* in the wrath of his grace.'[4] It is the 'purifying and cleansing ... element of the encounter with God'[5] and as such is instantaneous. What, then, is the meaning of praying for the dead, as every Catholic is encouraged to do and does do at a funeral mass? Küng says that it is 'certainly appropriate to pray for the *dying*',[6] but not for the dead. The funeral mass, therefore, is another little piece of harmless mythology, as are prayers for the dead in general.

In my opinion Rahner and Küng make a critical mistake in their treatment of afterlife in general and of purgatory in particular. Like Luther four centuries ago, they have reacted to the excesses and downright absurdities in the Church's treatment of purgatory by all but denying that purgatory exists. In doing so, they have belittled the significance of human choice and action. In life we expect to be held accountable for our actions, we expect to pay for our mistakes. Take away this expectation, and inevitably, like an invulnerable potentate, most of us would grow careless. Our moral choices would cease to matter to us much, for nothing would be riding on them.

Is there any wonder that many Catholics are turning, either consciously or unconsciously, to reincarnation as the answer? Instantaneous, total salvation for ordinary souls after a single undistinguished life strikes many Catholics as improbable. Instinctively they know differently. But what is the alternative to it? Must it be a succession of character-building earth-lives until, at long last, we are morally and spiritually ready for the presence of God?

There is an alternative. The Church, wisely, has provided minimal guidance in its deliberations on purgatory. She has provided little more than a skeleton for succeeding generations to flesh out according to their own lights. She has said that purgatory certainly exists, is a condition that those 'not yet free from imperfection' will find themselves in, and that the souls there 'can be helped by the prayers and other good works of the faithful on earth.'[7] As for the word 'purgatory', it is a relic of the Middle Ages. There is nothing sacred about it. It can be, and should be, discarded.

So I would begin a recasting of purgatory by changing the name. I suggest that it be called 'The Good Land', and for two reasons. First, I think that the condition of the ordinary, far-from-perfect person who was basically decent would be on average better than it was on earth: his new world would be 'good', not in the sense that there would be greater pleasure, but in the sense that there would be more understanding of what had gone wrong on earth and as a result, let us hope, more of a sense of purpose. It would be a place, in other words, where we would have the opportunity of getting down to business with a clearer sense of what was involved in our choices. Secondly, I think that it is extremely important to think of the after-death state along physical, or at least vividly symbolic, lines — to think of it, in other words, as a 'land'. Theologian John Heaney of Fordham University states the reason well: 'Religious psychologists have found that when people lose all symbolic images connected with beliefs, the result is not so much that there is a direct denial of the beliefs, but that it ceases to have any affective and effective meaning.'[8] He goes on to say that, when conceiving of the afterlife, 'we may allow ourselves such pictures as operative images while remaining skeptical about the literal truth of the details.'[9]

I would go further than Heaney. It is the unanimous teaching of Eastern religions that we have bodies in the next world. Furthermore, in all psychic literature — especially the large body of supposed revelations of conditions on the 'Other Side' that have come through mediums — there is the same claim. (These 'descriptions', while of dubious origin and value, are at least unanimous in their claim that the next world is vividly real and sensory.) Moreover, the near-death experience (NDE) so carefully studied by physicians over the last fifteen years has as one of its most striking features the sense of being embodied in a 'spiritual body'. Perhaps most importantly for Christians, St Paul teaches in the clearest terms that we will have spiritual bodies (see 1 Corinthians 15).

St Paul was of course talking about heaven, but that should not detain us; the point is that he conceived of the afterworld as one in which we have bodies. If St Paul is correct, then there is good reason to believe that the Good Land is a *real place*, and not just a metaphor. For what would be the purpose of having a body with all of its senses if there were no environment to be sensed? It is true that Rahner and Küng, with their Germanic love of abstraction, take a dim view of such 'crude' sensuality. Küng is quite sure that any after-death environment must be 'invisible'.[10] One wonders if it has seriously occurred to him that we might have spiritual bodies with all senses intact, if not heightened, and a spiritual landscape around us (whatever that might precisely amount to). No one, however, should feel compelled to join Küng in his anti-sensual bias. There is nothing 'spiritual' or 'advanced' about a teaching that cancels the validity of sensuous experience in this or any other world.

What is the Good Land like? Where does one turn for help? The

Bible is not very helpful. Dante is suggestive, but disarmingly medieval. And we have seen what two of the Church's most celebrated modern theologians have said. Where then? Catholic theologian Richard McBrien, taking a position long consistent with Orthodox teachings about purgatory, makes what I consider a helpful distinction. 'The kind of suffering associated with purgatory,' he says, 'is not suffering inflicted upon us from the outside as a punishment for sin, but the intrinsic pain that we feel when we are asked to surrender our ego-centered self so that the God-centered loving self may take its place.'[11] Is there anything more to say? Do we dare go any further?

I think that we must. My very tentative view of the Good Land is based on many sources, including my own sense of what seems 'intuitively right'. These sources include Protestant John Hick's benchmark theological study *Death and Eternal Life*;[12] the Buddhist scripture *The Tibetan Book of the Dead*;[13] the Jewish *Zohar*;[14] mediumistic classics such as *Swan on a Black Sea*,[15] a study of the Cummins-Willett Scripts so carefully analyzed by British philosopher C.D. Broad; the discerning ruminations of philosophers J.N. Findlay[16] and Frithjof Schuon[17]; the recent literature surrounding the widely studied near-death experience;[18] Church teaching, and much more.

With considerable trepidation I would describe the Good Land in the following way: when we die, we will discover that we are thoroughly ourselves, with all our good or bad habits intact. We will not experience hunger or sickness or any of the other ailments that are peculiar to the physical earth body, but we will experience the full range of emotions that we knew on earth. If we have hated someone, we will continue to hate him, and in the act of hating we will draw him (if he has died) to us. Reconciliation will often be harrowing; it may indeed be thoroughly hellish. All evasions and self-deceptions will be discovered, often to our profound mortification and sorrow. The whole point of living in the Good Land is to strip ourselves of illusions. Above all it is a place where we come to know ourselves: God does not have to judge us directly; He has made us in such a way that we will judge ourselves. Through this judgement we may gradually begin to understand; we may grow more compassionate, humbler, more forgiving, and finally more joyful. Or we may not. We may, if we prefer, further harden ourselves in our old, destructive habits. Hell is not so much a separate world as it is an unhappy state — a ghetto, if you will — within the Good Land. Many of us, however

— perhaps all of us in time — will discover that the Good Land is indeed very good, and that it leads to the presence of God that we all ultimately desire.

The 'geography' of the Good Land is not a matter about which I want to say much — although many ostensible accounts of the next world are available.[19] In any case, this is a matter of relatively little importance compared to other matters. Nevertheless, something must be said. I imagine the Good Land — at least for the basically decent person — as a place of clarity, color and luminosity. The landscape, far from futuristic or strange or ghostly, may be in many respects homey, comfortable and 'normal' — the sort of place where you can get work done without undue distraction. Loved ones who have died before us may be present from time to time. Always there will be helpers and teachers. Most importantly there will be tasks for each of us to do, all in the service of character development and purification.

Every person's experience will be different. Each will be as free in the Good Land as he was on earth — indeed freer. He may choose to alter his environment, or even his body, as he pleases; material substance over there will be malleable and will respond directly to the will. Perhaps he may even choose to re-enter the world of matter (reincarnate) to work on a particular problem or even to 'start over'; or he may choose to leave the narrow, too-comfortable, perhaps boring environment he finds himself in and seek new challenges in more advanced venues of the Good Land. He may study the Master Plan of the Universe (if something like that exists) or work at the very 'human' task of better communicating warmth and love. He may try to forgive a horrible evil done him, or he may try to develop an interest in theology or philosophy to fill the emptiness left by some earthside addiction. He may expand his knowledge of musical composition to include the unimaginable sonorities of that new environment. There will be no limit to the range of challenges available in the Good Land. He may choose to grow or to fritter time away — just as on earth. He will go at his own speed. To a frightening extent he will get what he wants — get it until he discovers what it is he *really* wants. This may take ages; it will rarely be quick and easy, for bad habits will perhaps be as hard to break in the Good Land as they were back on earth.

The Good Land will have many layers ('mansions'). The final destination will be the Godhead, the pinnacle of the Great Chain of

Being. When we finally choose that destination in earnest — and nothing will force us against our wills to make such a choice — we will find the way filled with unimaginable challenges, some of them harrowing, others exhilarating beyond our wildest fantasies, all of them meaningful and 'full of grace'.

Do we meet God along the way? The more advanced we are, the more present He will be to us. Perhaps we will first sense Him as a 'knowing light'[20] that suffuses our world, a light that attracts but does not push, invites but does not overpower — as much a nurturing, motherly presence as a fatherly. This light might be felt as intensely personal, Jesus' *Abba*, the very opposite of a distant or impersonal Absolute. As we progress, God might become more distinct, more concrete, more personal, more awesome, more loving, 'more infinite', more ravishing — and certainly less capturable in words, which will shatter in the presence of the Being they feebly approximate.

What about Jesus? He will be available in glory to anyone who calls on him — as will Krishna to his devotees, as will all the other personalities that the faithful have given to God, or, alternatively, that God has incarnated Himself in. Jesus will be there to love and succor, to advise and admonish — just as he was available to his disciples during his public life. And what about one's fellow Christians? If you desire to live among them, you need only will it — you might even be able to choose your denomination! There are many mansions in the Good Land.

Most Catholic theologians, I fear, will shy away from this much-too-brief account of the intermediate world. They will see dangerous pitfalls. Fine; I invite them to improve on the conception. The alternative is more of the same: a failure of nerve on the part of the Catholic Church to guide the faithful in a matter of extraordinary importance. Catholic theologians must speak in vivid imagery of the world to come. They must make new myths as freely as the ancients made their old ones. Modern men and women will never become so modern that they will no longer require the services of the imagination to mediate eternal truths. Intellectual abstractions work no better for modern people than for Jesus' first disciples, who were taught, let us not forget, in vivid parables. As it is, nothing that modern theologians — who should be as good at telling stories as at formulating universals — might say, however daring, could come close to matching the actualities that they seek to describe. They need never fear being more vivid than God.

I believe that many Catholics — many Protestants, for that matter — fail to see that they are souls in the making: divine projects, if you will, and, as such, deeply valued and loved by God. The decisions that we make here on earth are far more important than we suspect. Anything that drives this point home, as long as it does not motivate predominantly through fear, is good. The trouble with the notion of afterlife that older Catholics were raised with — eternal torture for one 'mortal sin', or a long agony of passive suffering in purgatory if they were lucky enough to die in the 'state of grace' — is that it motivated through fear. The trouble with much contemporary teaching is that it hardly motivates at all. This is especially true of the young. Typical graduates of Catholic high schools are bored to death with religion by the time they get to college, and often ditch their faith at the first excuse. The Church, for them, has become the dispenser of what Cardinal Newman called 'a languid, unmeaning benevolence'. They are not being challenged in a way that appeals to their imaginations.

The power and impact of a faith is directly proportionate to that faith's concreteness and vividness. One of the great distinctions of the Catholic Church over against most Protestant denominations is that it has always (at least until recently) understood this principle: along with Hinduism, which is notoriously difficult to uproot, Catholicism has given its blessing to images, pageantry, even ostentation — all in the interest of bringing sacred, ineffable reality down to the level of the faithful. Yet much of the modern Church remains mesmerized by the dubious abstractions of a few German theologians.

I believe that God's plan for humankind is profoundly exciting. Jesus' teaching that we must love God and each other is the greatest challenge that we will ever face, both in this life and in the next. The sooner we get started, the better it will be for us. It is the Church's mission to help people see this more clearly, more vividly, more compellingly.[21] A more plausible and attractive afterlife teaching in the context of the Great Chain of Being has always been crucial to its success, and will continue to be.

Notes

1. Archie Matson, *Afterlife*, Harper & Row, New York, 1975.
2. Karl Rahner, *Foundations of Christian Faith*, Seabury Press, New York, 1978, p.442.

3. Karl Rahner, 'The Intermediate State' from *Theological Investigations* Vol.XVII, Darton, Longman & Todd, London, 1981, p.123.
4. Hans Küng, *Eternal Life?*, Doubleday, New York, 1984, p.139.
5. *Ibid.* Küng here quotes with approval the Catholic theologian Gisbert Greshake.
6. *Ibid.*
7. *New Catholic Encyclopedia* Vol.11, McGraw-Hill Book Co., New York, 1967, pp.1034, 1035.
8. John J. Heaney, *The Sacred and the Psychic*, Paulist Press, New York, 1984, p.198.
9. *Ibid.*
10. Küng, p.144.
11. Richard P. McBrien, *Catholicism*, Vol.II, Winston Press, Minneapolis, 1980, p.1035.
12. John Hick, *Death and Eternal Life*, Collins, London, 1976.
13. *The Tibetan Book of the Dead*, trans. Francesca Fremantle and Chogyam Trungpa, Shambala Publications, Berkeley, 1975.
14. See Adin Steinsaltz, *The Thirteen Petalled Rose*, Basic Books, New York, 1980, for a particularly clear treatment of this difficult mystical text.
15. Geraldine Cummins, transmitter, Signe Toksvig, editor, *Swan on a Black Sea, A Study in Automatic Writing: The Cummins-Willett Scripts*, revised edn, Routledge & Kegan Paul, London, 1970.
16. See especially his *Assent to the Absolute*, Allen & Unwin, London, 1970, chapters I-III; also *The Transcendence of the Cave*, Allen & Unwin, London, 1966, chapters VI-X.
17. See especially *The Essential Writings of Frithjof Schuon*, ed. Seyyed Nasr, Amity House, New York, 1986, Part VII.
18. Raymond Moody's best-selling *Life After Life*, Bantam Books, New York, 1975, was the first of many books on the subject.
19. In my opinion, the most trustworthy accounts are F.W.H. Myers through Geraldine Cummins, *The Road to Immortality*, Ivor Nicholson Watson Ltd, London, 1932; Paramahansa Yogananda, *Autobiography of a Yogi*, Self-Realization Fellowship, Los Angeles, 1946, chapter 43; *Swan on a Black Sea* (see note 14 above); and Robert Crookall, *The Supreme Adventure: Analyses of Psychic Communications*, 2nd edn, James Clarke & Co. Limited, Cambridge, England, 1975.
20. See Jane Roberts, *The Afterdeath Journal of an American Philosopher*, Prentice-Hall, Englewood Cliffs N.J., 1978, chapter 10. This strange book, which purports to be a communication from the surviving William James, could be recommended even if it were sheer fiction.
21. With this in mind I wrote my illustrated fable *Sing Like the Whippoorwill*, Twenty-Third Publications, Mystic CT, 1987, which dramatizes the journey to and through the 'Good Land'. At present the publisher is vigorously promoting the book in all 1600 US Catholic high schools.

CHAPTER 6

Root Images and the way we see: the Primordial Tradition and the Biblical Tradition

Marcus Borg

Ideas matter. One would only expect an academic to say this, so let me add at once that some ideas do not matter very much. But some do, deeply affecting our lives. Of the ideas that do affect us, perhaps none does so as much as the root images of reality which lie deep in our psyches. A root image is a fundamental image of how reality is, our most basic 'picture' of reality. Perhaps most often called a 'world-view', it consists of our most taken-for-granted assumptions about what is possible. It is an idea (a mental construct) with immense power. Very importantly, a root image not only provides a model of reality, but also shapes our perception and our thinking, operating almost unconsciously within us as a dim background affecting all of our seeing and thinking. A root image thus functions as both an image and a lens: it is a picture of reality which becomes a lens through which we see reality.

Much of Huston Smith's work throughout his career has centered on the fundamental importance of root images. In particular, he has been concerned to describe and contrast two very different root images of reality: the pre-modern world-view, which he calls 'the primordial tradition', and the modern world-view. Though this emphasis can be seen in many of his publications, it is most systematically treated in *Forgotten Truths: The Primordial Tradition* (Harper & Row, New York, 1976).

Many scholars have described the contrast between the modern world-view and a more traditional world-view, of course, but

Professor Smith has done so with unusual lucidity and precision. And passion: he has persistently emphasized the pervasive effects of the modern world-view not only in our culture but also within the academy. One of the most far-reaching realizations of my own intellectual journey was the discovery of how deeply the modern way of seeing reality has affected my own mind, accompanied by a perception of how deeply it has affected the academic discipline in which I was trained and continue to work. For me, Professor Smith has been one of those 'bridge people', scholars in disciplines other than one's own who become significant in one's own work. Indeed, among such scholars, none has been more important to me.

In this tribute, I wish to describe the effect his treatment of the primordial tradition has had on my practice and perception of my own discipline of biblical studies. In particular, I will make the argument that the biblical tradition is a form of the primordial tradition, describe reasons why this has not commonly been given due regard in this century's scholarship, and then suggest the importance of taking this claim seriously.

Defining the Primordial Tradition
Whether one sees the biblical tradition to be a form of the primordial tradition depends, of course, upon how one defines the latter. Central to Professor Smith's description of it are three elements.

First, the most essential element of the primordial tradition is a map of reality as having more than one level. The key or fundamental claim is that reality has minimally two levels or layers, the visible (or 'terrestrial') world of our ordinary experience, plus another level, a world of 'spirit' or 'God' or 'being-itself', normally not visible and yet charged with energy and power, actual even though non-material, and 'more real' than the terrestrial or visible.

This basic division of reality into two levels is often elaborated into multiple levels (a 'third heaven', or a 'seventh heaven', etc.). Professor Smith speaks of four levels that are explicitly or implicitly affirmed in most pre-modern traditions: the 'terrestrial' plane of the visible space-time world; the 'intermediate' plane between the terrestrial and the higher non-material planes (the level of dreams, archetypes, good and evil spirits, etc.); the 'celestial plane' in which the gods (or God) are experienced as personal beings; and the level of the 'infinite', where the infinite 'ground' or 'source' is experienced without attributes or differentiation.

Secondly, the levels of reality are not completely separate from each other, but are connected. This notion of connectedness is seen in the nearly universal claim that the visible world has its source or ground in the non-visible: the two worlds are connected as creator and creation, as source and product, as ground and plant. Moreover, the two worlds are connected not simply at 'the beginning' in an initial act of creation, but continually: in each moment, the terrestrial world depends upon the other world for its existence. The other world 'floods' this world with its reality; the terrestrial vibrates with divine reality.[1] Connectedness is also affirmed in the notion of 'sacred moments' in which the other world is experienced, 'sacred places' which function as connectors between the two worlds, 'sacred times' which become openings to the transcendent, and 'sacred persons' who become connectors between the two worlds in exceptional or ritualized moments. In short, the other levels of reality are not completely separate from the terrestrial, but interpenetrate it.

In very simple language, these two characteristics of the primordial tradition are expressed in a current exhibition recounting the history of King's College chapel in Cambridge, England. The text accompanying the exhibition begins, 'The people who built this chapel thought of the universe, the whole of what there is, as twofold.' It then continues, 'These two worlds are not sealed off from one another', rather 'there are places which are thresholds between them' and 'people in whom the two worlds join' (then are listed Mary, Jesus, prophets, saints, bishops, and kings). In short, reality is minimally twofold, and there are connectors or mediators between the two worlds.

The third defining element of the primordial tradition is the claim that the other levels of reality are experienced or known. They are not simply elements of belief. In every culture known to us, there are people who have vivid subjective experiences of another world. These experiences cover a broad spectrum: moments of mystical union, visions, theophanies and hierophanies, nature mysticism, extraordinary dreams, good and evil spirits (Professor Smith even includes a vivid exorcism in his exposition of this point).[2] If the word 'shaman' is not defined too narrowly, this is the 'shamanic universe', a root image of a multi-leveled reality generated by intense experiences of an extraordinary kind. Thus the notion of other realms is not simply the speculative creation of our pre-modern ancestors, arising out of pre-scientific curiosity or primal anxiety, but is grounded in experience. Indeed, Professor Smith's four levels of reality can usefully be understood as a categorizing of the kinds of experiences people have. The primordial tradition, as a way of imaging reality, is the natural result of these kinds of experiences.

Thus the primordial tradition is most essentially constituted by three elements: a 'tiered' understanding of reality, with the levels connected in various ways, all capable of being experienced. This is the way people both pictured and experienced their 'world' prior to the modern period. As Professor Smith stresses, the primordial tradition was the virtual 'human unanimity',[3] a root image that was almost culturally universal.

Smith's characterization of the primordial tradition can also be clarified by means of contrast. The essential contrast, of course, is the way of imaging reality that constitutes 'modernity' and 'the modern mind'. Its central characteristic is a 'one-levelled' understanding of reality. Only the terrestrial plane is 'real'; only the visible world of our ordinary experience and as disclosed by science belongs to the category of 'what is'.

This one-layered root image flowed out of the new way of knowing that emerged in the Enlightenment, namely through observation and verification. The new way of knowing led rather naturally (though not necessarily) to an inference about what is real: only that is real which is knowable in this way. Epistemology shaped ontology, lens shaped image.

What began among a bold intellectual elite in the seventeenth and eighteenth centuries has become the dominant consciousness of our culture, the foundation of the 'modern mind'.[4] The polemic in Smith's writings is directed against this modern understanding of reality, as both image and lens. To use a metaphor important to him, the modern world-view sees only two dimensions of what is in fact a 'three-dimensional cross', only a world of space and time and not a world of spirit.[5] Or, to use an image which he borrows from Karl Popper, the modern way of knowing is like a searchlight scanning the night sky: it can illuminate only that which comes within its beam, and casts no light on that which is outside of its sweep.[6] In the modern mind, science as a way of knowing (which Smith describes with wonder and admiration) becomes 'scientism', the presumption that only what can be known in that way is real.[7] Thus the modern world-view denies, and in a sense cannot 'see', that which is most central to the primordial tradition.

To conclude this section on defining the primordial tradition, one further point merits mention. Describing the primordial tradition as we have may be considered a broad definition. Sometimes the notion is given a narrower connotation (perhaps unintentionally) by its association with 'the great chain of being', an association which Smith has frequently made himself. The association comes about by taking the notion of connectedness in the direction of plenitude and gradation: the notions that reality 'overflows', filling every possible potentiality; and that reality is 'gradated' from the top downward in a descending chain of being: the infinite, God, archangels, angels, humans, lower animals, rocks, etc. When this happens, something very like Neoplatonism results.

Yet it seems to me that it is a mistake to identify the primordial tradition very closely with the great chain of being. True, one might argue that the great chain of being is the most intellectually elegant expression of the primordial tradition; one might also argue that it is the esoteric core of most or all religious traditions. But to identify the great chain of being and the primordial tradition too closely conflicts with the claim that the primordial tradition is nearly universal; the implication that all pre-modern cultures are forms of Neoplatonism seems rightfully suspect. Rather, as a near cultural universal, the virtual 'human unanimity' found at the core of all pre-modern cultures, the primordial tradition embraces and is expressed in a vast array of cultural forms, indeed in as many forms as there are cultures, a root image underlying both esoteric and exoteric traditions. It is therefore not to be identified with any particular map of reality. Rather, as a root image it is a 'concept of structure', an underlying pattern whose elements can vary considerably in their specific content.

The Primordial Tradition and the Biblical Tradition

When the primordial tradition is defined in this broad way, then it becomes immediately apparent that it is the root image of reality which we find in the biblical tradition. The notion that there are minimally two levels of reality — the world of our ordinary experience and 'another reality' — lies at the core of the biblical tradition. It speaks of (and presupposes) a multiple-levelled understanding of reality. Though there is not much precision to the levels, the other world itself is portrayed as including different kinds of spiritual beings: angels, archangels, principalities, powers, cherubim, seraphim, councils of gods.

At the ultimate level of the world of Spirit and spirits is, of course, God. God is 'the lord of both heaven and earth'. As in the primordial tradition, God can be imaged both as the supreme being at the apex of the celestial plane, and as infinite encompassing Spirit. As a personal transcendent being on the celestial plane, God is spoken of as a distinct being 'up in heaven'. As the immanent omnipresent Spirit, God is spoken of as that 'in which we live and move and have our being' (Acts 17.28), as the Spirit from whose presence we can never depart (Psalm 139), as the one who fills both earth and heaven and the highest heaven (1 Kings 8).

As in the primordial tradition, the two worlds of the visible and the invisible are connected in many ways in the Jewish-Christian scriptures. The terrestrial world has its origin and ground in God: God is the creator of heaven and earth. Moreover, the created world is sometimes spoken of as the manifestation of God, as in passages which speak of God's 'glory' manifest on the terrestrial plane: 'The whole earth is full of God's glory' (Isaiah 6.4). 'Glory' in the Hebrew Bible is associated with the presence of God, and connotes 'radiant presence': thus, the earth is filled with the radiant presence of God.[8] God can show through the face of nature, and nature itself can become a sacrament, a vehicle of the sacred.

The two worlds are connected in other ways as well. As the institutionalized place of God's presence, the temple on Mount Zion was the 'navel of the earth', the *axis mundi* joining this world to the world which gave it birth. Other sacred places are referred to as thresholds or gates or doors into the other world, as in Jacob's exclamation after his night vision of angels ascending and descending on a fiery ladder: 'Truly this is the gate of heaven' (Genesis 28.17).

The two worlds are also connected in the extraordinary kinds of experiences which are reported throughout the biblical tradition. There are experiences of journeying into the other world. Paul speaks of being 'caught up into the third heaven' (11 Cor.12), and stories are told of Elijah, Ezekiel, and Jesus 'journeying in the Spirit'. Throughout both testaments, people have visions in which they momentarily 'see' into the other world. The book of Ezekiel's prophecies begins with, 'The heavens were opened and I saw visions of God' (1.1). The visions of the last book of the Christian Bible are introduced with the affirmation, 'I looked and behold in heaven an open door' (Rev. 4.1). Indeed, most of the major figures of the tradition are visionaries: Abraham, Jacob, Moses, the prophets, Jesus, Peter, Paul, John of Patmos. There are also theophanies and hierophanies, manifestations of 'God' or 'the holy'. Sometimes these may take visionary forms; at other times, they involve a momentary transfiguration of ordinary reality.

The accounts of the two most central figures of the tradition, Moses and Jesus, presuppose the root image of reality found in the primordial tradition in an especially clear way. Both function in the accounts as 'holy persons', i.e. people experientially in touch with the sacred who become mediators between the two worlds, delegates from the tribe to the other world, to use an anthropological characterization. Moses regularly ascends Mount Sinai (symbolically, the sacred mountain connecting the two worlds) where he encounters God, and becomes the revealer of the divine will. He is also mediator of divine power in the stories of the mighty deeds accompanying the exodus. He was one who 'knew God face to face and mouth to mouth' (Deut. 32.10; Num. 12.8).

The accounts of Jesus' ministry similarly presuppose the primordial tradition's map of reality. He had visions, and indeed undertook a vision quest (the forty-day fast in the wilderness). In his healings and exorcisms he became a connector between the realm of Spirit and the terrestrial world. Stories report that people experienced the 'cloud of the numinous' around him.[9] In his teaching, he spoke from the vantage point (and with the authority) of one whose perception had been transformed by the experience of another reality.[10] And, of course, the framework for the story of his life speaks of two worlds: born of a virgin by the Spirit and raised to the right hand of God after his death, Jesus came from the world of Spirit and returned to the realm of Spirit.

In short, at the heart of the biblical tradition is a root image of reality radically different from our own. Indeed, seeing the way the biblical tradition is permeated by the primordial tradition's image of reality as minimally two-fold yields a highly compact but illuminating definition of the former: Scripture is the story (and stories) of the relationship between the two worlds.[11] More precisely, the Hebrew Bible is ancient Israel's story of the relationship between the two worlds as perceived in her own experience, and the Greek New Testament is the early Church's story of the relationship between the two worlds as perceived in Jesus and their post-Easter experience.[12] It is a definition of Scripture which takes seriously what is in the texts themselves.

Biblical Scholarship and the Modern Root Image

Yet this understanding of Scripture has not, for the most part, significantly informed modern biblical scholarship. Indeed, quite the opposite is the case. To a large extent, the defining characteristic of biblical scholarship in the modern period is the attempt to understand Scripture without reference to another world. Born in the Enlightenment, which radically transformed all academic disciplines, modern biblical scholarship has sought to understand its subject matter in accord with the root image of reality that dominates the modern mind.

As noted earlier, a root image functions as both a picture of reality and a lens. When the biblical tradition is seen through the lens which accompanies the modern world-view, then the 'other world' is either denied or 'bracketed', that is, set aside. In the battle between supernaturalism and rationalism which reached its peak in the early 1800s, the reality of the other world (or at least its interaction with this world) was essentially denied. 'Rational' explanations — that is, 'rational' within the framework of a one-dimensional understanding of reality — were offered for texts which spoke of 'supernatural' phenomena. Treatments of the miraculous provide the best known instance of this. Texts reporting miracles were either understood psychosomatically or as mistaken perceptions of quite 'natural' events. They were to be understood wholly within the framework of interactions within the terrestrial world.

In biblical scholarship in our century, the aggressive denial of the two-foldness of reality has largely been replaced by a 'bracketing' or ignoring of the question. The major sub-disciplines which have emerged in the past several decades are those which can be done without reference to other levels of reality: studies of the way the biblical writers redacted the tradition which they received, the form and functions of various literary and oral genres, the rhetorical structure of texts, social factors shaping or reflected in texts, the development of early Christian tradition expressed in the texts, etc. All share in common the fact that they focus on the 'this worldly' aspects of the texts: their sources, forms, functions, social and historical 'rootedness', etc. They treat the kinds of questions and claims that are intelligible within the framework of the modern world-view.

All of this is legitimate. The texts do indeed have 'this-worldly' features. Indeed, in an important sense, the texts are completely 'this-worldly': they are human creations, the products of historical communities and individuals over a long expanse of time. Biblical scholarship's focus on the this-worldly aspects of the texts has been immensely illuminating, interesting and important. Yet, for the most part, modern biblical scholarship has left something out. Though the texts as texts are completely 'this-worldly' they often speak about another reality, the 'other world' of the primordial tradition. In modern scholarship, what the texts say about that other reality is seldom the subject of study.

The effects of modernity can be seen not only in the types of sub-disciplines which have emerged, but also in the dominant modes of interpretation operative in biblical scholarship through much of this century. The two most influential hermeneutical approaches in mainstream Protestant biblical scholarship have both stressed the historical and this-worldly meanings of the texts.[13]

Within that scholarship, the interpretation of the Hebrew Bible was dominated by a 'covenant-historical' model. What is important, it was affirmed, is what the Old Testament says about the world of history. Indeed, the centrality of history in the Old Testament was seen as its defining characteristic. Sometimes this emphasis was even seen as unique, allegedly distinguishing it from all other religious traditions (and thus also from the primordial tradition). What mattered was not what the Old Testament might say about another world, but its concern with historical existence in this world.

To some extent, of course, this emphasis flows out of a central feature of the Hebrew Bible: it is organized around a historical narrative involving the experience of a people through time. It does assign more importance to historical and political existence than many religious traditions do. But one suspects that the hermeneutical emphasis upon history is also because of the importance that the world of history has come to have in the modern period: it is the world we think of as 'real', the visible world of space and time. We are led to see the texts in a particular way by our root image of reality.

Within New Testament scholarship, a similar dynamic can be seen.

Here the most influential hermeneutic permeating the discipline has been existentialist interpretation, seminally (and also most fully) represented by Rudolf Bultmann. Bultmann's work has an ironic dimension. More clearly than most, he recognized the very different world-view found in the texts of the New Testament; his famous essay speaking of the 'three-storey universe' has become a classic.[14] But then, in a hermeneutical move which graphically exemplifies the modern mind, he sought in his program of demythologizing and existentialist interpretation to translate that language into what it says about life in this world. Language about another world is to be understood in terms of its reference to human existence, its actualities and possibilities. The other world is vividly recognized, only immediately to be demythologized.

As with the covenant-historical model for interpreting the Hebrew Bible, this hermeneutic does illuminate central features of the texts. In a sense, the language of the New Testament does need 'demythologizing'. Its cosmology of heaven above and Hades below is simply part of an earlier world-view. Language about another world is a different kind of language and is certainly not to be taken literally. Moreover, to a large extent the New Testament is sharply focused on human existence, its bondage and liberation. The existentialist interpretation of Paul is very impressive. Much of the message of Jesus can be powerfully understood in this way, as existentialist interpretation of his wisdom teachings (parables, aphorisms, proverbs) shows.

Thus the two dominant hermeneutics are not mistaken in what they affirm. Rather, their limitation lies in what they overlook. By seeking to translate biblical language about another world only or primarily into language about human existence in history, they effectively eliminate that language as language about another world, or about experiences of another world. Yet it is possible to take this language about another world seriously, even though not literally. To a large extent, it is the language of the 'imagination', that part of us that creates and responds to symbols and images. The crucial question is, 'What are these images and symbols about?' Are they simply an oblique way of talking about existence in this world? Or are they a way of speaking about realities and energies that people have actually experienced? It is this latter possibility that is largely overlooked. In much of mainstream biblical scholarship, what is 'demythologized' is not simply language about another world, but the very notion of another world at all. What disappears is what is arguably most central to the texts: the world of Spirit.

Modern biblical scholarship's concentration on the this-worldly characteristics, functions, and meanings of the texts points to the fact that what is at work is not simply a collection of modern methods, but also a lens, a way of seeing. That lens is, of course, the one that accompanies the modern root image of reality. It enables us to see much, but at the same time circumscribes what we look at. We pay attention to what it says is real. That which falls outside of that image of reality, which is not contained within the perimeter it inscribes, is not 'real'. The modern lens calls our attention to particular features of the texts, but leads us to overlook or avoid others. It defines what the legitimate areas of study are: those which can be addressed within the canons and spirit of modernity.

Re-viewing Scripture through the Lens of the Primordial Tradition

In short, the dominant thrust of biblical scholarship since the Enlightenment has been the effort to understand the biblical tradition within the framework of the modern world-view. We have been attempting to see *their* world through *our* lens. However, what is needed as an essential complement to the rich results of modern scholarship is a way of seeing the biblical texts that does not immediately reduce them to their this-worldly dimensions. We need to 're-view' the biblical tradition with a different lens, one that reflects and refracts the radically different understanding of reality contained in the texts.

Of potentially great value in this effort is an emphasis which has emerged strongly in biblical scholarship in the last decade: the interdisciplinary study of the 'social world' of the biblical texts.[15] Using insights and models derived from the social sciences and cultural anthropology, these studies seek to re-create the 'social world' or 'life world' of the communities whose experience the biblical tradition reports.

Some of these studies limit themselves to illuminating an aspect of the social world of the texts, as when studies of peasant societies or purity/impurity societies are used to disclose and explore similar dynamics in much of Scripture. Even these sharply focused studies illustrate the value of a different lens: we are led to 'see' things we

41

otherwise might not see if we looked only through our cultural lens.

But it is especially when 'social world' is defined in a comprehensive sense that we can see the value of this approach and the importance of the primordial tradition to it. When 'social world' is defined as the *total* social environment of a people, it includes their shared root image of reality. In the case of the biblical tradition (and most pre-modern traditions) that shared root image of reality was of course the primordial tradition. Moreover, the model of reality limned by the primordial tradition was not simply one element in a belief system, but it was the image of reality which structured their life world — their perception, experience, thought, practices, social organization and political institutions. It was foundational to their way of seeing and being.

Taking this alternative model of reality seriously enables us increasingly to see their world through their lens. Doing so completely is impossible, of course; we never cease to be twentieth-century persons. But by imaginatively reconstructing their mental and experiential world, we are enabled somewhat to see from within their perspective. It is an exercise in 'passing over' from one culture to another; not just seeing one culture through the lens provided by another, but the ability to enter into another perspective and to 'see' from that vantage point.

Re-viewing the biblical tradition through the lens provided by the primordial tradition would generate questions in addition to those which have dominated modern scholarship. Texts which report paranormal religious experiences could be studied not only for their literary structure or redactional history, but also for what they may say about religious experience, and the role of that experience in generating the tradition. Vision texts could be studied not only for their literary characteristics and historical rootedness, but also for what the vision may be saying about experiences of another reality.[16] Healing and exorcism texts could be studied not only for their redaction and literary form, but also for what they may say about an experiential tradition.[17]

It is important to note that taking material like this seriously does not require an ontological affirmation. One does not need to affirm the ontological actuality of another world in order to take seriously the fact that people had experiences which they believed to be experiences of another world. One may ask, 'What do these texts say about those experiences?', while still leaving the ontological question in brackets; that is, unresolved. However, taking this material seriously does require a momentary bracketing of the modern world-view. So long as we do not set aside the modern root image, our vision remains limited by it. Our own image of reality circumscribes what we can *imagine* the texts to be saying.

Some ways of seeing and some models of reality enable us to see more than others. The primordial tradition provides a way of seeing the biblical tradition that enables us to see more clearly the world of the texts. It is a world very different from our own, one not simply or exhaustively to be understood in categories drawn from our world. There is an 'otherness' in the texts — not only the otherness of a distant culture, but the otherness of an image of reality radically different from our own. An approach to the texts which does not see this does not see them fully.

Operating within us at the level of the imagination, a level deeper than the discursive intellect, root images of reality involve the imaging or intuiting of a whole *Gestalt* in light of which everything else is seen. As the root image of reality of the biblical writers themselves, the primordial tradition enables us to see Scripture through their lens rather than simply through our lens: as the story of the intersections between the two worlds, a narrative of creation and history, of epiphanies and incarnation, of encounter and response, all occurring in a world which is filled with the glory of God.[18]

Notes

1. For Smith's powerful description of Pascal's famous vision of fire as a moment when reality as a whole 'vibrated' with a radiance that was both transcendent and immanent, see *Forgotten Truth*, p.33.
2. *Ibid*, pp.43-6.
3. *Ibid*, pp.x, 5, 18.
4. In Smith's own words, 'the final definition of modernity' is 'an outlook in which this world, this ontological plane, is the only one that is genuinely countenanced and affirmed'. *Forgotten Truth*, p.6.
5. The 'three-dimensional cross' is the central image (and title) of the second chapter of *Forgotten Truth*, pp.19-33.
6. *Ibid*, pp.8-9.
7. *Ibid*, p.16.

8. The passages which speak of God's glory being manifest on the terrestrial plane are probably not enough to establish the notion of plenitude; though the notion of 'gradation' can be found in a few texts, there is no indication that it was a central conviction of the biblical writers.

9. A point stressed by Rudolf Otto in *The Idea of the Holy*, Oxford University Press, New York, 1958, pp.155-9.

10. For an account of the ministry and message of Jesus within the framework of the primordial tradition, see my *Jesus: A New Vision*, Harper & Row, San Francisco, 1987, especially chapters 3, 4 and 6.

11. This definition of Scripture as the story of the relationship between two worlds is very consistent with the work of Mircea Eliade, another 'bridge person' important in the development of my perception. See especially his *The Sacred and the Profane*, Harcourt, Brace & World, New York, 1959; *Myth and Reality*, Harper & Row, New York, 1963; and his technical study *Shamanism: Archaic Techniques of Ecstasy*, Pantheon, New York, 1964.

12. 'Scripture as Story' is a growing hermeneutical movement in contemporary biblical theology. For a popular-level introduction, see John Shea, *Stories of God*, Thomas More, Chicago, 1978.

13. Until recently, mainstream biblical scholarship was primarily Protestant and, to a lesser extent, Jewish. For the most part, Roman Catholic scholars entered the stream only after World War II.

14. Originally published in German in 1941, the essay may be found in H.W. Bartsch, ed., *Kerygma and Myth*, Harper & Row, New York, 1961, pp.1-16.

15. So important is this emphasis that it is one of the central characteristics of the resurgence in historical Jesus studies. See my essay 'A Renaissance in Jesus Studies' from *Theology Today* Vol.45: 280-292, October 1988.

16. Not all biblical vision texts should be taken as reflecting actual visionary experience; some seem to be consciously contrived literary creations designed to carry a particular message. But, unless we are inclined to deny that visions 'happen', it seems likely that some vision texts do reflect actual visionary experiences.

17. A few studies have already done this. In my own field of historical Jesus studies, two important recent studies are Geza Vermes, *Jesus the Jew*, Macmillan, New York, 1973; and James Dunn, *Jesus and the Spirit*, Westminster, Philadelphia, 1975. Vermes takes seriously the gospel texts which locate Jesus in the experiential stream of charismatic Judaism, with its paranormal phenomena of healings, exorcisms, visions and auditions. Dunn treats many of the 'Spirit' texts in the gospels as reflecting actual experiences of Jesus. In the field of Pauline studies, James D. Tabor's *Things Unutterable*, University Press of America, Lanham Md, 1986, locates Paul's ecstatic experience in 11 Cor.12 in the context of other 'heavenly journey' texts. But such studies are few compared to the vast number that basically bracket the fact that the texts contain a root image of reality radically different from our own.

18. In a personal note to Professor Smith a few years ago, I described *Forgotten Truth* as 'the best work in religious apologetics' known to me. By that I meant something very specific. His work is not religious apologetics in the common sense of seeking to persuade one of the truth of a particular religious tradition, often at the expense of other traditions. Rather, by expositing the root image of reality common to the primordial tradition and by exposing the modern root image as a limited way of seeing, his work makes religious traditions in general credible by making their central claims *imaginable*.

CHAPTER 7

To hear the stars speak: ontology in the study of religion(s)

M. Darrol Bryant

> *Knowledge is a shoreless ocean in which the knower's*
> *soul is a signpost.*
>
> *Khwaja Abdullah Ansari (1006-1089)*
> *Intimate Conversations with God*

The title of this exploration points to a central issue that arises in the believing heart of a human being and in the work of a contemporary student of religion. For the believing human being it is the question of relating the truth given in one's own tradition to the truth that resounds in traditions other than one's own. For the contemporary student of religion it is the question that arises from years of study of religious traditions where one is continually confronted by varied beliefs, rituals, disciplines and ways that point to dimensions of reality that transcend the mundane. In this latter context, those transcendent dimensions of reality lay claim upon the student of religion not only to be acknowledged as part of the religious tradition one is attempting to understand in relation to its history, inner development, and cultural context, but *as such*. The modern study of religion has, however, by and large refused to acknowledge the claims of the transcendent as it is mediated through the study of diverse religious traditions of humankind. Instead, we have chosen the strategy of segmentalizing and bracketing as, in part, our way into another tradition on its own terms, but also as a way of protecting ourselves and our discipline from the troubling realities with which religions have ultimately to do.

But before we proceed, allow me this qualification: there is much in

46

the strategy of segmentalizing and bracketing that needs to be affirmed. Ninian Smart, one of our foremost scholars of religion, has written that 'one of the great achievements of modern scholarship is the invention of the modern study of religion.'[1] I agree. Moreover, Smart goes on to locate what he calls 'crosscultural bracketing' at the 'heart of the modern study of religion'.[2]

And even here I find myself in agreement with him as he explains the centrality of learning to 'walk in another's moccasins' to the modern study of religion. It has been this methodological strategy which has allowed the study of religion to become something more than distorted commentary on the religious life and faith of another from an assumed vantage point of cultural, religious or philosophical superiority. The practice of bracketing, writes Smart, 'involves trying to present the beliefs, symbols and activities of the other . . . from the perspective of that other.'[3] Such a discipline of structured empathy, of learning to truly enter into the religious life of human beings is essential to the modern study of religion. It is so fundamental that I take it as a given for the contemporary scholar of religion.

However, the practice of 'walking in another's moccasins' cannot be wholly divorced from taking seriously that towards which the other walks, namely the Ultimate. For the Plains Indian, when we walk in our moccasins we walk on Mother Earth, and for the Blackfoot, in the presence of Napi.[4] And even in our sleep, our dreams, the Indians believed, unfold as glimpses of the Great Spirit within which all life unfolds.[5] Likewise, the Bushmen of Southern Africa not only endure in one of the harshest climates known to human beings, the Great Kalahari, but they also hear the stars and find the infinite in the mantis.[6] And when the *bhakra(s)* watch the dances of Krishna and Radha they are not only being entertained in the here and now, but are also being lifted up into the Eternal Play (*lila*) where the fullness of our being resides.[7] When the counsel of caution in our study, the injunction not to enforce a frame of reference inappropriate to the study of different peoples and religions, or even our own, is transformed into an ontology of ignorance concerning that towards which the believer walks, then we have refused to walk the crucial second mile where real compassion and new dimensions of understanding might arise.

This is not to deny that there is great wisdom in counselling restraint, in learning to leave questions open, in waiting upon the results of further enquiry before rushing to premature judgements.

Often such a strategy involves circumscribing the intent of our study, of focusing now only upon the historical setting in which a particular religious tradition or practice unfolds, or upon particular aspects of a given tradition. But what I want here to call our attention to is the obvious dynamic present to the whole range of humankind's religious venture, namely that it seeks to relate the human to a dimension of reality that transcends the historical and cultural contexts our methods can easily engage. What place, if any, should those dimensions have in the study of religion?

Again, there is no easy answer. But having said that, it does seem to me wise to turn to such questions from time to time. The reasons are twofold: first, as I have already suggested, the very stuff of religion demands it. And secondly, the integrity of the discipline requires that from time to time we offer a report on where we are on this question — a report card, if you will.

II

Let me further note that these questions have been prompted anew in me by my recent sabbatical (1986-7) in India. I had gone to India to deepen my familiarity with the great traditions of the subcontinent. While there I tried to spend as much time as possible in the many religious communities that constitute religious life in India. I visited temples, mosques, gurdwaras and churches, and spent long hours talking with Hindus, Muslims, Sikhs, Buddhists and Christians. During those months I visited Vrindaban and Varanasi, seeking to allow those traditions of Hindu faith and piety to enter my life and consciousness, I travelled to Dharamsala to visit the Tibetan Buddhists and share in their meditation, I sat in mosques in Delhi as the faithful gathered for prayers, I felt something of the anguish of Sikhs at this present moment, and I learned something of Indian Christianity in Kerala and Tamil Nadu. As I sat in Vrindaban watching a festival of dance centered on Krishna and Radha, or went from temple to temple on Diwale, I became aware not only of the necessity of understanding the religious life of the devotee, the *bhakta* in its historical and cultural context, but also of acknowledging those glimpses of the divine that beat upon my heart and mind. Is it enough to just describe this life in relation to the self-understanding of a Hindu? Of a Buddhist? Or a Sikh? Or a Muslim? Was not I, as a scholar of religion and a human being, also under some obligation to acknowledge, at least inwardly, what was being mediated to me through their faith and practice and ritual?

These questions are, of course, too large to be easily answered. But the experience points, I believe, to the issue that we in the study of religion are called to address, and it is here, I believe, that we have much to do. That issue is, of course, the truth of that to which religion points and that which is mediated to us through the faith, rituals, and gestures of men and women in the great traditions. It is in religious life, believers from every tradition report and scholars of religion acknowledge descriptively, that the human and divine meet, where the eternal is present to the temporal, where the longing of the spirit for the ultimate is most dramatically disclosed. But the difficulty that confronts us in the study of religion is, first, to acknowledge that Beyond, and then to find a language adequate to express, at least in part, what we encounter in religion and suitable to the demands of scholarship. This is not just a problem of right words, but more importantly of the right views of things within which the words and acts of religious life resonate and direct us, *and* in the view of things within which we hear what is spoken in word and gesture within the traditions being studied. The problem with the modern study of religion is that it unfolds with a *modern* view of reality that is, in principle, hostile to the truth known in religion. For in the modern view, reality is wholly explicable from within, there is no Beyond that must be appealed to in order to understand what is. Nor is there any Beyond that is mediated in the religious life of humankind. How then can we understand religion when the implicit ontology or view of things that we bring to the study of religion rules out *a priori* the ontologies of the religious traditions within which religions unfolds? In such a situation, the implicit ontology of a given religion is not only cast into radical doubt — an ever present possibility — but is rendered nonsensical.

In part this difficulty rests in the reluctance of the modern study of religion to deal with the ontological aspects of its subject, of its implicit or covert submission to what Huston Smith has called 'scientism'; that is, the reduction of reality to the space/time co-ordinates of modern science. Clearly here the religious traditions confront the modern scholar with a dilemma: either to ignore those dimensions of religion which exceed the constraints of scientism, or to run the risk of being considered, in the context of modern scientism, outdated and outside the paradigm of modern scholarship.[8] The signal contribution of Huston Smith to the study of religion involves the recovery of what he calls the 'primordial tradition', or what we might here call the multi-layered account of reality to be found within the religious history of humankind. Smith is well known for his celebrated, now classic, introduction to the world's religions: *The Religions of Man*. But in his later *Forgotten Truth: The Primordial Tradition*, Smith retrieved the question that the modern study of religion has been at such pains to avoid, or at least 'bracket': the question of truth. In his *Forgotten Truth*, Smith not only demonstrates that religion unfolds within a shared ontology or account of reality, but he had the audacity to affirm that that ontology was true and an improvement over the impoverished account of reality bequeathed to us in modern science. In crossing the boundary from the study of religion to the affirmation of its truth, Smith led the way into what I would call the post-modern study of religion.[9]

Before proceeding, it is necessary to clarify two phrases that I am using here: the modern study of religion and the post-modern study of religion. By the 'modern' study I mean that approach to the study of religion that assumes the truth of that modern account of the way things are, that claims that reality is exhausted by what is made available to us in the modern paradigm of knowledge; that is, through the empirical sciences. In this approach the Beyond is, at best, bracketed, at worst denied. But my point is that such an approach to religion precludes an encounter with the depth dimensions of the religious traditions where they point to the Beyond, or transcendent dimensions of reality. In what I here call the 'post-modern study of religion' there is an attempt to move beyond the restrictions placed upon the modern study of religion by its covert assent to 'scientism', by reopening the question of the Beyond in relation to the study of religion. In the post-modern approach, then, we have become aware that the assumptions of the modern paradigm need not be presumed and we are thus free to explore again the depth dimensions of the religious traditions, and especially their ontologies or world-views.

Thus in that post-modern study of religion to which Smith points us, we move beyond the reductionist presuppositions that characterized modern study; that is, the assumption that only those dimensions of religious life that are explicable within a scientistic view of reality were legitimate. In its post-modern study we can begin to explore those dimensions of religious life that unfold within what Huston Smith has called 'the primordial tradition'. In *Forgotten Truth*,

Smith turned again to the world's enduring traditions of religious life, but this time 'to see how they converge'.[10] The convergence that Smith discerns obviously does not reside in the foreground of each tradition or its contents. Rather what he saw was that they were 'structurally very much alike'.[11] This structural similarity that cut across the traditions, or perhaps better, underlay the traditions, is most evident in Smith's account of the multi-layered understanding of reality and of human being found across traditions.This great unanimity, Smith argued, has been especially obscured for us by the account of the 'way things are' that emerged within modern science.

While modern science, Smith contends, shares with the more traditional accounts of reality a hierarchical structure, there the similarity ends.[12] For modern science, the macro, meso and micro-worlds are accessible only in terms of quantity. Reality becomes that which we can measure and enumerate; space, size and strength of forces become its keys and the focus of attention. In the traditional hierarchy of earth, higher planes and lower planes, or heaven, earth and hell, however, the units of measure differed. There the issue was quality, the significance of being in the order of things. Life was to be lived out in relation to 'a Great Chain of Being' that linked each to all, the worlds above and below to the human world between. But for the modern account of the way things are, an account that views all there is as a spatio-temporal continuum, the traditional view with its recognition of a different ontological status for things, persons, angels and gods was nonsense. Thus, as Smith notes, 'science challenged by implication the notion that other planes exist.'[13] And since that challenge was not effectively addressed — and it could not be on the premises of modern science itself — the traditional view was eclipsed. And with that eclipse came the pervasive confusions and uncertainties that have surrounded values, purposes, meanings and quality in the modern era. For, as Smith rightly observes, 'modernity' is 'an outlook in which this world, this ontological plane, is the only one that is genuinely countenanced and affirmed.'[14] But such a view is, Smith is careful to point out, an unwarranted consequence of modern science, it is science transformed into 'scientism'. This distinction is crucial to his argument — and to ours here as well.

When the dimension of reality illumined by modern science is taken to be *the full account of what is*, then science has been transformed into what Smith calls 'scientism', a method of investigation into an ideology. Here it is important to quote Smith more fully.

> With science itself there can be no quarrel. Scientism is another matter. Whereas science is positive, contenting itself with reporting what it discovers, scientism is negative. It goes beyond the actual findings of science to deny that other approaches to knowledge are valid and other truths true.[15]

Thus for Smith it is this extra-scientific extrapolation that is at issue, the denial of other approaches and truths. His is not a contemporary Luddite mentality. Rather he is concerned to track down the philosophical roots of our contemporary cultural distress. And, for Smith, those roots lie in the abandonment of the primordial tradition that sustained the human longing for purpose, value, and meaning: for being illumined from Beyond.

When some ground is thus cleared, Smith turns to the exposition of the primordial tradition primarily in relation to two key conceptions: levels of reality and levels of selfhood. The point here is that the different religious traditions shared a common account of the way things are that included a multi-layered account of reality and of humanity. In that shared ontology, reality is 'terrestrial, intermediate, celestial, and infinite', [16] and likewise humanity is 'body, mind, soul, and spirit.'[17] One can quarrel with Smith's terminology and his illustrations from the several traditions, but his general account is, at least to me, persuasive. What is central here is not, in my view, the details but a recognition that religious life unfolds in a more complex ontology than the modern one we so often implicitly assume, even in the modern study of religion. It is this implicit consent to a view of things that renders religious claims not only open to doubt, but nonsensical, that has led to the reluctance of modern students of religion to deal with the transcendental aspects of the traditions studied. But if we take Smith's analysis seriously, we have the beginnings of another way to understand religious life and activity. It is a way that at least grants the integrity of the ontology within which religious life has unfolded.

Smith's account of the primordial tradition reminds us that we moderns are the great dissenters, the ones who have dissented from 'the human unanimity'.[18] That we need to relearn the language and ways of that longer tradition and its view of things is, or at least should be, obvious to the student of religion who has experienced, as I have, the inner conflict between what seemed to be the demands of the discipline to conform to scientism and the demands of the traditions studied to recognize dimensions of self and reality that transcended the material stratum of modern science. If Smith is right — and I think he is — then we have to revise our understanding of reality and the human. We need to do this not only because that view of things found in the primordial tradition is true, but also because it is only within such a framework that we, as scholars of religion, can do justice to that we are committed to study. Consider, for example, the moving incident that Laurens van der Post recounts in his *The Heart of the Hunter*. The incident occurs on the evening after his party met a small group of Bushmen that had suddenly appeared out of the blazing heat of the Kalahari desert of Southern Africa. They were without food or water, but doggedly moving towards the lightning that had appeared on the horizon the night before. After receiving water and food, the Bushmen had camped nearby and van der Post had gone to visit them.

Then suddenly, ahead in a band of absolute black with no fire to pale it down, I thought I heard the sound of a human voice. I stopped at once and listened carefully. The sound came again more distant, like the voice of a woman crooning over a cradle. I stood with my back to the horizon bright with portents of lightning, waiting for my eyes to recover from the glare of our great campfire. Slowly, against the water-light of the stars lapping briskly among the breakers of thorn and hardwood around us, emerged the outline of a woman holding out a child in both her hands, high above her head, and singing something with her own face lifted to the sky. Her attitude and the reverence trembling in her voice moved me so that the hair at the back of my neck stood on end.

'What's she doing?' I whispered to Dabe [a Bushman raised among Europeans who was part of van der Post's party], who had halted without a sound, like my own star-shadow beside me.

'She's asking the stars up there,' he whispered, like a man requested in the temple of his people to explain to a stranger a most solemn moment of their ritual. 'She's asking the stars to take the little heart of her child and to give him something of the heart of a star in return.'

'But why the stars?' I asked.

'Because, Moren,' he said in a matter-of-fact tone, 'the stars there have heart in plenty and are great hunters. She is asking them to take from her little child his little heart and to give him the heart of a hunter.'

The explanation moved me to a silence which Dabe mistook. Afraid, I suspect, that like most of the people he knew in his life of exile I would scorn a Bushman's belief, he wanted reassurance immediately.

'But why don't you say something, Moren?' he asked . . . 'Surely you must know that the stars are great hunters? Can't you hear them? Do listen to what they are crying! Come on! Moren! You are not so deaf that you cannot hear them.'

I hastened to say, 'Yes, Dabe, of course I hear them!' But then I was forced to add, 'Only I do not know what they are saying. Do you know?'

Reassured, he stood for a moment, head on one side, while the light of another flash from the horizon flew like a ghost moth by us. Then, with the note of indulgence he could not resist using on me when he felt his authority not in doubt, he said, 'They are very busy hunting tonight and all I hear are their hunting cries: "Tssik!" and "Tsa!" '[19]

This incident aptly illustrates the quandary we, in the study of religion, often find ourselves in. As 'modern' men and women we could dismiss the whole incident as an example of 'primitive superstition'. Because we know — don't we — that stars do not speak, nor is it possible for the 'little heart of her child' to receive that starborne 'heart of a hunter'? My point, however, is not to argue this issue on such grounds, rather my point is the impoverished way that we understand what is happening if we do not allow our 'modern' view of things to be opened up by such an encounter. Or perhaps better stated: we need to ask about the view of things, the implicit ontology, within which the woman's words and gestures unfold. For here the universe 'speaks' and she, and her child, are part of its interdependent web. If we were to insist on understanding this incident on our implicit 'modern' terms, we could say little. But if we were to attempt to understand it in terms consistent with the primordial tradition, then we could perhaps move closer to its truth. For, as Huston Smith sought to remind us in *Forgotten Truth*, both the human self as 'body, mind, soul and spirit', and reality as 'terrestrial, intermediate, celestial and infinite', are more complex and multi-layered than our reduced modern view allows.

Now it would be clearly preposterous to think that these lofty issues concerning the nature of reality could even be addressed here. I leave that for others. But it is possible here to see something of the implications of different accounts of the way things are — for ourselves and the study of religion. What I hope I have been able to make clear is that we in the modern study of religion have, more often than not, fallen victim to a modern account of the way things are that has profoundly altered our perception of the religious life of humankind, and that the alternative ontology offered by Huston Smith — not as his own but as the cumulative wisdom of the human race discernible in its manifold religious traditions — offers a far richer and more adequate view for unfolding the very content of what we encounter, as students of religion, in the religious life of humankind. In that perspective we could, perhaps, learn again to hear the stars speak.

III

If, as argued above, it is necessary to find ways to acknowledge the truth of the Transcendent given to us in the study of the religious traditions of humankind, where do we begin? We have already seen in Huston Smith's *Forgotten Truth* one consequence, namely a recovery of the shared ontology within which religious life unfolds. There will no doubt be other consequences that will arise as well, indeed some of those have begun to emerge. Wilfred Cantwell Smith, for example, has argued that 'there is a transcendent dimension of human life — so far as I can see, there has always been, from paleolithic times. Most human beings on earth over the centuries have been aware of this and have lived their lives less or more vividly, less or more effectively, in terms of it.'[20] He then goes on to assert that 'the history of religion is simply the process of humankind's double involvement in a mundane and simultaneously a transcendent environment.'[21] For W.C. Smith, this conviction has emerged, he tells us, from his very study of the history of religious life. Another starting point, most eloquently articulated by Raimundo Panikkar, begins with the transcendent depths of the experience of *intrareligious* dialogue. Here one discovers a way into 'the almost universal conviction that reality is ordered ... It is a divine Reality, say most of the human traditions.'[22]

What is significant here — and this is true of Huston Smith, W. Cantwell Smith and Raimundo Panikkar — is the principle that what I call a post-modern approach to religious life must grow out of the religious heritage of humankind itself. This principle, namely that the study of religion must be unfolded according to principles inherent in the religious traditions themselves, is crucial. It holds out the promise of neither reducing the phenomenon of religion to ontologies that are inherently hostile to religious life, nor misconstruing the dynamics of religious life towards the Beyond. This circular argument is not vicious, but necessary. It is analogous to the arguments found in other fields of inquiry: principles for the study of literature must emerge from the study of literature, those in biology from the study of living organisms, etc. When this principle is recognized then we have shifted the study of religion to its proper ground: the manifold encounter with the Transcendent that is the story of the religious life of humankind.

The discipline of the study of religion has, however, both an inner and an outer front — as well as a past and future. On the outer front we read texts, study rituals, observe practices, count noses, observe changes over time, interview devotees, and engage in many other practices. But is there a corresponding inner discipline appropriate to these activities? Here we normally speak about the scholarly virtues of objectivity, empathy, truthful exposition, rigorous attention to detail, openness to the phenomenon, and so forth. And these are central to our work. But there is, I would like to propose, another dimension to this inner discipline as well, namely an inner spiritual discipline. Here I obviously want to play on the dual meaning of discipline as an outward practice and as an inner practice. We tend to pay attention to the former and ignore the latter despite the fact that we, as all human beings, have to struggle with these different dimensions of our life and work. But in each 'discipline' we find these two inter-related aspects. We can readily see, for example, that the working biologist must develop not only the experimental practices of his discipline, but also a set of inward or spiritual disciplines appropriate to his discipline, namely rigorous attention to method, a willingness to heed the results of inquiry, a certain inward distance and objectivity, etc. But we in the study of religion are strangely reluctant to acknowledge the importance of spiritual discipline for the study of religion when we should be most aware of its importance. We seem to fear, I suspect, that here we cross a boundary that separates the study of religion from its practice.

But there is a place where our lives as believers and scholars intersect and meet: in our love for truth. Thus it is appropriate that we as scholars cultivate those disciplines given to us in the religious traditions in order to prepare ourselves inwardly to cling to the truth wherever and as it is given to us. Likewise, our lives as believers in a given tradition will be altered and transformed as we practice the outer discipline of reading the texts of communities other than our own, and empathically enter into their experiences of the truth as it has been manifested to the other. I have certainly felt both the pain and joy of this inward dialectic in my own journey in the study of religion and as a believing Christian. It is in the torn heart that our love of the truth is refined and strengthened. While those disciplines of the inner life must arise within particular communities they can, at least to an extent, be shared across traditions — or at least it seems so to me. But enough: let me sketch a proposal for an inward discipline appropriate to the study of religion as the encounter with the manifold expressions of humankind's life in relation to the Beyond.

My proposal takes as its point of departure Bonaventure's masterful *Itinerarium Mentis in Deum*, which Professor Ewert Cousins has translated as *The Soul's Journey into God*.[23] This thirteenth-century masterpiece sought to instruct its readers in the art of contemplating God. The art Bonaventure conceived as a journey in two senses. First, it is a journey in that one passes through 'stages of ascent' on the way towards God. But secondly, it is also a journey *through* different aspects of creation, the senses, the natural powers, grace, goodness, being and ecstasy. Central to the journey was the contemplation of the 'footprints' or 'vestiges' of Divine presence to be found both at the different stages of the journey and in the different dimensions of life being contemplated. Thus no stage or dimension of life is left unmarked by the divine if one cultivates the spiritual capacities to see and read them aright. But Bonaventure warns his readers that 'the mirror presented by the external world is of little or no value unless the mirror of our soul has been cleaned and polished.'[24] The interplay of the inner and outer are intimately linked for Bonaventure as he moves through the journey of the soul into God.

Perhaps we need to supplement Bonaventure's journey of ascent and learn to *contemplate God through his vestiges in the religious life of humankind*. The inner discipline appropriate to our outer practice, I want to suggest, involves a preparation of the heart to see the religious life of humankind in ways that acknowledge its own central dynamic towards the Beyond. That different traditions have differing conceptions of that Beyond or Ultimate is so obvious that it hardly needs mention, except to say that the aim of such contemplation is not this or that particular conception of the Ultimate. It is rather the inward disposition and willingness to listen to the tradition at their deepest levels. While the Beyond is itself never the direct object of our study, nor even of our contemplation, it is the dynamic present within the tradition that its beliefs, rituals and practices seek to mediate. And unless we cultivate the inner discipline of a willingness to acknowledge what is mediated we miss the heart of the outer practice. Hence we need to cultivate a discipline of allowing the dynamic to shine in and through the beliefs, rituals and actions in order to rightly appreciate the tradition itself. It is, I believe, the inner discipline that will keep us from falling victim to an implicit cultural ontology or ideology that insists that there is no Beyond to acknowledge.

Contemplation is not to be confused either with conceptualizing or with discursive reasoning. Rather, it is the act of holding a certain reality before one and allowing it to shine forth in one's consciousness. Its aim is to deepen openness and encourage receptivity, to allow a certain reality to resonate in one's soul before it is refracted in our faculties of reasoning, willing, or feeling. It is more to be grasped by a whole, than to grasp the whole. It is to elevate and enlarge consciousness in ways appropriate to the object of contemplation. Bonaventure likens the journey to the life of prayer and commends a prayer of Dionysius, a major figure in western mysticism, to his readers:

> Lead me, Lord in your path,
> And I will enter in your truth.
> Let my heart rejoice
> That it may fear your name.[25]

This discipline of prayer is not a substitute for acquaintance with the religious heritage of humankind, nor is it a substitute for intellectual discernment. Rather as a spiritual discipline, it makes clear the necessity to be inwardly prepared for the journey, to open ourselves to wisdom and insight so that we might perceive these vestiges of God present in the religious life of humankind aright. Here it is not a matter of building up an argument — though there is certainly no objection to that as well — but of honing our capacities of receptivity so that we may acknowledge aright what wishes to shine through to us in the religions of humankind.[26] Moreover, it is not at all assured that we will hear aright, or perceive aright, what is given to us in these vestiges. Beyond the spiritual discipline of prayer lies the community of believers and scholars which are bound to receive what one prayerfully hears and to subject it to rigorous examination. Rather here we have the discipline that must mark the path.

Beyond this Bonaventure suggests some principles that may be relevant to this contemplation. These are the same principles that Bonaventure mentions in urging us to contemplate God in his vestiges in creation. These are: origin, magnitude, multitude, beauty, fullness, activity and order. As one contemplates the religions under each of these headings, one discovers features of their life that hitherto remained hidden. It is not that they were not there, but because we did not attend to them aright, namely as vestiges of God left to guide us to the One that is above, we missed these crucial aspects of their reality. Consider, for example, the question of their origin in God or their beauty or multiplicity. Here all the vast array of human religious experience, ritual and doctrine come into view in ways that move us beyond historical relativism and towards (to use Frithjof Schuon's phrase) their Transcendent unity.[27]

Of course, such contemplation will in its preliminary stages be mediated through the images and patterns given to us in our own traditions, but we can also gradually learn to heed aright the images and patterns given to us in traditions other than our own. At the height of this ascent we might move beyond the realm of images altogether in order to glimpse the Light itself, the Light that gives to the images and patterns of the respective traditions their own luminous character. For it is, finally, that Light that is the Truth that we were dimly seeking, though perhaps even unacknowledged at the outset, when the journey had yet to begin.

IV

In summary, then, I have offered here a five-part argument in relation to the place of ontology in the study of religion(s):

1. The modern study of religion has, for all its achievements, been caught within the assumptions of modernity, especially the denial of the Beyond.

2. This situation needs to be overcome if the study of religion is to attain to its proper task of illuminating the religious history of mankind.

3. Huston Smith's critique of 'scientism' and recovery of the primordial tradition points us beyond the modern to the post-modern study of religion. The virtue of his contribution is that it allows the student of religion to take seriously the depth dimensions of the religious traditions and to see them within the context of a richer and more differentiated understanding of the way things are.

4.   In order to take full advantage of the possibilities opened up by Huston Smith in relation to the exploration of ontology and truth within the religious traditions, the post-modern student of religion must develop an inward spiritual discipline appropriate to the vital dynamics of the religious traditions towards the Beyond.

5.   That inward discipline involves the contemplation of all religious traditions as the meeting place of the Beyond. Such a discipline will reorient scholars and scholarship and enhance the possibilities for a more fruitful discussion concerning the depth dimensions of the religious traditions. It will, I believe, contribute to our learning again to hear the stars speak.

Notes

1. Ninian Smart, *Religious Studies and the Western Mind*, Macmillan, London, 1987, p.3.
2. Smart, p.3. As will become clear, I trust, my objection is not to the procedures or methodological strategies of the modern study of religion, but to the implicit ontology within such study. Or, to put it another way, my concern is to find ways to acknowledge the views of reality that we encounter in the study of religious traditions, and to give to such views their rightful place in our study.
3. Smart, pp.3-4. My contention is, curiously, that we have not taken the issue of 'bracketing' the truth claims encountered in the religious traditions themselves to the point of recognizing the necessity to become aware of the assumptions concerning reality that we, *modern* students of religion, bring to our study of traditions. Those assumptions are not, any longer, primarily those arising from our own religious traditions that preclude our entering into the experience of the 'other', but rather the assumption that the experience of the other is finally empty since there is no Beyond to which it relates. This, it seems to me, is the implicit assumption of the modern student of religion that needs most to be bracketed. For the process of bracketing is properly a way of keeping at bay those assumptions on the subject that preclude a proper encounter with the other, not *a priori* judgement about the other, or the Beyond that the other claims to be related to in their religious life and practice.
4. For an account of the rites and beliefs of the Oglala Sioux, see *The Sacred Pipe, Black Elk's Account of the Seven Rites of the Oglala Sioux*, recorded and edited by Joseph Eppes Brown, Penguin Books, Baltimore MD, 1971. This book is an excellent example of the study of religion that does not subject

the experience of the Oglala to 'modern' or 'scientistic' assumptions.
5. This view of dreams was pervasive across traditions. For a brief review of this history, see James Gollnick *Dreams in the Psychology of Religion*, The Edwin Mellen Press, Lewiston NY, 1987, especially pp.15ff.
6. See Laurens van der Post *The Heart of the Hunter*, Penguin Books, Harmondsworth UK, 1965.
7. For a fine study of this tradition, see David Kinsley *The Divine Player, A Study of Krishna*, Motilal Banarsidass, New Delhi, 1979.
8. Similar issues underlie the continuing discussions concerning the place of the study of religion in the modern university. For an important contribution to this discussion, see George Grant 'Faith and The Multiversity' from *Technology and Justice*, Anansi, Toronto, 1986, pp.35-77.
9. Huston Smith, *Forgotten Truth, The Primordial Tradition*, Harper & Row, New York, 1977. Smith does not use the terminology proposed here, namely the 'post-modern study of religion'. But to the extent that Smith seeks to move beyond the modern paradigm of knowing, even though it involves, ironically, a recovery of an earlier tradition, it seems appropriate to describe what emerges from his approach as 'post-modern'. Smith's earlier study, *The Religions of Man*, Harper & Row, New York, was published in 1958.
10. *Ibid*, p.ix.
11. *Ibid*, p.ix.
12. *Ibid*, pp.2-3.
13. *Ibid*, p.6.
14. *Ibid*, p.6.
15. *Ibid*, p.15.
16. *Ibid*, pp.34-59.
17. *Ibid*, pp.650-95.
18. *Ibid*, p.x.
19. Laurens van der Post, *The Heart of the Hunter*, pp.42-3.
20. Wilfred Cantwell Smith, 'Theology and the World's Religious History' from *Toward a Universal Theology of Religion*, ed. Leonard Swidler, Orbis Books, Maryknoll NY, 1987, p.59.
21. *Ibid*, p.59.
22. For a fuller exposition of Raimundo Panikkar's views, see *The Intra-religious Dialogue*, Paulist Press, New York, 1978. This quotation is from Raimundo Panikkar, 'The Invisible Harmony: A Universal Theory of Religion or a Cosmic Confidence in Reality' from *Toward a Universal Theology of Religion*, p.144.
23. Bonaventure, *The Soul's Journey into God*, translated and introduced by Ewert Cousins in *The Classics of Western Spirituality Series*, Paulist Press, New York, 1978.
24. Bonaventure, p.56.
25. Bonaventure, p.60.

26. Of course, everything depends on this 'aright', but it is not possible to unpack this term fully here. However, a couple of comments may be appropriate. First, I am not suggesting that the discipline of attending to the religious traditions to discern the Divine is a substitute for the open forum of public and scholarly debate concerning right conceptions and understandings of what is encountered in the study of religion. Rather, this discipline proposed here proceeds in the order of experience and then public debate and discussion in the order of ideas. At the same time, I am persuaded that the orders of ideas and experience are, to a degree, intertwined. And, further, that we in the study of religion have had our encounter with the religious traditions distorted (is this the right word?) by notions about religion that preclude hearing them aright. Thus the discipline proposed here seeks to redress this situation by encouraging a predisposition in the order of experience to hear what is deepest in the traditions themselves. If this discipline can be cultivated, I believe we then could have a much more fruitful discussion at the public level about right conceptions and understandings. But nothing concerning those right conceptions is here proposed. Secondly, it is appropriate to acknowledge that our attempts to see and hear aright will, in part, be mediated through those images and convictions that one's heart clings to as a matter of faith. Thus as a Christian, the image of God given in Jesus as the Christ, will affect what I see and hear, but it will also be altered by what I see and hear. The particular is one's way into the Beyond, just as the Beyond comes to us in the particular. There is a dialectical process here. But at the outset I, as a Christian, must acknowledge my indebtedness to that Image in whom the Beyond was given in my tradition. Here there emerges a benevolent God who creates, redeems and sanctifies the whole human race on its pilgrimage to the Ultimate. Hence the central Christian criterion for discerning the presence of God in the religious life of humankind is the Cosmic Christ made known in Jesus as the one who lays down his life for the Other, a criterion that stands over Christianity as well. The Cosmic Christ known in the death and resurrection of Jesus as the Christ is not a cookie cutter criterion, but must be apprehended as a living reality through the experience of death and resurrection in one's own heart and life. Such considerations are not inappropriate in the context of a cross tradition practice of the discipline proposed here.

27. See Frithjof Schuon, *The Transcendent Unity of Religions*, Harper & Row, New York, 1978. It is appropriate that the introduction to this volume by Schuon was written by Huston Smith.

CHAPTER 8

The Last Days in Judaism, Christianity and Islam

Victor Danner

All of the great religions, and even many of the so-called primitive or archaic traditions, have teachings of an eschatological nature that refer to the events that occur in 'the last days', namely the period immediately preceding the Day of Judgement. In the Semitic religions that we are about to examine on precisely this question of the last days, there are two great parameters, as it were, to sacred history: the Garden of Eden and the Day of Judgement. The loss of the first leads inexorably to the terminal climax of the latter.

The numerous Prophets and Messengers who intervene in the course of mankind's earthly cycle to restore a measure of spiritual equilibrium create an undulatory movement in the succession of declines and rebirths from the initial Fall to the final denouement, so that we cannot really say that the decline is a purely downward movement from beginning to end. Nevertheless, at a certain point the great universal regenerations that major revelations bring to particular segments of mankind cease altogether; for, if they were to continue indefinitely, there would obviously be no end to the wave-like, up-and-down effect that the constant intrusions of divine revelations generate in human societies throughout their earthly cycle of existence. The momentum of the Fall, in other words, would not eventually lead to the Day of Judgement. Thus, the cessation of major celestial messages, signalling that Heaven no longer will intervene dramatically to slow down the cumulative momentum of the Fall, must be discoverable somewhere in the historical manifestations of religious teachings in the past; otherwise we have a right to assume that perhaps another major revealed message establishing a new religion is in the offing.

63

The last major revelation that occurred within historical times is the Islamic message, which is the fourth and final dispensation within the overall Abrahamic cycle, Judaism and Christianity being the second and third dispensations. Muslims regard the Islamic religion as a throwback to the message of Abraham, who was neither a Christian nor a Jew, as the Koran would have it, but a *Hanif* ('a pure believer'),[1] remnants of whose monotheistic message (the *Hanafiyyah* or 'the pure belief') could still be found in the early days of the Prophet, when he met some of the last *Hunafa* (pl. of *Hanif*) in Arabia, who were lost in the prevailing paganism of the ancient Arabs.

Indeed, the Koran speaks of Muhammad as the Seal of the Prophets (*Khatim an-Nabiyyin*),[2] by which is meant that he seals the entire line of Prophets and Messengers going all the way back to Adam, who was the first Prophet; and thus there will be no Prophet or Messenger after Muhammad. The religion of Islam is, therefore, the final revelation to be sent mankind before the coming of the Hour.

With those two theses, the one touching on the closing of the Prophetic cycle by Muhammad and the other on the finality of the Koranic revelation, we have the historical signs, so to speak, pointing to the cessation of celestial messages. Thenceforth, the gradual erosion of spiritual values amongst greater and greater numbers of believers, including the Muslims, will lead by inevitable causality to the events surrounding the last days, which constitute in their totality the eschatological resolution of the entire range of problems set in motion by the Fall, and only temporarily arrested by the descent of fresh revelations establishing religious structures for different collectivities in the world.

Before going any further, we might pause here to say that the Semitic religions under consideration are not the only ones to have this view of history from the Garden of Eden to the Day of Judgement. Other religions have analogous teachings, but they differ in this: that they break down the overall cycle of mankind's history into more detailed ages. Take, for instance, the Graeco-Roman ages of mankind: the Golden, the Silver, the Bronze, and the Iron Ages.[3] These all involve a gradual decline in the spiritual and even the physical nature of man, so that, at the end of the Iron Age, the decadence is complete. Or consider the Hindu *Maha Yuga* ('Great Cycle'): it is subdivided into four ages; the *Sattva Yuga*, the *Treta Yuga*, the *Dwapara Yuga*, and the *Kali Yuga*, with the gradual decline in spirituality from one age to the next leading to the cataclysms that mark the end of each age.[4] We are now in the *Kali Yuga*, which will end in a cataclysm greater than the previous ones. The *Sattva Yuga* of the Hindus and the Golden Age of the Greeks and Romans correspond to the Garden of Eden of the Semitic religions, and the conditions surrounding the closing moments of the *Kali Yuga*, when spiritual ignorance is triumphant, have a ring about them that sounds similar to what we hear in the Semitic traditions. There is even a messianic element in Hinduism and Buddhism analogous to what we find in Judaism, Christianity and Islam. The *Kalki Avatara*, the tenth and final *Avatara* of Hinduism, closes the ages; the *Maitreya-Buddha*, the celestial Buddha of great compassion, is the Messiah of the Buddhist world.[5]

It goes without saying that the perspectives of these different religions, determined for the most part by their particular revealed messages, can be quite different. Thus, for example, both the Hindus and the ancient Greeks have transmigrational teachings that are non-existent in the Semitic religions. Transmigration implies the existence of pre-human and posthumous states of existence for the individual soul. The Semitic religions have posthumous conditions similar to the Heavens and Hells of Hinduism and other non-Semitic traditions, but they do not have pre-human states of existence for souls caught in the web of transmigration (*samsara*, in Buddhism and Hinduism). Both Buddhism and Hinduism maintain that for souls in transmigration, rebirth in the human condition is 'hard to obtain', since it is only from this central state that one can consciously seek salvation.

While the Semitic religions also stress the centrality of man because he alone can actively save his soul, whereas the animals and other species are peripheral in relation to him, they teach that the soul is freshly created by God and projected into its human habitation at a certain moment when the embryo in the mother's womb has attained the requisite perfection. The newly-created soul has thus not migrated from a previous state. Nor, for that matter, do the Semitic religions have an indefinite number of mankinds going that have no transmigrational teachings, there is only one mankind that moves from the Garden of Eden to the Day of Judgement. In Hinduism, one single 'Day of Brahman' has one thousand *Maha Yugas*, each of which contains within its overall cycle a different mankind, a rather breathtaking and bold concept based on the interrelationships between the impersonal law of causality (*karma*), which affects everything, and the world of transmigration (*samsara*). By contrast, the Semitic religions fasten their attention on only one humanity, so to speak, and on the Heavens and Hells, to say nothing of the limbos and purgatories, that await mankind at death or, in a more definitive fashion, on the Day of Resurrection.

But whatever the distinctions between the Aryan and the Semitic religions might be in the interpretation of the details of mankind's cyclical unfolding from the Primordial Age to the ultimate climax embodied in the Day of Judgement, it is clear that they are analogous in their general drift, and this can only be the result of the fact that cosmic laws operate in the same fashion everywhere, even though the modes of expressing those laws vary from religion to religion.

It is likewise obvious that all of these traditional cyclical theories are the exact opposite of the evolutionary theses that have arisen in the West since the days of such nineteenth-century thinkers as Charles Darwin, Charles Lyell, Thomas Huxley and Herbert Spencer, all of whom played a major role in applying evolutionary theories not only in the biological field, as in Darwinism, but in the social, political, moral and other domains as well.[6]

Sooner or later the concept of progress, which antedates evolutionism, joined forces with the latter and provided a kind of ameliorative element, so that evolutionism took on the guise of successive improvements, culminating in modern man and his civilization. Allied to that was the thesis of uniformitarianism, largely the work of Charles Lyell's geological theories, which would have it that the processes now at work in Nature can account for geological formations without having to call into the picture any catastrophism, such as the Biblical Flood, which earlier geologists had referred to when explaining the strata of the rocks and other natural phenomena. The two, evolutionism and uniformitarianism, became the fundamental pillars of modern civilization. They provided the philosophical and scientific postulates that governed all of the ideologies of the nineteenth and twentieth centuries down to our times. Everything, eventually, was explicable in evolutionary terms; everything evolved, including God, although in general His presence was not necessary in explaining the origin of things, and for that reason evolutionism, in all of its guises, led directly to the great secularist societies of our times.

As a result, to understand the traditional cyclical teachings of the different religions, one has to step out of the evolutionary matrix of modern culture and see things from a completely different perspective. If anything, the traditional cyclical notions are decidedly catastrophist in nature, and for that reason they are closer to the views of catastrophism than to those of uniformitarianism. It is true that one will find religious people who seek to combine the two contradictory theories on mankind's development, the evolutionary and the creationist, and for that reason they are called theistic evolutionists, for they assume that theories of evolutionism are descriptions of how God works in creating the different species. But to do this they must compromise the integrity of Scripture, to say the least.

It is not, however, this aspect of things that is of interest to us, but rather the fact that the difference between the millennial cyclical theories we find in the world's religions, on the one hand, and the evolutionary ideologies within the thinking of modern man, on the other, is so great as to amount to two utterly distinct perspectives on man and the universe.

Modern secularism would be unthinkable without the underlying evolutionary ideologies of one type or another. In other words, a completely secularized society would be one in which evolutionism accounted for everything; but that is an impossibility, given that there would always be an individual who rejected evolutionism as such. The attempt of the communist party in the Soviet Union to create a society based on the purely evolutionary ideology of Marxist-Leninism has been only a partial success, even with all the education and repressive measures introduced in Russia after the downfall of the monarchy and the Church. The creation, by the way, of vast secularist societies in both the capitalist and communist worlds is no doubt indicative of the triumph of evolutionism in all of its aspects over the mind of modern man.

Yet, even this triumph, with all that it implies for the religious cultures of mankind, is one of the many 'signs of the times', so that it too plays a major role in the eschatological unfolding of the events in the last days, and it too must have a causal bearing on the cyclical tendencies of the day. If all the religions were sound and healthy, their institutional frameworks in society would be sound and healthy too, in which case there would have been no Russian Revolution, and so the presence of a one-world secularist civilization that is fundamentally anti-religious must therefore constitute an important phase in the history of mankind. By the same token, extreme secularism breeds its exact opposite, fundamentalism, which we find now in the

Jewish, Islamic and Christian worlds, and since this in turn has a considerable influence on the march of events, we shall have to return to it later on, when examining Zionism.

To see exactly how the doctrine of the last days is interpreted in the Jewish, Christian and Islamic traditions we can do no better than to examine quickly how each one perceives the events of those times. After that, we shall pick up once again the thread of Christian fundamentalist thinking on Jewish nationalism, or Zionism, in order to understand how fundamentalism in the Christian world affects directly the events in the Holy Land for better or for worse, and how this influence ultimately brings the entire Islamic world into the picture. It is certainly ironic, to put things mildly, that biblical prophecies can be construed in favor of political nationalism, in this instance that of the Jews, but that is what the Christian and Jewish fundamentalists have done; and in doing so, they have inadvertently, or perhaps consciously, precipitated the sequence of events that are supposed to take place as this age of mankind draws to a close.

In the Muslim world, the rise of fundamentalism, which is a reaction against the increasing secularism of the times, is on the contrary anti-Zionist by definition; for it sees the invasion of Palestine by Jewish Zionists and the creation of the State of Israel as attempts to wrest Palestine from *Dar al-Islam* ('the world of Islam'). Since Muslims, whether fundamentalists or traditionalists, have their own eschatological teachings that revolve in the main around the land of Palestine, the establishment of the State of Israel and the power that Jewish nationalism has demonstrated in the Near East are not seen as minor historical events, but are viewed instead against a background of Koranic verses and prophecies made by the Prophet Muhammad that fall within the purlieus of everything relating to 'the end of time', as the Muslims say. As a consequence, the three religions are inextricably locked together as they move towards the terminal point of their earthly careers.

Judaism is the oldest of the three Semitic traditions we are examining, but it is not the oldest of the monotheistic messages, for it was preceded by Abrahamic monotheism, and Islamic teachings maintain that all of the Prophets and Messengers going back to Adam were monotheists. The Jewish tradition bases its teachings regarding the last days on a number of elements, such as Scripture, the Talmud, and the interpretations of the great rabbinical authorities of days gone by, such as Maimonides of medieval fame.[7] Perhaps the most salient

68

feature of Jewish eschatological doctrine is the central role of the Messiah, who has a strong political coloration about him that is bound up with the notion of an earthly kingdom over which he presides, a kingdom — or perhaps one should say an empire — that presumably will radiate over all the world from its spiritual capital in Jerusalem. That the messianic concept of the Jews is of hoary antiquity needs no further commentary than to mention in passing that even the disciples of Jesus were heavily influenced by the political characteristics of the Messiah's reign, and thought for a while that Jesus, being the Messiah, would restore to Israel its independent kingdom.

The loss of Jewish independence with the Babylonian Captivity in the sixth century before Christ and the subsequent Greek and Roman imperial control over the Holy Land, had accustomed the Jews to thinking of a political role for their coming Messiah. Jesus Christ, as the suffering servant who was humiliated by the Sanhedrin and put to death through crucifixion, was completely lacking in the attributes of power and majesty associated with a triumphant and lordly Messiah. In certain forms of Jewish thought, it is true, the doctrine of the coming of the Messiah is stripped of its political trappings and given a spiritual interpretation in the sense that it is God as Divine Presence who descends after the purification of the earth and mankind, to dwell amongst His creatures.[8] While a spiritualized version of Jewish messianism is no doubt a valid interpretation, it could not supersede such a firmly held religio-political belief that had been circulating for so long amongst the Jews, both learned and simple.[9] With the destruction of the Temple of Jerusalem in the year 70, as predicted by Jesus if the Jews rejected him and put him to death, there began another massive dispersion of the Jews from Palestine. The Temple had been the heart of the Jewish religion for centuries on end.

True, the first Temple, that of Solomon, had been destroyed by the Babylonians; it was rebuilt by Zerubbabel, and this second Temple was replaced by a third in the time of Herod the Great, who was ruling when Jesus was born; but in any case, for long centuries the Jewish tradition revolved around the Temple of Jerusalem. After the first Temple was destroyed, the rabbis in the diaspora formulated a version of Judaism that permitted the Jews to exist within a religious framework even without the actual physical presence of a Temple. This rabbinical Judaism of the Pharisees came to life when the third Temple was destroyed by the Romans, and from thence on guided the destinies of the Jewish people, especially after recension of the Talmud had been made by the sixth century. It is they who kept the teachings on the coming Messiah alive amongst the Jews scattered in many lands.

The Prophets of Judaism speak of the restoration of the Jews back into their homeland, the so-called ingathering of the exiles; they speak also of the future restoration of the Kingdom under a scion of the house of David, the future Messiah, who would rule from Jerusalem and spread the monotheistic message of Judaism throughout the lands of the Gentiles. Eventually, the Jewish tradition would refer, not to one Messiah, but to two of them: the Messiah son of David, and the Messiah son of Joseph; the latter is a warrior-Messiah who would fall in battle, while the former is the victorious Messiah who ushers in the supremacy of Israel, when all nations would accept the tutelage of Heaven. The suffering Messiah, who engages in battle the forces of Gog and Magog, bears the same relationship to the Messiah son of David as the *Mahdi* ('the rightly-guided') in Islam does to the *Masih* (the Messiah, who is Jesus at his Second Coming). That the Messiah is of the Davidic line and incarnated in an actual person shows that the main tenor of Jewish messianic thinking was towards the political, not the idealistic, version of messianism. On the other hand, both the suffering and triumphant Messiahs of the Jewish tradition coalesce in the person of Jesus, as understood in Christianity, who, at his First Coming, embodied the suffering servant, while at his Second Coming he will be the majestic and triumphant Messiah; and he too is of the Davidic lineage.

But this interpretation is of course rejected by centuries-old rabbinical Judaism, which sees in Jesus Christ a false Prophet, to say nothing of the calumnies it has hurled against him and his mother, the Virgin Mary. As a result, the possibility that the Christ is the actual Messiah of Jewish eschatological doctrine, in the spiritual sense of messianism, has been continuously denied by the Jews since the very inception of Christianity. Now, it is a tenet of Christian teachings on the last days that the Jews in the end will recognize Jesus Christ as their Messiah. This so-called 'conversion of the Jews' is a notion based on Scripture and the writings of the Fathers of the Church and later figures.[10] It is an extremely powerful element, as we shall see, in the speculations of the Christian fundamentalists of our days who support Jewish Zionism.

With respect now to Christian eschatological views, these are drawn from the prophetical verses of the Old and New Testaments, from such books of the Church Fathers as St Augustine's *City of God*,[11] and from medieval authorities. Contrary to what is generally assumed, numerous details on the events preceding the Second Coming of Christ abound in both the Oral and Written Tradition of the Church; but our intention is merely to give an overall view, not the specifics and step-by-step particulars. The first lesson that these data teach us is that the messianic hope in Christianity has two phases of strongly contrasting natures that correspond to the First and Second Comings of Jesus. In the first, he appears as a humble, suffering servant who was put to death by his own people; in the second, the Parousia, he descends as the majestic Messiah of Davidic descent, who comes this time to judge the nations, and therefore to judge the Jews and the Gentiles together. His Kingdom is the Heavenly Jerusalem that descends at the end of time, and that is so spiritualized in the New Testament descriptions that we are obviously in the presence of an altogether different world,[12] the one that exists after this present world has been completely purified by fire and the Day of Resurrection come to pass.

Before the Parousia, which is the dramatic celestial response to the horrendous tribulations that smite both mankind and the cosmos in the last days, there is the reign of the Antichrist. This is an actual government with a real person at its head, one who radiates infernal powers and sets himself up as God. He is 'the abomination of desolation' spoken of by Daniel,[13] so that the concept of a person in the end time who attacks the people of God and seeks to magnify himself is also a part of Jewish belief, but of course he is not specifically referred to as the 'Antichrist'. Antiochus Epiphanes, the Seleucid tyrant who desecrated the Temple in Jerusalem in the second century before Christ, is a type of the abomination of desolation, in Jewish and Christian thinking.

In the Christian belief the Antichrist is a Jew, as he is in the Islamic tradition; but it is difficult to say whether he reigns from a Temple in Rome or in Jerusalem, or perhaps in both places. His government will be the most totalitarian regime ever witnessed, and it is on account of this that 'the great tribulation' referred to in the New Testament[14] will be the expression of his invincible hand. His coming will follow the ingathering of the Jews in Palestine, bringing to an end their diaspora; but whether this means that all Jews, or only many of them, will return to the Holy Land is another question. In some

Christian interpretations, a rebuilt Temple of Jerusalem will be his seat of power. Since he will preach a new religion that will attract vast numbers, we can only assume that his doctrines will be a subversion of the teachings of the Christ, for he will be a kind of inverse image of Jesus Christ in all respects. Because his reign will see such unimaginable persecutions and tribulations, its length will not be long. In the beginning of his reign he will seem like a man of peace; then, in the second half, he will unleash over the heads of the Jews and the Gentiles his terrible powers of deception and persecution unto death. While initially the Jews will greet him as their long-awaited Messiah because of his apparently peaceful message,[15] at the end, after he has exterminated great numbers of both Jews and Gentiles, and after the return of both Henoch and Elijah as witnesses against him in their preaching, the Jews will recognize that their Messiah is indeed the Christ himself — this is the point at which the Jews cease their rejection of the Christ and believe in him.[16] The descent of the Christ results in the destruction of the Antichrist and his forces; then the Day of Judgement follows, which involves the spiritual restoration of the universe; the descent of the Heavenly Jerusalem, an almost mystical vision that hints at the coming of a golden age, brings the entire momentum of the Fall to an end — sin is no more, and therefore death is no more.

When we turn to the Islamic eschatological doctrines, we move into a different spiritual climate, so to speak. This is due to the fact that Islam is a purely monotheistic religion with no God-Man perspective, to begin with, and with no emphasis on any particular ethnic group. The Christocentrism of Christianity necessitates a strong emphasis on the divine function of Jesus Christ as Judge at the end of the cycle, so that his role is central; the ethnocentrism of the Jews necessitates an almost political stress on the functions of the Messiah, whose primary duties relate to the Jews as a Chosen People, even though he has some influence on the Gentiles. We see neither of these two perspectives in Islam, which therefore can more appropriately be described as theocentric, in the sense that there is no God-Man, on the one hand, and that no particular people can claim a quasi-divine right as the Chosen People, on the other.

In Islam, the teachings on the last days derive from the Koran, the *hadiths* ('statements') of the Prophet Muhammad and his Companions, and from the rather vast corpus of Sufi literature that comments on the previous two sources.[17] For Islam also the principal eschatological theater is Palestine, even though the entire world goes through the major and minor 'signs' that will appear as the age draws to a close. Islamic doctrine, like the Jewish and the Christian, speaks of a great decline in faith as the end approaches. But there is a figure who appears on the eschatological scene, called the *Mahdi*, as mentioned above, who is a descendant of the Prophet Muhammad and a warrior-like chief who restores a temporary reconciliation between Heaven and earth. The major scenes of his activities are in the Meccan and Palestinian regions, and he is obviously contemporaneous with that other eschatological personality, the Antichrist, called in Arabic *ad-Dajjal* ('the Impostor'). The *Mahdi* is said to have a government and to engage in great battles, even against fellow Muslims who have fallen away from the faith; but his greatest fighting will be against the Antichrist. This latter does not have the tremendous importance that the Christian tradition gives to him throughout the ages, perhaps because even the Prophets and Messengers are treated in the Koran with a certain relativization: their function is merely to deliver the celestial message, and that is all. If they are treated with a certain disregard, it is largely because the Koran wants to focus attention on the majesty and absoluteness of *Allah*, not on His Prophets and Messengers, for they come and go in this world according to cyclical needs, and they all deliver the same type of monotheistic message to a mostly recalcitrant humanity. That being the case for the Prophets and Messengers, the Antichrist is likewise given short shrift. He comes with a new religion that represents subversion: he has a Heaven and a Hell, according to what the Prophet Muhammad has said, but his Heaven is Hell and his Hell is Heaven. Thus, Islam also takes note of the fact that he comes with a new religion to seduce vast numbers; and the Islamic tradition likewise says that he will have impressive powers, which are really satanic miracles that will deceive great numbers.

For the Muslim, the Antichrist will operate in the Palestinian area, but it does not follow that he will reign from Jerusalem. He destroys the *Mahdi*, the warrior chief, who resembles the Messiah son of Joseph of Jewish beliefs. The Antichrist, for his part, is destroyed by the Christ and this eventually leads to the Day of Resurrection and the definitive assignment of mankind to either the Heavens or the Hells, according to case. In Islamic eschatology, the purification of the universe is also alluded to and we are left with the feeling that this restoration of all things is the end of the cycle.

Such, then, are the main eschatological features of Jewish,

Christian and Islamic thought. It is of great importance to remark that Jesus Christ figures in both the Christian and Islamic worlds, as does the Virgin Mary, whereas in rabbinical Judaism of the last twenty centuries, both Jesus and his mother are in general relegated to the roles of veritable impostors, as Talmudic passages and the *Toledot Yeshu* (*Life of Jesus*) would have it.[18] How is it possible that such saintly figures as both Jesus and his mother Mary should occupy lofty positions in the Islamic spiritual cosmos and yet be treated as if they were the exact opposite in the minds of the Jews for such a long period of time? To answer this, we must recall that the Koran was revealed in the early part of the seventh century after Christ, and that by then the Talmud had been put together in both Babylon and Jerusalem, the Babylonian version being much more authoritative because it was more comprehensive. The Koran, which is the Scripture of the Muslims and therefore seen by them as the Word of God transmitted through the vehicle of the Prophet Muhammad, numbers both Jesus and Mary amongst the saints. Jesus was both a Prophet and a Messenger; his mother, who is also called the Virgin Mary in the Islamic tradition, is sometimes referred to by theologians and religious scholars as having the function of a Prophetess. In Islam, Prophets and Messengers are without sin; they might, on occasion, commit an imperfect deed, but that is not the same as committing an actual sin. They are indeed said to possess 'impeccability' (*'ismah*), and this is one of the items in the orthodox formulations of Islamic dogma. The Prophet Muhammad, accordingly, is but the seal of the line of Prophets and Messengers going all the way back to Adam, and the number of them is considerably greater than the twenty-seven or twenty-eight mentioned in the Koran; but the point is that all of them, without exception, are saintly persons who cannot sin.[19]

There is, however, something else particular to both Jesus and Mary, something that even Muhammad himself did not possess, and that is the fact that both were born without the touch of the devil, according to a *hadith* of the Prophet, a privilege that others in their rank do not possess. From this, as well as from certain other Koranic verses on Mary, one can deduce the Islamic version of the Annunciation and the Immaculate Conception.[20]

The Koran holds it against the Jews that they have slaughtered the Prophets sent to them, that they maltreated Jesus, and that they calumniated the Virgin Mary.[21] Whether this calumny was expressed orally by the Jews of the Medinian area in the days of the Prophet

Muhammad, or whether the reference is to specific Talmudic passages that are in effect judgements against the integrity of Mary, not to mention Jesus, is neither here nor there, for both sources go back to a long-standing hostility in the Jews against the Founder of Christianity and his mother. What the Koranic revelation attempts to do amongst Muslims is to reassert the integrity of both Jesus and Mary that the Jews had violated egregiously both in their oral and written statements. This is the reason why the Koran is rather harsh at times in its judgements against Jewish behavior.

Another corrective that the Koran drives home again and again in the many verses referring to Jesus as the Messiah (*al-Masih*) is that Jesus is indeed the Messiah awaited by all believers of the Abrahamic dispensation. This also is an article of faith found in both the Shi'ite and Sunnite creeds, and both make a similar distinction between the *Mahdi* and the *Masih*. As Messiah for the Muslims, however, Jesus does not have the divine attributes found in Christian beliefs, nor can he have them, for the absoluteness of *Allah* precludes any possibility of sharing the divine nature with other beings. It is only *Allah* who judges at the end of time; it is not the Messiah himself, who does not distribute reward or punishment, nor can he have any share in the divine nature whatsoever. Even so, it is clear that in Islamic eschatological thinking, the Christ has functions of a certain cosmic grandeur that are unique to him. Add to this the special traits of his mother, the Virgin Mary, which Islam obviously stresses in opposition to the opinions of the Jews, who is a Prophetess born of an Immaculate Conception, and who is loftier than all the women of the universe, and one realizes that although both Jesus and Mary are not divine within the Islamic perspective, they are certainly treated with particular emphasis because of their special natures.

Having examined rather summarily the eschatological views of the three Semitic religions, it remains now to see what has happened to these beliefs in our own days. Apart from those believers who still cherish the traditional teachings of their religion, there are two other camps who have come upon the scene in more recent times, and these are the modernists and the fundamentalists. Since we have already discussed the evolutionary ideologies of the nineteenth and twentieth centuries, which are to be found in all kinds of thinking after Darwin's day (biological, social, political, economic, artistic, theological, geological and so on), we need not rehearse what has already been said. Suffice it to say that the modernists in the Jewish,

Christian and Islamic worlds are all those who are imbued, to one degree or another, with evolutionary thinking and beliefs. Formerly, these beliefs coalesced in the dogma of Progress, but of late, especially after the discovery that modern science and technology produced evil fruits in the form of pollution, depletion of natural resources, and the like, the modernists are less certain about Progress than before; but they retain, in the other strata of their minds, a strong evolutionary perspective that governs all of their thinking about religion, Scriptures, dogmas, morality, rituals, and so on.

It would be vain to attempt to classify modernist versions of religion amongst the Jews, Christians or Muslims. In extreme cases, as in the so-called 'liberation theology' of the modernist Catholics, the Marxist-Leninist bias of their evolutionism is too evident to ignore. While Jewish communism, Christian communism and Islamic communism might all sound like contradictory ideologies, and even actual contradictions in terms, their partisans exist and are characterized more by their evolutionary views of a social, political and economic nature than by their actual understanding of the traditional intellectual and spiritual doctrines of their religions. Yet, as said previously, because of their very evolutionism (whatever its particular nature might be), they contribute in their own ways to the overall disequilibrium of the world around them. It is largely because of their presence in the midst of these religions that we see the reaction to them, and especially to their natural propensity towards secularism, in the rise of Jewish, Christian and Islamic fundamentalism. Since the Christian fundamentalists are intimately bound up with Zionism, and the latter with the ingathering of the Jewish exiles, which is a process connected with the latter days, we can now turn to Christian eschatological belief and what effects this actually has on the contemporary scene.

Christian Zionism, to put things simply, antedates Jewish Zionism, and not vice versa as is commonly thought.[22] Already, in the seventeenth century during the days of Oliver Cromwell's puritanical regime, there was a call amongst the Puritan divines for believers to help the Jews return to their homeland by way of accelerating the Second Coming. In the nineteenth century, a Christian movement arose in England in the guise of a teaching called pre-tribulationism. According to this reinterpretation of Scripture and tradition, the Jews, although in a state of complete perfidy and iniquity for having rejected Jesus, must nevertheless be helped to return to Palestine so as

76

to fulfil Scripture on the ingathering of the exiles. Not only that, but from the pre-tribulationist view the Jews were destined to play a major role in the dissemination of the Christian message once they returned to Palestine and went through certain terrible experiences; indeed, after the tribulation of the Antichrist and their newly found faith in Jesus as their Messiah, they would become the major missionaries for Christianity the world over. But before they could assume such a missionary role they had to go through the tribulation alongside the lukewarm and insincere Christians. The sincere Christians, for their part, would not have to go through the tribulation of the Antichrist for the simple reason that they would no longer be in this world. They would have been 'raptured' out of this world through a secret coming of the Christ that would spare them the rigors and sufferings that the tribulation would impose on everyone else amongst Gentiles and Jews. This secret coming is distinct from the actual Second Advent of the Christ after the tribulation, in which these Christian Zionists also believe. Because they feel that they will be spared the sufferings of the tribulation caused by the Antichrist, they are called 'pre-tribulationists' to distinguish them from the traditional Christians throughout the centuries who have believed that Christians as well as Jews, not to mention other peoples, will all go through the trials together, at the end of which the Christ descends; and these are called 'post-tribulationists'. Similarly, the Christian Zionists are known as 'rapturists' because they stick fast to the idea that they will undergo a secret rapture before that fearful period of the Antichrist. Finally, they are also known as 'dispensationalists' because of their dividing up the Bible into different dispensations.[23]

With the return of the Christ and the conversion of the Jews, the fundamentalists see the inauguration of the millennium, or the period of a thousand years mentioned in the Apocalypse. Jerusalem will become the focal point of world attention because of the radiance of its spiritual light; the Jews will scatter all over the world proclaiming the message of the Christ. Only at the end of the millennium will the final struggle between the forces of good and evil take place, with the good triumphing in the end. There is here an echo of the sacred political messianism of the Jews, and the fact that the Jews have such a dominant part in the millennium has given to the whole concept a powerful Jewish cast.

By way of clarifying things, we might recall that the traditional

Church has always upheld a post-tribulationist position, on the one hand, and what came to be called an amillennial attitude on the other. Amillennialism was eventually adopted by the Church under the influence of such Fathers as St Augustine, who taught that the millennium meant the period between the First and the Second Coming of the Christ. The great struggle between light and darkness comes towards the close of the millennium, and is crowned triumphantly with the Parousia. St Augustine, like some of the earlier Church thinkers, had previously given a rather crass and even materialistic view to the millennium, which meant that formerly he had believed that the millennium would begin with the Second Coming. That teaching, known as pre-millennialism, was abandoned and the Church, both in its Catholic and Protestant camps, became firmly amillennial; and then in the nineteenth century, with the English and later the American evangelicals of Zionist bent, pre-millennialism reared its head once again, this time in the company of the pre-tribulationists. Needless to say, in the writings of some of these fundamentalists, the picture of the millennium can be intensely optimistic and even full of details on the idealistic life of those future lives.

Pre-tribulationism would have been simply a minor Protestant evangelical sect of England and America if it had not set out to influence the English Government first and then later the American in favor of a Jewish homeland in Palestine. These Christian Zionists became a powerful force in the formulation of English foreign policy. Their Zionism made it possible for the Jews, now affected by the nationalistic sentiments that were current in nineteenth-century Europe, to think of having their own State and to begin making moves to bring about the realization of their Zionist ambitions. Not that this affected most Jews, quite the contrary, the majority of Jews were not interested in a national home in Palestine, for they were content in living under the conditions of the diaspora as they had done since the Babylonian Captivity in the sixth century before Christ, when their rabbis had created that form of Judaism that can live outside the precincts of Palestine and even without the existence of the Temple. After the destruction of the Temple by the Romans, this form of rabbinical Judaism became the only type Jews would know for centuries down to our times.

Nevertheless, Jewish nationalism grew in power as Judaism, succumbing like Christianity to the dissolving forces of skepticism and disbelief that an increasingly secularist civilization generated, began to diminish as a cohesive belief holding all Jews together. Zionism sooner or later became the actual unifying ideology that held both believing and atheistic Jews together. It had a dynamism of its own, like all nationalistic movements, that not only competed with Judaism but actually used the Jewish Scripture to back its claims to the Holy Land. This was an intoxicating ideology that came into existence precisely at the time that the Christian Zionists were beating the drums to help the Jews return to the Holy Land.

Without the Jews the Christian Zionists could accomplish nothing to bring about their eschatological program; without the Christians the Jewish Zionists likewise were powerless to get hold of Palestine. Both camps, however, had to face the fact that Palestine was part and parcel of *Dar al-Islam*, or the Islamic world. It was under the control of the Ottoman Turkish Empire and had been for centuries on end. Most of its inhabitants were Arabs, mostly Muslims, the rest Christians; but a small minority of Jews could also be found there. The First World War provided the opportunity that the Zionists, both Christian and Jewish, were looking for, and it came in the Balfour Declaration of 1917, promising the Jews a homeland in Palestine. Of course, it was assumed that Great Britain would inherit not only Palestine but also other parts of the Ottoman Empire. The Ottomans had fought on the side of the Germans, and at the peace conference ending the war the English got precisely what they wanted. Great Britain remained the patron of Jewish nationalism up to the Second World War, when the American Government took over that function under pressure from both Jewish and Christian Zionists in the United States, and it has remained to this day the foremost bastion of Zionism outside Israel itself.

For the evangelicals the Jews are simply the means to an end, the end being the Second Coming. Perhaps it is best to say that both sides use one another; the Christians use the Jews to make sure that each step of the way towards the coming of the Messiah is carefully realized; the Jews use the Christians, initially the English and then the Americans, because they constitute a massive financial, military, diplomatic and economic support without which the Jewish State of Israel could not exist. Neither side has any illusions about the other. What the fundamentalists have expected from the Jews for well over a century has gradually but surely been realized: first, the Jews have returned to the Holy Land, thus fulfilling the Biblical prophecy having to do with the ingathering of the exiles; second, they have taken over the land and — what is of prime significance — now possess Jerusalem. The fall of Jerusalem at the hands of the Jews in 1967 meant that the eschatological timetable was on schedule. The remaining events, such as the rebuilding of the Temple of Jerusalem, the coming of the Antichrist, the great tribulation, the conversion of the Jews, and the Second Coming of Jesus are all now but a matter of time. The power that the Christian fundamentalists have to influence public opinion, the Congress of the United States, and the American Presidents is considerable and constitutes a veritable public relations program on behalf of the State of Israel. It is therefore quite wrong to assume that only Jewish Zionism affects the American Government.[24]

The capture of all of Jerusalem by Israeli forces in 1967 also affected the Muslims, for whom the Dome of the Rock (*Qubbat as-Sakhrah*) is the third holy place, after Mecca and Medina. According to the Islamic tradition, the Prophet's Night Voyage (*Isra'*) from Mecca to Jerusalem ended up in his Ascension (*Mi'raj*) through the Heavens to the Divine Presence. A sacred footprint of the Prophet is enshrined in a grill on the boulder under the cupola. That same Rock is said to have been where the Prophet Abraham was to have sacrificed his son Isaac; it was there that the Holiest of Holies could be found in the Temple of Jerusalem; and of course the Christ spent part of his mission on earth in the Temple area now occupied by the spacious grounds surrounding the Dome of the Rock. This shrine, therefore, commemorates the four Semitic religions, Abrahamism, Judaism, Christianity and Islam.

Until the capture of Jerusalem by the Jewish troops in 1967, the warfare between the Jews and the Arabs had been seen by the Muslims outside the Arab world as largely two secularist nationalisms in conflict over the same land, not as an Islamic conflict. Arab nationalism, like Jewish nationalism, was essentially secular and comprised an ideology that united both Christian and Muslim Arabs together; and, indeed, the foremost theoreticians of Arab nationalism were the Christian Arabs. Jewish nationalism, we have already seen, is a powerful secular force that unites both religious and irreligious Jews. But with the capture of Jerusalem, the entire Islamic world came into the scene, for the Jews now claimed that Jerusalem would be theirs forever, and backing them up were the Christian Zionists. Amongst the latter could now be found extremists who were propounding the thesis that to accelerate the eschatological flow of events the Dome of the Rock should be destroyed and the Temple rebuilt in its place, a proposal that evidently ignores the sacred nature of the Dome of the Rock for the Muslims. Even if it is never carried out, it shows to what extent fundamentalists are prepared to go to make sure that everything is kept moving towards the eschatological peaking point.

Now, what of the Islamic world in all this? We have already mentioned that fundamentalism (whether of the revolutionary sort, as in Iran, or of the conservative type, as in Saudi Arabia) is a reaction against modernism. The failures of nationalistic ideologies have resulted in the intensification of fundamentalist, or revivalist, forms of Islam, which must be distinguished from traditional Islam. The two can sometimes be confused, but what characterizes traditional Islam is precisely its union of the spiritual Path (*tarigah*) and the Law (*shari'ah*), the two dimensions of the revealed message embodied in the Koran and the Sunnah ('Norm') of the Prophet Muhammad, whereas the fundamentalists reduce Islam to the *shari'ah* on the one hand, and then reinterpret the Law on the other, in ways that are at times frankly anti-traditional and even heretical, as we can see in Iranian 'revolutionary Islam'. We must not, consequently, put the traditional and the fundamentalist Muslims into the same camp. Moreover, some of the fundamentalist movements of Islam, while claiming to return to the *shari'ah*, are in effect merely variants of Western evolutionary ideologies of different types, to which they append the epithet 'Islamic', such as 'the Islamic republic' and the like. This means that, far from being opposed to modernist Muslims, some of the fundamentalists share with them a number of Western modes of thought of a political, social, educational, economic and moral nature, ignoring the entire intellectual and spiritual tradition of Islam. Very often the fundamentalists are just as violently opposed to the traditional Islamic doctrines and institutions as are the modernists.[25] The latter, for their part, embrace all categories of thought coming from the West, and one will find every conceivable ideology flowing out of modern Western evolutionism as from a common source.

The traditional Muslims, the fundamentalists and the modernists are nevertheless all united in their opposition to Jewish imperialism, which they equate with Zionism, and they make a clear distinction between secular Jewish nationalism on the one hand, and Judaism on the other. The latter, for Muslims, is a religion revealed by God, as is the Christian message; and this notion, on the universality of revelation, is embedded in the Koran, which pictures the same divine source, *Allah*, as the revealer of all monotheistic celestial messages. When Zionism first arose as a political system with definite goals in the Holy Land, it was rejected by many orthodox Jewish rabbis. Most of them have succumbed to the powerful nationalistic fervor that characterizes world Jewry at the present time. But in Israel and elsewhere, there are still orthodox Jews who reject out of hand the Zionist claims of creating a 'Jewish' State, all the more so in that many of these Zionist Jews in Israel are no longer pious or even believers in the tenets of traditional Judaism.[26]

Similarly, amongst Christian fundamentalists, there are many who reject Zionism completely, for they regard the Jewish State as an illicit creation of the Jews even though they might see in that Zionist accomplishment one of the many 'signs of the times'. That the Jewish State is indeed one of the 'signs of the times' is precisely the opinion of the Muslims, who judge the Zionist accomplishment in the light of the eschatological criteria provided by the *hadiths* of the Prophet Muhammad. In general, however, the Muslims have been less aware of the powerful Christian Zionist support for Jewish nationalism than they have been of Jewish Zionism. More recently, Christian Zionism has appeared within the Catholic church after the second Vatican Council, so that we can now speak of an evangelical Zionism and of a Catholic Zionism.

That there are now tens of millions of Christians, both in the United States and elsewhere, who feel that we are living in 'the last days', and that maximum support must be given the Jews to realize their nationalistic aspirations and goals in Palestine because this has a direct bearing on the Parousia, is assuredly a strange interpretation of Scripture. What is even stranger is the belief held by these evangelicals of pre-tribulationist stamp that they will actually be raptured out of this world before the coming of the Antichrist, leaving the affairs of the entire world in the hands of the Jews in the Holy Land, so that the future of mankind lies exclusively in Jewish control, for better or for worse: for better, because eventually they will recognize Jesus Christ as their Messiah; for worse, because initially they will be deluded by the Antichrist, whose one-world government and religion will be centered in the Temple of Jerusalem. The eminently Jewish trait of the future is one of the outstanding peculiarities of dispensationalism. Still, the evangelical opponents of Christian Zionism ask a very pertinent question of the rapturists: What would happen if, instead of being raptured out of this world before the tribulation, they too had to go through it, as the traditional teachings would have it? Would they lose their faith in Jesus as a result?

With those remarks we can see that a strong dosage of illusion lies in the thinking of both the Christian and Jewish Zionists, and that both sides reinforce each other's illusions considerably. For the evangelical pre-tribulationists, a goodly number of their goals for the Jews have been realized gradually in the twentieth century. It is almost as if they have been calling the tunes in the eschatological program. With every success, they have been emboldened to consider their rapturist beliefs as being incontrovertible. It never seems to occur to them that pragmatic success in this world does not necessarily imply that one's beliefs are true. Moreover, the traditional Christian belief never looked forward to some future Jewish Kingdom presided over by Jesus. The Church has always considered itself the new Israel, meant for both Gentiles and Jews; it looked back at the message of salvation brought by the Christ, and when it anticipated the blessed hope of the Parousia in the future, that also embraced both Jews and Gentiles. As for the Jews, their use of Old Testament prophecies on the ingathering of the exiles to back up their Zionist political goals ignores the purely religious nature of the messianic era as well as the terrible events that befall all mankind, Jew and Gentile, before the coming of the Messiah.

Yet, when all is said and done, even these illusions contribute in their own way to the cosmic drama whose closing moments are being played out before our very eyes, and whose end, the victorious triumph of Heaven, has always been affirmed in the Old Testament, the Gospels, and the Koran.

Notes

1. The Koran says: 'Abraham was neither a Jew nor a Christian, but rather he was a pure believer [*hanif*]' (3:67). See also Koran 6:61: 'Say: Verily my Lord has guided me to a straight path, the true way, the religion of Abraham, who was a pure believer [*hanif*].'
2. 'He is the Messenger of God and the Seal of the Prophets' (Koran 33:.40).
3. Gary W. Trompf's *The Idea of Historical Recurrence in Western Thought*, Berkeley, 1979, gives the best account of the cyclical concepts of Antiquity.

4. In the English translation of the *Vishnu Purana* (2nd edn, Calcutta 1961), which is the most comprehensive of the Puranas of Hinduism, the cosmological teachings of that religion, as affecting the cycles of mankind and the descent of the Avataras, are thoroughly explained.

5. See the article 'Maitreya' from *The Encyclopedia of Religion*, New York, 1987, Vol.9.

6. Jeremy Rifkin, in *Algeny: A New Word — A New World*, New York, 1987, says on p.63: 'It is no secret that Darwin's theory of evolution has been exploited over and over again to justify various political and economic ideologies and interests.' See also Huston Smith, 'Hope, Yes; Progress, No', *Forgotten Truth*, New York, 1977, chapter 6; and Titus Burckhardt, 'Evolutionism' from *Mirror of the Intellect*, Albany, 1987, pp.32-45.

7. Joseph Klausner's *The Messianic Idea in Israel*, New York, 1955, is certainly the most thorough-going account of Jewish messianic teachings. Of the thirteen articles of the Jewish creed written by Maimonides and that are included in the Daily Prayer Book, the twelfth is: 'I believe with perfect faith in the coming of the messiah, and though he tarry I will wait daily for him.'

8. See Isaiah 2:2-4 for this spiritualized view of messianic times; the fourth verse contains this famous description of things in those days: 'They will beat their swords into plowshares and their spears into pruning hooks. Nation will not take up sword against nation, nor will they train for war anymore.'

9. On this, see Jeremiah 23:5-6. ' "The days are coming," declares the Lord, "when I will raise up to David a righteous Branch, a King who will reign wisely and do what is just and right in the land. In his days Judah will be saved and Israel will live in safety. This is the name by which he will be called : The Lord Our Righteousness." '

10. St Paul, in Romans 11:25, provides the scriptural basis for this belief, which has been held since the beginning of Christianity: 'Israel has experienced a hardening in part until the full number of the Gentiles has come in. And so all Israel will be saved, as it is written: "The deliverer will come from Zion; he will turn godlessness away from Jacob. And this is my covenant with them when I take away their sins." '

11. See, for example, St Augustine, *The City of God*, Bk. 20, chapter 30, on the events of the last days. John Henry Newman, in his 'Advent Sermons on Antichrist' from *Tracts for the Times*, London, 1838-40, pp.1-54, gives a comprehensive view of the Latin and Greek Fathers on this subject.

12. The characteristics of this Heavenly Jerusalem can be found in Galatians 4:25, 26; Hebrews 12:22; and Revelation 3:12, 21:2, 21:10.

13. Daniel 11:31; 12:11.

14. Revelation 7:14.

15. The Christian thesis that the Jews will accept the Antichrist is based on this utterance of the Christ: 'I have come in my Father's name, and you do not

84

accept me; but if someone else comes in his own name, you will accept him' (John 5:43).

16. The coming of Elijah in the end days is a tenet of Judaism; see Malachi 4:5-6 on this. In Christianity, both Elijah and Henoch return at the end of time.

17. The eschatological doctrines of the Koran are to be found in the innumerable verses of the Meccan Surahs on the Day of Judgement; and for the *hadith-literature* see the English translation of Tibrizi's *Mishkat al-Masabih*, Lahore, 1975, Bk. 26, a collection of *hadiths* from numerous sources on the last days.

18. The article on 'Jesus' from the *Jewish Encyclopedia*, New York, 1902-5, says that Jewish legends concerning Jesus are found in the Talmud and Midrash, and in the life of Jesus (*Toledot Yeshu*) of medieval origin: 'It is the tendency of all these sources to belittle the person of Jesus by ascribing to him illegitimate birth, magic, and a shameful death', Vol.7, p.170. The *Toledot Yeshu* was translated by Solomon Bennet as *The Gospel According to the Jews Called Toldoth Jesu, the Generations of Jesus*, London, 1923, wherein both Jesus and Mary are dealt with in calumnious fashion.

19. According to a *hadith* found in Tibrizi's *Mishkat al-Masabih*, Bk. 26, chapter 17, the number of Prophets from Adam to the days of the Prophet is 124,000, and the number of Messengers is 315. The Messengers found religions, the Prophets revive them and prophesy; but the two functions can occasionally be found in one and the same person, such as Jesus and Muhammad, who were Prophets and Messengers.

20. On the Annunciation: 'Behold! The angels said: O Mary, God gives thee glad tidings of a Word from him: his name is the Messiah, Jesus son of Mary' (Koran 3:45). On the Immaculate Conception: 'And she who guarded her chastity: We breathed into her of our Spirit, and We made her and her son a sign for all the world' (Koran 21:91).

21. See Koran 4:155 on the charge that the Jews slaughtered the Prophets unjustly; and 4:156 for their 'grave calumny' against Mary. Koran 4:159 maintains that everyone, including the Jews, will eventually believe in Jesus: 'There is not one of the People of the Book but will of a certainty believe in him before he dies, and on the Day of Resurrection he will be witness against them.'

22. For the rise of Christian Zionism, and especially of pre-tribulationism, in Britain and America in the nineteenth century, see Robert H. Gundry, *The Church and the Tribulation*, Grand Rapids, 1973, pp.185-8. On American pre-millennialism, see Timothy P. Weber, *Living in the Shadow of the Second Coming: American Pre-millennialism, 1975-1982*, Grand Rapids, 1983.

23. As in the Scofield Reference Bible, with notes and comments by Dr C.I. Scofield, which came out in the first edition in 1909. Since then, millions of copies of this work have been printed. Scofield divided up mankind's history into seven 'dispensations', beginning in the Garden of Eden with

'Innocence' (Genesis 1:28) and ending with 'Kingdom' (Revelation 20:4), referring to the coming Messianic dispensation. To see this dispensation-alist theology applied as commentary to a particular book of the Bible, see John F. Walvoord's *The Revelation of Jesus Christ*, Chicago, 1966. On a much more popular plane, Hal Lindsey's famous work *The Late Great Planet Earth*, Grand Rapids, 1970, a book that sold over eighteen million copies in the 1970s, is indicative of how far-reaching an influence this brand of Christian Zionism has been in America.

24. On the rather impressive influence that Christian Zionism has on the American Government in its dealings with the State of Israel, see Ruth W. Mouly, *The Religious Right and Israel: The Politics of Armageddon*, Chicago, 1985.

25. For present-day Islamic thinking, see John Voll, *Islam: Continuity and Change in the Modern World*, Boulder, 1982; and John L. Esposition, ed., *Voices of a Resurgent Islam*, New York, 1983. Seyyed Hossein Nasr, in his *Islam and the Plight of Modern Man*, New York, 1975, gives a contemporary Muslim's view from the traditional intellectual perspective.

26. See a Jewish rabbi's rejection of Zionism in Gary V. Smith, ed., *Zionism: The Dream and the Reality*, London, 1974, p.13. However, Jewish fundamentalism at the present day is a mixture of Judaism and ethnocentric nationalism, the latter compromising Judaism to a remarkable degree. In Jewish fundamentalism, as in Christian Zionism, the same tendency to hasten redemption is evident, except that for the Jewish Zionist-fundamentalists, redemption is for the Jews, whereas for the Christians it is for the Jews and the Gentiles at the Second Coming. Both Jewish and Christian Zionists of an extremist bent see the Islamic sanctuary of the Dome of the Rock as one of the major stumbling-blocks in their program for the future, which is understandable since the Messiah, at least in Jewish thinking, must occupy the Temple of Jerusalem. The latter, if it is rebuilt, must first be preceded by the destruction of the Islamic sanctuary, and this, as is only too evident, would bring the entire Islamic world into the picture.

CHAPTER 9

The Interpretation of Symbol in René Guénon

Marilyn J. Gustin

In pondering the extensive symbolic studies of René Guénon, this question arose: is he the only one who can interpret symbols in this way, or could others learn from him, follow his methods, and build on what he founded? The answer is not as obvious as it may seem, since some of Guénon's followers think that only 'traditional initiation' into certain spiritual realities enables the accurate interpretation of symbols, because specific doctrinal understanding is necessary.[1]

But after an extensive study of Guénon's work[2] it seems to me that theoretical studies of symbols can be made, following the information that Guénon has given and using the methods that can be discerned in his own work. I do not mean to suggest that his approach to symbolic interpretation is the only legitimate one, but it is intriguing enough that further use of it seems eminently worthwhile.

The question was not foreign to Guénon himself. Scattered throughout his works are indications of what he thought would disqualify the would-be interpreter of symbols, as well as necessary qualifications. Among the former are: interest in erudition for its own sake; taking corporeal reality as the sole reality;[3] a purely social or moralizing interest;[4] improvisation;[5] analysis taken alone.[6]

The positive qualifications include: intellectual intuition and the ability to see beyond forms;[7] a 'sense of the marvellous';[8] being at least in the process of spiritual growth;[9] the possession of basic doctrinal information, because symbolism is an exact science.[10]

Even with all these considerations, Guénon has said that symbol is for everyone, because each can interpret it at the level accessible to him and in accord with personal capacities.[11] The highest significance will remain veiled for some, but be fully revealed to others.

Guénon surely did not intend that the direction of his work would dead-end with his death. With his cautions in mind, I have offered here some basic information about symbols according to Guénon, and indicated the primary procedures of interpretation which are discernible in his symbolic studies. It is a sketch, taken from my more complete study. My hope is that it may whet the appetites of some to turn to Guénon's own work for themselves.

First we must ask what Guénon understands a symbol to be, and for that it is necessary to glance at his view of the structure of reality.

For him, everything is, in its own way, a manifestation of the One Principle, the Absolute. There are many degrees of reality, hierarchically ordered and thus nearer to the Principle or farther from It. The precise nature of each thing derives from its relationship to the Principle and from its place within the whole hierarchy. Or one might equally well say that a thing's place in the hierarchy derives from its own particular nature. Thus there are coherent and harmonious inter-relationships among all things, by virtue of their relation to the Principle.[12] On this basis, each thing symbolizes the Principle in its own manner, in its own order.

The inter-relationships of things, viewed vertically (that is, from a given order to a higher or lower one), show qualitative correspondences. It could not be otherwise, since each bears its own relation to the Principle through the hierarchical orders above itself. Thus the correspondences are built into the nature of all reality. This fact for Guénon is the Law of Correspondences and it is the Law on which all symbolism is grounded.[13] The implications of this Law of Correspondences are several.

The first is that anything can be rightly taken as a symbol. Everything, expressing the Principle in its own order, expresses also all the orders which lie above itself, between itself and the Principle. (This spatial symbolic language is Guénon's own and must not be taken literally.) Thus each thing, according to its nature, symbolizes the corresponding 'thing' in all orders transcendent to itself. Since everything has a place within a given order, it may be said to have a place on a vertical line to the Principle. 'Everything' is here taken exactly: concepts, facts and events of nature, historical events and social customs, laws, the human figure — actually every thing, since each thing expresses the nature, or some aspect of the nature, of all that is more profound than itself in its own vertical line to the Principle.[14] This symbolizing capacity, opening to all higher orders, is in fact each thing's reason for being and the inter-relating laws are the same for all.[15]

Guénon says there is an order which must be respected when considering the vertical relations of symbols. First, never can a lower thing be taken for the higher itself, for the result is bound to be serious error. The lower must remain lower and be seen for what it is.[16] Then, a given symbol can never be taken to symbolize anything in the order below itself, though it can be symbolized by the lower. This is why there is no physical thing which symbolizes another physical thing, and why nothing else symbolizes physical things: they are already the lowest.[17]

The symbolic value of a thing, further, does not in any way diminish the reality it bears in its own natural order, its place in the hierarchy. All things have the degree of reality accorded them by the hierarchical order to which they belong. Thus a natural phenomenon, say, the sun, is no less a physical object out there in its own place. An historical fact is no less actual. But seen more profoundly and more truly, it expresses that which is beyond it. Indeed, Guénon insists that factual significance is greatly enhanced by the thing's expressiveness of the higher.[18] For Guénon, the symbolic value is clearly the more important, because 'it is only by symbolism that the things of this world are attached to higher realities.'[19] It is the symbolic meaning that gives things their real significance.[20]

So for Guénon no symbol is arbitrary. Its symbolizing capacity is its very nature and it could not be otherwise. For the same reason, no symbol is invented and no symbol can be individual in origin. As Guénon is fond of saying, symbolism is of 'non-human' origin.[21]

These are, then, the major implications of the Law of Correspondences as Guénon sees them. The correspondences themselves also require some comment. Correspondences occur between things in the same order and between different orders or degrees. They can often be recognized as analogous, since each part of the Universe is 'always and everywhere analogous to the whole,'[22] and therefore to each other. This is the Law of Analogy.

These analogies are sometimes of form, but more frequently and more reliably, analogies are to be sought among functions and relationships. Thus two things which have a given relationship in one plane are analogous if that relationship remains the same when viewed from another plane.[23] For example, when considering ternary symbols, i.e. sets of three that belong together, one cannot take the 'three-ness' alone as indicating correspondence. One must be sure that the relationships among the three terms are the same on another plane.[24]

Yet some correspondences are not analogical[25] and many are inversely analogical. This latter notion is especially important for the interpretation of symbols.

An inverse analogy is like a reflection in water: the shapes are the same, but reversed. This is the true meaning, says Guénon, of the well-known Hermetic statement, 'As above, so below'. He also refers here to the statement in the Gospel of Matthew 20:16, 'So the last will be first, and the first last.'[26] Guénon insists that when the Law of Analogy is strictly applied, every true analogy is inverse. When moving toward a higher order, the move is analogical, but specifically inversely analogical when moving from the sensible to the non-sensible, from the exterior to the interior, from manifestation to the non-manifest or principial.[27]

Here are two examples. The heart is the center of the being, its principle. The physical heart is the most hidden, the innermost of the body. But the principle of the being is in reality the greatest of all, encompassing all. Likewise the point is spatially all but nothing, yet it is the principle which produces all space by reproduction of itself only.[28]

'Every true analogy must be applied inversely,' Guénon says.[29] Yet in his own interpretations what may be called 'direct' analogies are sometimes used. For example, Guénon speaks of the Divine Word expressing itself in Creation and this being 'comparable analogically' to thought being expressed in words.[30] There is no inversion here, but a direct analogy. This kind of example is not rare.

When Guénon studies particular symbols, his basic observation is that symbols are multivalent. By this he does not mean primarily that many meanings are attributed to symbols. He means that symbols by their very nature have many inherent meanings. Likewise inherently, the meanings can never be contradictory or totally unrelated to one another. All meanings of a symbol are wholly coherent and mutually expansive.[31] Interpretation based on such an observation is, then, never a matter of creating meanings but of discovering the inherent significance within the symbol itself. It is precisely in their multivalence that their value is to be found. So the interpreter's task is to search out their multiple senses.[32]

The multivalence of symbols is grounded in the reality that each thing is by nature related to all other things. The multiple senses and the concepts that may be drawn from them are indefinite in number since they move through all worlds to the Infinite. But Guénon hastens to affirm that this leads to no laxity. Symbolism is an 'absolutely mathematically'[33] exact form of expression. Again, such an affirmation is grounded in the nature of symbol: of itself, the symbol means what it means and could not mean otherwise.

There is a similar absolutism in Guénon's idea of symbolic meanings in different cultures. He recognizes easily that there are cultural differences in interpretations. But he believes that multivalence has limits, that some interpretations can simply be erroneous. Guénon is not interested in erroneous interpretations, except to correct them, no matter how many cultures may share the interpretation in question.

In Guénon's work, one finds describable kinds of multivalence and reasons for it, all based on the inherent multivalence just considered. One range of meanings depends on the universal hierarchy. A given thing, as symbol, implies all that is above it in the hierarchy, through all orders of reality up to and including the Principle itself.[34] This is the reason it is so excellent a means of expression for metaphysical ideas. The symbol means always more, there is always more to discern, suggesting and aiding conception of even the inexpressible and infinite Principle.[35]

A second range of relationships which figure in his interpretation, but which he does not describe explicitly, are those of a symbol with other things in its own order. Strictly speaking, Guénon would not say that a symbol can symbolize things in its own order, but even so, similarities and relationships on the same level can contribute to the fuller understanding of a symbol. Meanings implied in this way are also indefinite in number, since Guénon says the full extension of a being on one level includes indefinite modalities.[36] There is then a 'horizontal' multiplicity of significant relationships in addition to the 'vertical' multivalence.

Vertical correspondences and their attendant multiple senses cannot be uncovered arbitrarily. This work is governed by the laws of analogy. A shift from one order to another in the universal hierarchy is called by Guénon 'transposition'. A symbol may be given one meaning in its own order. Then it may be transposed to orders beyond its own, fuller and analogical meanings being revealed in the process. Transposition can occur repeatedly and indefinitely upward, through degrees of increasing universality, since the orders up to the Principle are indefinite in number.[37] This is a function of discernment rather than invention.

Guénon's analogical transpositions are consistently inverse when he moves from the manifest to the principial orders. For example, Guénon notes that there is an inverse analogical relation (not a likeness) between the human, conditioned by a certain level of existence, and the total being which is unconditioned. The human is the individual synthesis of all the elements of the individual order. Unconditioned being is the principle of all manifestation. 'Conditioned' and 'unconditioned' are analogically inverse to one another, but their synthetic or principial quality is similar in their respective orders.[38]

However, it does seem that some interpretations which Guénon calls transpositions are not inversely analogical. Examples are not rare. Thus the untying of the knot is understood at the level of individual man to be his death to the physical state, i.e. the 'loosening of the collection' which makes a man. In a higher order, the untying of the knot is the loosening of all connections, the freeing into total deliverance from all manifested states.[39] This is a direct analogy rather than an inverse one.

Whether by direct or inverse analogy, there is no question about Guénon's constant use of transposition, 'through all the domains which one can envision',[40] without ever leaving reality, since reality itself is structured the same way. Transpositions may be followed to whatever degree is required by the immediate use of the symbol, from the smallest physical object up to the whole of the Principle.[41]

Inasmuch as symbols may be transposed into many orders of reality, revealing ever more meanings, it is clear that these meanings can be 'stacked up' as it were, each one remaining true. Guénon calls this aspect of interpretation 'superposition', noting repeatedly that these superposed senses may well be different, but can never be mutually exclusive.[42]

Here is an example of superposition, interesting for its use of both direct and inverse analogy: Guénon considers the waters of Genesis 1 and shows the consistency in superposition that results from accurate transposition. At the highest level, all the waters represent Universal

See Maurice
Bacaille
Bible, Quran & Science

Possibility, both manifest and non-manifest. The separation of the waters here refers to the non-manifest (upper waters) separated from the manifest (lower waters). On the next lower level all waters are all possibilities of manifestation; when separated the upper waters are formless manifestation and the lower waters are formal manifestation. Next lower, taking all waters as all possibilities of formal manifestation, the upper waters become subtle manifestation and the lower waters gross manifestation. Each transposition here is directly analogical.[43] But the gross manifestation of water is the element itself. That is the lowest, weakest. Viewed metaphysically it is the most powerful, as we have already seen. This latter relationship is inversely analogical. The pattern of the transpositions is consistently directly analogical, while the lowest and the highest meanings are inversely analogical. All the meanings are included in the single symbol, water. That is superposition.

Guénon adds that superposition sometimes results in fusion of symbols, so that many meanings are visually indicated in one configuration. A frequent traditional symbolic use is a circular figure with twelve inscriptions or twelve divisions. He calls attention to the Round Table with twelve people seated around it, then the round zodiac inscribed on such a table, with the twelve zodiacal signs referring to the astronomical zodiac, which being of nature is itself also symbolic. These appear everywhere, often gathered into one complex or fused figure.[45]

Guénon does not pursue it at this point, but knowing others among his interpretations, one could proceed: the circle implies a center. So one could consistently (conceptually if not practically) 'fuse' all the symbolic meanings of center (including that of the Principle Itself) into the round figure. Further, knowing that the Round Table was meant to receive the Holy Grail, all of the very complex Grail symbolism could be added. Going on, one might suggest temporal symbolism, the year of twelve months, with all of its implications. Although the figure becomes impossible to draw, by proceeding thus one begins to sense how far such a possible superposition of meanings might go without ever leaving the basic form of a circle with twelve figures. Surely some applications made in this way might be secondary to the primary intention of the symbol, but legitimate because the correspondences are there.

This is by no means to be understood as an 'evolution' of symbols, which is not possible, Guénon says. The intrinsic meaning of symbols does not change with arbitrary human effort. Since a symbol is not human in origin, one cannot add new meanings that are not borne within it by its very nature. No theory of symbols 'evolving' or acquiring new meanings is acceptable to Guénon, because it puts something into symbol that was not there in itself.[46]

A phenomenon noted by Guénon is that symbols quite often bear double, even apparently opposed, meanings even within one traditional form.[47] Guénon takes this fact itself symbolically, saying that since symbols are within the realm of manifestation, their double meanings may refer to the duality inherent in manifestation.[48] Guénon is nothing if not alert to discerning symbolic significance at every level of fact.

All traditional forms include symbols with double significance, easily observed. The serpent provides an accessible example. In Christianity, the serpent refers to evil in the Garden of Eden, but to wisdom when it rises from the Eucharistic cup. In Egypt, the serpent is wisdom and power as the uraeus on the pharaonic crown, but threatening in other settings. In this example, the two meanings are apparently opposed, i.e. 'maleficent' and 'beneficent' as is often the case.[49]

Guénon says that symbols can never be finally contradictory, because reality demands coherence. What appears oppositional on one level is in reality only the exterior aspect of an actual, more inward complementarity.[50] Further, since every symbol leads toward the unity that is the Principle, such a complementarity is somewhere midway between the multiplicity of manifestation and the Principial Unity.[51] Where such an opposition appears, it implies a demand to seek the more unifying relationships.

Guénon demonstrates a number of ways in which this may be done. The first is to look beyond the obvious meanings for the single principle that may unite them, whether this principle comes from the same traditional form or another. The two serpents entwined on the caduceus, for example, usually mean life and death, but are in reality a single power 'double in its manifestation'.[52] One might add that in the Christian tradition, the power of wisdom, perverted, could be understood to be evil.

The intention behind the uses made of symbols may indicate a double meaning as well as its reason for being. Here the uniting idea is likely to be, as above, the power which is single but can be used in opposing ways or for opposing purposes. Magic or sorcery calls on the influences inherent in symbols. So does ritual. The same symbolic process is aimed at qualitatively opposite results in these two uses.[53]

Real complementarity in apparently opposed symbols may also be found in analogical transposition to another level. On a lower level, the symbol of darkness means chaos, indeed threatening; on a higher level, it is non-manifestation, devoutly to be sought. The relationship here is inverse, but the common factor is 'indistinction'.[54] The indifferentiation in chaos becomes symbolic of the Principial Unity, also undifferentiated. Darkness bears both meanings within itself, complementary to each other by inverse analogy.

When transposed like this, some apparent dualities become equivalents. Others may turn out to be arranged hierarchically, the one becoming the immediate principle of the other.[55]

Resolution by a higher order is not the only explanation Guénon offers for double or opposed senses. He also notes the role a symbol fills in a given usage. A cord may unify or it may prevent access, a bridge can be crossed in two directions.[56] It is not only that a figure may be viewed from two angles, but that one figure in itself actually can function in more than one way, yielding both beneficial and threatening senses. When the cord unifies, it is to be welcomed; when it defends, presumably the one who approaches is repulsed. A bridge may be crossed into heaven, but it also provides the means for regression to earth.

The context of a symbol can change its meaning from maleficent to beneficent. A river bank, when the clear task is to cross the river toward it, usually bears a beneficent quality. One is happy to be headed in that direction. But when the river flows toward the ocean as its goal, the task is to arrive there. Then the banks become threatening, to be avoided.[57]

One may also approach this issue of role by noticing whether a symbol relates to a lower or higher state. The whale of Jonah, for example, when seen from the boat (i.e. the lower state) is maleficent indeed. But when viewed from the shore (the higher state in this case) the whale is beneficent, for it has saved him.[58]

Symbolic meanings may sometimes be reversed by circumstantial or temporal changes. Taking Babylon symbolically: Bab-Ilu, in its own traditional form, means 'gateway to heaven' or even sometimes 'house of God'. But when times bring changes, when the traditional form is lost or the symbol taken over by another traditional form, the 'gateway to heaven' comes to refer to confusion.[59]

Guénon himself has pointed out that the double meaning of symbols makes the interpretation of symbols very 'delicate', and demanding of precision.[60] Further, he insists that these double meanings are commonly misinterpreted and can give rise to considerable error, sometimes deliberately. For that reason, he is careful to point out double meanings in individual studies.[61]

From all of the above discussion of symbolic multivalence, it is clear that the meanings of any symbol are affected by the viewpoint from which one examines it. For Guénon, that viewpoint must be explicitly chosen to avoid confusion in the interpreter as well as the student.[62]

First one must note the order to which the symbol itself belongs, then choose the order which is to be taken as its referent for immediate interpretive purposes. Is the metaphysical significance (referent) of a mineral in question? If so, then inverse analogy should be applied and this particular meaning discerned.

Another choice of viewpoint has to do with the particular tradition within which the symbol appears. Does the interpreter stand in the same traditional form or in another? Here Guénon gives the example of Jerusalem, in the Judaic tradition understood to be the Center of the World. Seen from within that same tradition, Jerusalem actually is the Center which is the Pole or Axis of this world, and those who belong to this tradition will so interpret it. But if one steps outside this tradition, Jerusalem can no longer be considered the actual Center (since now the actual Center might be, say, Mecca), but it can just as well be taken to symbolize the Center.[63] Again these two possibilities are not mutually exclusive.

Yet another possible viewpoint is whether the referent is the esoteric (metaphysical) realm or the exoteric (religious) realm.[64]

These are three angles of view from which a symbol may be interpreted without confusion. They are the primary standpoints taken by Guénon in his interpretive studies.

There remains one further complex aspect of the multivalence of symbols: their degeneration, misunderstanding, misinterpretation, and deliberate abuse. For Guénon, these difficulties do not lie in the symbol as such, but in the interpreters.

Symbols do sometimes degenerate, or more precisely, the interpretations of them degenerate with times and circumstances. Such degeneration primarily has to do with loss of knowledge of the reality of symbolism or with the loss of the principle of a particular symbol. Sometimes one of the qualitatively lesser senses of a symbol remains while the higher meanings are forgotten. When these things occur Guénon speaks of the symbols as having degenerated. An example he gives is the exclusively magical use of symbols.[65]

A further degeneration may be apparent when something that was traditionally understood symbolically comes to be used merely as ornamentation. One case in point is the necklace, meaning the chain of all worlds, but now only decoratively used.[66] Guénon says that everything used as ornament originally had symbolic connections and intent, however forgotten that may have become.[67]

Degeneration of symbols then is usually based on a misunderstanding which leads to other consequences, including the actual deformation of symbols, with a resulting increase in misunderstanding.

Degeneration and misunderstanding, when involuntary, are one thing. But Guénon insists that sometimes symbols are knowingly subverted. He warns that one must distinguish carefully between these two cases, since the latter is significant, while the former may frequently be shrugged away. He is not thoroughly explicit about how to discern it, but there are a few indications. One must look at the intention behind the given interpretation, first of all. This involves not only content of the symbol itself, but motivation betrayed in the context. One must try to see whether the form of the traditional symbol has been distorted and exactly how. That is not easy since false interpretations can be given to traditional symbols without changes in their form, remaining plausible precisely because of that. The analogies do exist and they can be misread, either by those who merely want to support their own notions or by those who purposefully wish to distort.[68]

No matter how far-fetched the interpretation, all is never lost. The symbol always and forever retains its own proper meaning, as it retains its rightful place in the universal hierarchy with its rightful significance. Meanings can indeed be unperceived or misperceived, but no deviations can affect the real meanings of a symbol.[69] Since symbols are of reality itself, the spiritual influence which they bear can always revivify them and fully restore what has been lost, for those who have the inner eyes to see.[70]

Nowhere does Guénon describe his methods of interpretation. Therefore it is necessary to explore his own interpretive processes, ferreting them out of his symbolic studies.

One notices immediately that Guénon follows many procedures in no consistent order. He follows his principles and uses his tools in the order and manner dictated by the necessities he perceives in the immediate study, much as a surgeon uses his instruments, according to the needs of the moment. Awareness of specific needs depends on previous information, on intuition and probably also on experience.

The most striking feature of Guénon's practice is his constant gathering of symbols from every traditional form to which he has access. This means not only the best known 'religious traditions', but also the Greeks, the Celts, the alchemists, the Hermetic and Masonic traditions, the ancient Egyptians, and occasionally others. (Notably little present in his work are Buddhism, Eastern Orthodox Christianity and shamanism.)

The only 'test' of validity to which these choices across ages and cultures seem to be submitted by Guénon is the Law of Correspondence. Certainly he is not always willing to accept the meaning ascribed to a symbol by its own particular tradition, although he very often does. He searches for more light in other traditions, aiming always for the higher idea that may unite them all.[71] Similarly, when he finds several symbols in one tradition which express the same idea, he presses them to their highest single possibility, supporting the interpretation with symbols from any tradition available.[72] Thus the possibility of demonstrating universal implications might be said to provide a kind of principle of selection for Guénon.

In many studies, Guénon begins by noting the relation of the symbols under consideration to their own traditional form, then immediately gathers symbols from other traditions, seeking and explaining connections and relationships as he goes.[73] He seeks harmonies, appropriate connections, to expand, complement, enrich and complete the symbol with which the study began.

Because of the network of inter-traditional associations which Guénon builds, usually without explaining himself, he has been accused of syncretism. His clearest response is given in the 'Preface' for *Symbolism of the Cross*. There he says that syncretism is basically superficial and fragmentary, the elements having been gathered in haphazard fashion, so that they cannot be unified into a coherent whole. Synthesis on the other hand is a gathering viewed from within, i.e. from the standpoint of the higher idea or principle to which all these elements relate. It requires the capacity to see beyond forms.

The key is that the symbols chosen in synthesis all express the one primordial doctrine and the Unity of the Principle, resulting in a harmonious, organic coherence.[74]

In the search for symbols which correspond to each other, it is quite obvious to begin by looking for similarities of form. Guénon often examines similarities and differences among forms. Occasionally these may look highly coincidental to the casual interpreter. For example, Guénon draws a connection between the divinatory cup belonging to Joseph in Genesis 44:5 and the Grail cup which Joseph of Arimathea is said to have taken to Britain after the resurrection of Jesus.[75] The same name, perhaps similar cups — these connections of form hint to Guénon that more may be found here.

Sometimes an important element or even the principal element of form in a symbol may be invisible. For example, in the symbol of the ladder, the central pole is missing, but implied by the dual stands (two currents of force) and the rungs (levels of being).[76] The clue in such cases is that all parts of the symbol's drawn form imply a relation to that part which is not drawn.

Discerning the chief element of a form is not always easy, even when it is visible. Guénon studies some heraldic and funereal marks of the fourteenth century which look very much like the number 4. Form alone would indicate quaternary symbolic connections. Guénon says that they are indeed quaternary, but not because they look like the number 4! The determining element of this form is the inclusion of two lines at right angles, forming a cross. The cross is definitely a quaternary figure in all its associations.[77]

Some forms may be quite different from one another, but have a related or identical spiritual significance,[78] like the symbol of the carpenter's square and that of the cross. The connecting factor here is a particular possibility of arrangement: the square can be quadrupled and laid so that the unmarked portion is cruciform.[79]

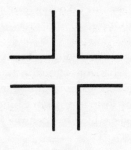

Occasionally the forms of symbols are modified, whether deliberately or ignorantly. Then the question is what to do with the modified symbol. Guénon takes the modifications seriously, since there may be legitimate reasons for them in particular cases, cultures or ages.[80] Sometimes on examination they mean nothing, as in the two directions in which the arms of the swastika are drawn.[81]

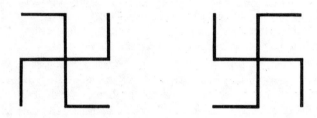

In another case, a change might add or subtract something from the primary meaning.[82] Modifications may be quite complex and Guénon looks for the basic scheme of the symbol.

Guénon's fullest study of symbolic form is his examination of the three-dimensional cross, in which the form is expanded by many additions without departing from the basic figure. Each addition has its own significance. This use of form is an aid to the imagination, based on human need for sensory representation, and as the ideas become increasingly complex, so does the form in which they are represented, while very carefully keeping intact the analogies between the idea and form.[83] Visual imagination is much challenged but the concepts remain graspable.

The more one explores issues of form, the more obvious it becomes that similarities alone do not determine correspondences or meaning.[84] More relationships, sometimes many more, must be discerned.

The most important element of that 'more' is function. Guénon says that when symbols share the same function, a correspondence is indicated.[85] There is a nice example in which Guénon rejects the connection suggested by form in favor of a functional one. The Greek delta looks like a triangle, which by itself might suggest connections between the delta and the whole complex of ternary symbols. But the delta holds the fourth place in the alphabet and functions numerically as a four, and so belongs to quaternary symbolism.[86] Quite generally function supersedes form as an interpretive indication.

Function very often refers to a symbol's function in its own traditional form. Beginning with his selected symbol, Guénon tries to understand its function and thereby its significance in its own proper tradition. Then he looks into other traditions for the symbols which perform the same or similar functions there. These indicate harmonious relationships between the traditions and may also augment the significances of the symbols.

Symbols having similar functions may or may not look alike. The rainbow looks very much like a bridge and indeed both are used to connect worlds. That far, form and function are parallel. But their respective functions are not identical. The rainbow is usually a sign of communication between worlds, as in the Judaic tradition. The bridge enables passage from one world to another, as in the Islamic tradition. The difference in function lends depth and nuance to their respective interpretations.[87]

Things which have a similar function in nature often have similar symbolic meanings. Guénon studies arms as symbols, then notes that their meanings are much like the symbolic meanings of animals' horns or of spines on thorny plants. Where is the correspondence? All are weapons: arms for humans, horns for the animals which bear them, spines for the plants. So weapon-symbolism is coherent in several natural orders (human, animal, vegetable), and arms, horns and spines correspond to each other, because of function.[88]

The placement of a symbol within its context is another indicator of meanings. The largest context is reality itself, which is the same for all symbols. The largest specific context is the particular traditional form in question. The examination of a symbol's place here frequently points to the symbol's function in relation to other elements of the tradition. Then the interest in function plays its usual role.

Another kind of context is the symbol's relation to the universal cycle. The precise placement here is difficult, but since there are laws governing cycles, some determinations can apparently be made. Guénon sometimes asks whether the symbol corresponds qualitatively to what might be expected of a particular phase of the cycle. For example, he says that while both mountain and cave can correspond to the center of the world, the mountain is the more 'primordial' since it is accessible to all. The accessibility of Truth to all is a quality of the first phase of the Manvantara. Similarly, the cavern has a more hidden quality, just as the Center and the Truth would have in a later phase of the universal cycle.[89] The forms of cave and mountain are different, the functions the same, and the cyclical context explains how that can be.

The immediate context of a symbol may be physical, as in a design or a building. Or it may be verbal, as in symbolic word studies, or within a legend, or in scripture. Or the context of one symbol may be a larger complex of symbols, like the zodiac or a cathedral. The first aim of examining such contexts is to discover the underlying idea which may link symbols and throw light on their individual meaning. The symbolism of the Holy Grail is exceedingly complex,[90] but noteworthy on our immediate point is Guénon's use of legendary context: the Grail is said to have been carved from an emerald that dropped out of Lucifer's forehead when he fell from heaven.[91] This context connects the Grail to the third eye of Shiva and especially to the sense of eternity which it represents, and which fallen Lucifer lost, and which the Holy Grail is said to restore.

One of the most complicated procedures which Guénon follows, and one which he uses frequently, is the examination of etymologies and other verbal connections. In these interpretations he treats words as he does other symbols: they have multiple possibilities and do not refer exclusively to their usual denotation. He says that all language, both written and spoken, has essentially the same quality as all symbols: the capacity of a physical fact to express truths which are beyond the physical.[92] Thus even in language there is nothing arbitrary, the names of things always being related in a decipherable way to their natures, pointing toward the universal harmony of all things.[93] Such broad symbolic possibilities are especially characteristic of 'sacred languages' and an important reason for their careful preservation by traditional cultures.

It should be noted that Guénon does not explicate the guidelines he uses for etymological connections. He does not explain how he finds the roots he uses or discovers their meanings. One wishes that he had been less allergic to academic methods of documentation. Guénon certainly expresses concern that etymologies be true and not contrived.[94] At the same time, he is frequently explicit that he follows principles which modern etymologists do not use, but which are contained in the 'traditional science' of words and letters.[95]

Most obviously, Guénon traces the words under study to their roots, gathered from a number of languages. He searches for the general thrust of their meaning, the sense of the root.[96] When in form and meaning they are the same or very near in more than one language, he takes that to indicate symbolic relationships. Then they, like other symbols, can bear significance in other orders than their own.[97]

Whether or not his etymologies would pass strict scholarly examination, he uses another technique which is 'unknown to modern philologists'[98] and it could cover a multitude of etymological misdeeds. This is called 'phonetic assimilation', or sometimes 'phonetic convergence'. It means simply that words or their roots sound alike, having letters in common, and that therefore they may be taken to correspond as symbols, even if etymologically distinct. He insists that the reasons for this kind of similarity are often very profound and it should therefore not be ignored, but that the 'secrets' of this work are almost completely lost today.[99] Nevertheless, Guénon seems to know and follow at least some of these unknown guidelines. A simple example here is that 'Grail' is almost like 'grasale', which means vase, and also like 'gradale', which means book. Both vase and writing are connected to the Grail in other, larger symbolic complexes and this phonetic similarity is both a clue and a corroboration.

Further, Guénon says that sacred languages are so constructed that the same letters, differently arranged and yielding different literal meanings, bear symbolic relationships. Anagrams are symbolically related and the nature of the relationship should be sought. Among many, there is this example: in Sanskrit, *harda* means heart, and *dahara* means cavity. Since there are wide-ranging connections between heart and cave as symbols, he finds here again both clue and corroboration.[100]

Guénon finds significance in the very forms of the letters in sacred languages, especially those used for scriptures,[101] such as Hebrew, Arabic, Sanskrit and Greek. Likewise, he takes account of the ideographic content of letters,[102] obvious in Chinese or Egyptian, perhaps less so in Hebrew or Sanskrit. The principle here is attributed to sacred science and not well explained.

The metaphysical principle behind such great emphasis on words and letters is found in the Islamic, Kabbalist, and Rose-Cross traditions. It is, simply stated, that every letter is one of the divine ideas or essences which together form the manifested world. Thus each letter holds an ultimate significance.[103]

In sacred languages, each letter is also a number and so each word has a numerical value. When the numbers of letters or words are equivalent, they bear equivalent or corresponding symbolic meaning. Even when the roots are different, if the numerical values are the same they are to be interpreted together.[104] (The interpretation of numerical values is immediately lost if words are transliterated.) These correspondences of letter and number connect the whole symbolism of numbers to that of words, and Guénon notes especially that the Kabbalist science of numbers is based on letters.

Guénon tells us that none of these methods should ever be taken alone. One can be sure of profound correspondences only when connections are of more than one type. Then, whatever the nature of the connections (verbal, formal, functional or other), he piles them up to show the coherent meaning inherent in them all.

Traditional symbols seem to be gathered in groups or sets. For purposes of this discussion, I am calling these sets 'classes' of symbols. Guénon refers to these classes and offers a few statements about their inter-relationships. Chiefly, he repeatedly warns that they must not be confused. There are definite correspondences to be perceived between classes, since all symbols and all types of symbols refer finally to the Principle. It has seemed to me that interpretation would be considerably aided if one were aware of some of the major classes from the outset.

Two classes are spatial symbols and temporal symbols, connected but not identical. Space and time are used in our present world as symbols because they are basic determinations of this world's nature and thus these two classes may represent one reality. The multiple states of being, for example, can be suggested by spatial hierarchy or by temporal cycles, neither of which is a literal description. Thus when one moves to the viewpoint of another domain, say that of formless manifestation, time and space are no longer determinations but are still valid as symbols. This can be so precise that space or time can symbolize the corresponding particular determinations of other worlds or states of being.

Spatial and temporal classes include other classes as well: symbolic or sacred geography (the placement of buildings, cities, ritual establishments, spiritual centers); historical facts as a kind of temporal symbol, their nature corresponding to time in this world and to parallel realities in higher worlds. Historical facts also are related to cyclical phases. There are also links between history and geography, as there are between time and space. Another class of symbols connected to spatial symbols is geometrical symbolism. The link is the three-dimensional cross, a geometrical representation of the six directions of space. This connection enables the discernment of correspondences between all the ideas most easily expressed in geometrical forms and all those best expressed in other spatial terms. But geometry is also the basis of all forms and all figured symbolism, including letters, numbers, and all kinds of graphics. So spatial symbolism can be broadly inclusive of almost all visual symbolism.

Another parallel to the geometrical symbol is the arithmetical symbol, as revealed by the symbolic correspondence between the point and the number one. Each, by reproduction of itself, produces everything else in its own order. So from spatial symbolism, one moves to arithmetical symbolism and the connections remain strong.

There are similar parallels between vegetable symbols and mineral symbols. Vegetable symbols include all things that grow and their products. Minerals include stones, precious gems, all subterranean products. For example, minerals refer to the Principle by being an inversely analogical representation of immutability; trees represent It by suggesting the Pole which connects all levels of reality from the mineral to the Principial.

Two frequently mentioned classes of symbols are the polar symbols and the solar symbols. The two are not the same, but there are subtle and complex connections between them. Polar symbols are 'of a more elevated order' since they revolve around the axis or center of the world (universal), which connects all worlds (hierarchical degrees or orders), thus representing the Principle quite directly.

Solar symbolism is connected with the sun, representing the Principle as that which enlightens this present world, but keeps a certain distance, as is consistent with cyclic development.

The connections between these classes have been introduced over long ages and are extremely complex. One way of connecting solar and polar classes is to note that the solstices of the sun constitute the pole of the year, that is, of the temporal world, which implies a correspondence to the spatial world where the polar symbols predominate. There are other, more complicated connections as well.

Space requires that this sketch close here. It is hoped that it is enough to suggest the broad foundation which Guénon has offered and on which further symbolic work in the same vein may be erected. If a would-be interpreter is willing to study what Guénon has done and to continue from there, it seems to me that his/her work could bear fruit which even Guénon might acknowledge.

Notes

1. Jean-Pierre Laurant, *Le sens caché selon René Guénon*, Editions l'Age d'Homme, Lausanne, 1975, pp.115, 128, 141.
2. Marilyn J. Gustin, 'The Nature, Role and Interpretation of Symbol in the Thought of René Guénon', Ph.D. dissertation, Graduate Theological Union, 1987; available from University Microfilms.
3. René Guénon, *Man and His Becoming According to the Vedanta*, trans. Richard Nicholson, 1st Indian edn, Oriental Book Reprint Corporation, New Delhi, 1981, p.155.
4. René Guénon, *Aperçus sur l'Initiation*, 2nd edn, Editions Traditionnelles, Paris, 1953, p.200; *Mélange*, Editions Gallimard, Paris, 1976, p.104.
5. René Guénon, *Initiation et réalisation spirituelle*, Avant-propos Jean Reyor, Editions Traditionnelles, Paris, 1952, p.100.
6. René Guénon, *Les Principes de Calcul infinitesimal*, Editions Gallimard, Paris, 1946, p.130.
7. René Guénon, *Symbolism of the Cross*, trans. Angus McNab, Luzac & Co., London, 1958, p.xi; *The Reign of Quantity and the Signs of the Times*, trans. Lord Northbourne, Penguin Books Inc., Baltimore, 1972, p.167.
8. Laurant, *Sens caché*, p.136.
9. Guénon, *Initiation*, p.200.
10. René Guénon, *Symboles fondamentaux de la science sacrée*, Michel Valsan, ed., Editions Gallimard, Paris, 1957, p.28.
11. Guénon, *Fondamentaux*, p.34.
12. René Guénon, *Man and His Becoming*, pp.100-101; *Cross*, p.xii.
13. Guénon, *Cross*, p.13; *Fondamentaux*, p.35.
14. Guénon, *Quantity*, p.162; *Fondamentaux*, p.411.
15. Guénon, *Introduction to the Study of Hindu Doctrines*, trans. Marco Pallis, Luzac & Co., London, 1945, p.134; *Man and His Becoming*, p.154, note 3.
16. Guénon, *Cross*, p.128.
17. Guénon, *Initiation*, p.173.
18. Guénon, *Fondamentaux*, p.416.
19. René Guénon, *Etudes sur la Franc-maçonnerie et le Compagnonnage*, 2 vols., A. Andre Villain, ed., Editions Traditionnelles, Paris, 1984, Vol.1, p.101.
20. René Guénon, *Lord of the World*, trans. Shaffer, Chieke and Blake, Coombe Spring Press, North Yorkshire, England, 1983, p.66.

21. Guénon, *Initiation*, p.57; *Fondamentaux*, pp.35-6.
22. Guénon, *Cross*, p.12.
23. Guénon, *Man and His Becoming*, p.40.
24. René Guénon, *La Grande Triade*, Editions Gallimard, Paris, 1957, pp.18-19.
25. Guénon, *Maçonnerie I*, p.295; *Fondamentaux,*, p.319.
26. Guénon, *Fondamentaux*, p.242.
27. Guénon, *Man and His Becoming*, p.41; *Cross*, p.128; *Fondamentaux*, p.436.
28. Guénon, *Fondamentaux*, p.219; *Cross*, p.130.
29. Guénon, *Cross*, p.7.
30. Guénon, *Fondamentaux*, p.37.
31. Guénon, *Initiation*, p.205; *Fondamentaux*, p.444.
32. Guénon, *Fondamentaux*, p.43.
33. Guénon, *Hindu Doctrines*, p.131.
34. Guénon, *Cross*, p.xiii.
35. Guénon, *Initiation*, p.205.
36. Guénon, *Cross*, p.57.
37. Guénon, *Triade*, p.202.
38. Guénon, *Cross*, p.8.
39. Guénon, *Fondamentaux*, p.342.
40. Guénon, *Fondamentaux*, p.441.
41. Guénon, *Man and His Becoming*, p.90.
42. Guénon, *Fondamentaux*, p.139.
43. Guénon, *Man and His Becoming*, pp.56-7, note 3.
44. Guénon, *Fondamentaux*, p.387.
45. *Ibid*, pp.42, 115.
46. *Ibid*, p.54.
47. René Guénon, *Formes traditionnelles et Cycles cosmiques*, Avant-propos Roger Maridort, Editions Gallimard, Paris, 1973, p.168.
48. Guénon, *Quantity*, p.242.
49. *Ibid*, p.245.
50. Guénon, *Fondamentaux*, p.363.
51. Guénon, *Quantity*, p.243.
52. Guénon, *Fondamentaux*, p.159; *Triade*, pp.46-7.
53. Guénon, *Fondamentaux*, p.401.
54. Guénon, *Réalisation spirituelle*, pp.205-6.
55. Guénon, *Fondamentaux*, p.417.
56. *Ibid*, p.380.
57. *Ibid*, p.345.
58. *Ibid*, p.174.
59. Guénon, *Lord*, p.62, note 8.
60. Guénon, *Fondamentaux*, p.44.
61. Guénon, *Lord*, p.17.

62. Guénon, *Cross*, p.102.
63. Guénon, *Lord*, p.37.
64. Guénon, *Cross*, p.102.
65. Guénon, *Fondamentaux*, p.393; *Hindu Doctrines*, p.93.
66. Guénon, *Fondamentaux*, p.368.
67. Guénon, *Triade*, p.46, note 1.
68. Guénon, *Lord*, p.52, note 11; *Quantity*, pp.246-7; *Fondamentaux*, p.307.
69. Guénon, *Fondamentaux*, p.307.
70. Guénon, *Maçonnerie I*, p.271; *Initiation*, p.205.
71. Guénon, *Fondamentaux*, p.229.
72. *Ibid*, p.96.
73. Guénon, *Fondamentaux*, p.297, but evident everywhere in his studies.
74. Guénon, *Cross*, pp.x-xi.
75. Guénon, *Fondamentaux*, p.293.
76. Guénon, *Fondamentaux*, p.339.
77. *Ibid*, pp.397-8.
78. *Ibid*, p.343.
79. Guénon, *Cross*, p.55, note 2.
80. Guénon, *Fondamentaux*, p.337.
81. Guénon, *Cross*, p.56.
82. Guénon, *Fondamentaux*, p.337.
83. Guénon, *Cross*, p.92.
84. Guénon, *Fondamentaux*, p.430.
85. *Ibid*, p.286.
86. *Ibid*, p.430, note 2.
87. *Ibid*, Chapter LXIV passim; *Lord*, p.6.
88. Guénon, *Fondamentaux*, p.206.
89. *Ibid*, p.223.
90. Cf. Guénon, *Lord*, Chapter 5, and *Fondamentaux*, Chapters III and IV.
91. Guénon, *Lord*, p.26.
92. Guénon, *Initiation*, p.117.
93. Guénon, 'Word and Symbol', p.64.
94. Guénon, *Fondamentaux*, p.310; *Initiation*, p.191.
95. Guénon, *Initiation*, p.191; *Fondamentaux*, p.149.
96. Guénon, *Fondamentaux*, p.449.
97. *Ibid*, p.204; *Lord*, p.40, especially note 6.
98. Guénon, *Fondamentaux*, p.149.
99. Guénon, *Initiation*, p.191.
100. Guénon, *Fondamentaux*, p.442.
101. *Ibid*, p.70.
102. *Ibid*, p.222.
103. Guénon, *Fondamentaux*, p.71.
104. *Ibid*, p.70.

CHAPTER 10

The Middle Realm

Ben Johnson

Among the most profound Western scholars of religion of our century is Huston Smith, who burst upon our consciousness in the 1950s with his successful television series and later book entitled *The Religions of Man*. His long tenure at the Massachusetts Institute of Technology brought him into dialogue with some of the foremost scientific minds of the nation, and set him at the task of thinking through the interface of science and religion. This era bore fruit in his *Forgotten Truth* (1978) and his collection of articles, *Beyond the Post-Modern Mind* (1982).

Although Smith is himself a devout Christian and brings the sensitivity of a child of missionary parents, his special contribution is among god(s), people and the world — as an empathetic inquirer rather than as an advocate or a disinterested agnostic. His particular contribution among thinkers is that he takes the 'god(s)' component of the tripod with as much seriousness as he does 'the people of the world'.

Smith eschews that materialism of the West which reduces the formula to 'people and the world'. He does this not by recourse to tradition as authority — whether to an authoritative scripture or an authoritative institution, but by inviting us to join him in examining what is real both in psychology and in cosmology. Through these doors Smith reopens the 'god(s)' question as a natural concomitant of examining the world as it is. Further, he demonstrates that this wisdom is not a *discovery* but a *recovery*. It has been lost only to the secular West. It is alive in Eastern religion and in received Western intellectual tradition. Hence his title *Forgotten Truth*.

I wish in this essay to explore a portion of the tradition that Smith does little with except to acknowledge, that is, the existence of non-physical beings — non-human, non-animal — known throughout the ancient world, in non-Western cultures, and in Western sub-cultures.

My interest is similar to that spirit of inquiry I find in Smith — *what is true about the world?*. I have come at the issue as an issue of interpretation vis-à-vis the Hebrew and Christian scriptures. These documents, from Genesis through Revelation, treat of angels and demons (the latter especially in the Gospels and Acts). Are these, as most contemporary philosophy, theology, and exegesis would have us believe, real only within the primitive imagination of the biblical characters and authors? Or might they testify to a broader range of reality than western materialism knows?

In his essay 'Excluded Knowledge',[1] Smith offers the following brief comments:

> Human life is so obviously psyche and soma, body and mind, that the terrestrial and intermediate planes are usually best considered together. Nevertheless, the intermediate plane does contain ingredients that exceed its manifestly human ones that phenomenology attends to. These additional ingredients have the looks of a hodgepodge, a grab bag — they constitute the world of tarot cards, tea leaves, and premonitions, as someone has characterized it. The animate denizens of this world are gods, ghosts and demons; the 'little people' of various descriptions; the 'controls' of spiritualists, mediums, and amanuenses; departed souls in limbo, purgatory, and the Tibetan bardos — in a phrase, discarnates generally. Some of them are so suspect that I am embarrassed even to list them, but one man's mush is another man's meaning, so in view of the difficulty of producing reliable criteria for sorting out what has at least some factual basis, it is best at this point to be egalitarian. So much nonsense goes on in the name of this intermediate or psychic plane that it takes a bit of courage to say, as did both Margaret Mead and Gregory Bateson, that something does go on.

I share Smith's commitment that it is one world we live in. I am perhaps more optimistic than he about the possibility of making some sense of it.

Contrary to the phenomenologists, I do not accept the notion that we construct our own reality. Reality may be significantly filtered, influenced, shaped, even blocked out by the conditioning of our perception. But the range of reality itself has the priority, not our receiving apparatus. It is to Smith's great credit that he has given an intellectual frame for comprehending this realm back to us.

Over a period of two decades I have collected anecdotal data about this intermediate plane, about individuals and their reports of voices, visions, dreams which suggest a broader range of reality than western scholarship can tolerate without recourse to the assumption of hallucination. I have found these reports to come from all sorts and conditions of women and men, on the whole people of apparent sound mental health.

These people differ from seekers after hidden wisdom (represented most recently on the popular level by Shirley MacLaine, *Out on a Limb*, 1983), in that they had not consciously sought such experience.

For most of them, it has happened only once. It did not mark them as especially religious or especially sensitive. While the type of experience sometimes emerged in a life crisis, these cases by no means cover all situations.

I will offer three examples of the type of experience of which I speak.

A. John ... is a skilled worker in an Eastern U.S. city. He is a Lutheran of Hungarian descent. One night when he arose to make his way to the bathroom, he saw a strange woman of distinctive dress in the hall. He awakened his wife, who was not able to see what he saw.

A few days later he was working as a calligrapher for a folk festival, and noticed that for one participant he wrote the same last name as his own. When he turned to see the owner of the name, the man was a spitting image of himself, except larger. In talking with the man he discovered that they were cousins, and had in common an uncle who had once been a Roman Catholic priest in Cleveland.

Some time later John was interviewed for a job in Cleveland. The job did not work out, but since he was in the Cleveland area he resolved to see if he could find the church where his uncle had been pastor. The first Catholic parish he came to had a priest who met him at the church door. The priest said, 'Yes, your uncle served this parish. Wait here in the sacristy until I've finished some duties and then I'll chat with you.'

John waited in the sacristy. As his eyes became accustomed to the semi-darkness, he was amazed to see the woman who had been in his house that night. It was a statue of St Elizabeth of Hungary. John, who had grown up as a Lutheran, had never heard of her before.

B. A father and son drive across the prairie in Nebraska. As they go along they see a beautiful panorama of clouds over a rise of hills in front of the setting sun. Upon the clouds they see three crosses.

C. A mother and son are driving home from town in Iowa in the evening. As they travel they notice a bright light on the horizon. Approaching closer they realize that the burning of their country church is causing the brightness.

They pull over to watch the burning with a great deal of sadness. Soon the outer frame of the church burns away and reveals the structure. Upon a crossbeam they see the figure of Jesus standing. Then the supporting beams drop away but the center beam with Christ standing upon it remains. And they receive the message that what was burning was a building, not the church. The people are the church.

These examples are only a few of many such reports which I have collected. They are the extraordinary experiences of ordinary people. The first case is difficult to dismiss as wish fulfilment, in that the recipient had not even heard of St Elizabeth. In a world open to the possibility of such phenomena, we might most naturally conclude that she sought him out because he was Hungarian. In the other two experiences we have the rarer examples of simultaneous visions to relatives. Nothing was extraordinary about the recipients and no extraordinary actions followed them.

How common are such experiences? What do they mean to those who experience them? Who experiences them? What do they say about the reality in which we live?

In an effort to gain some answers to the first three questions I joined forces with Milo and Mark Brekke to carry out a survey of the St Cloud, Minnesota, church population on a given Sunday. Over thirty Christian churches were invited to participate. Twelve churches (Roman Catholic, Lutheran, Presbyterian, Independent) did. The participating congregations represented approximately 6000 worshippers over 12 years of age. The survey was completed between October 1st and November 10th, 1986. The form used in the survey is attached as an appendix (see page 288). Detailed analysis is currently under way. The following preliminary observations can be shared.

1. Over 600 of the 2000 participants claimed at least one extraordinary experience during their lifetime.

112

2. Such experiences were no more common among Roman Catholics (who have historically been cautiously approving of such experience) than among Lutherans (who have been traditionally suspicious of such experience).

3. By and large those who claimed to have undergone such experiences thought them to be both positive and self-explanatory.

4. Except for a small number of the respondents of our sample who identified themselves as charismatic, almost all of the rest claimed only to have had one to three such experiences in their lifetime. (There may emerge under closer scrutiny a small grouping who are not charismatic Christians but who, without seeking such experiences, have had them more often.)

Prior research by Andrew Greeley has demonstrated that the recipients of such experience are in the upper range of mental health and above average in educational level.[2] Popular surveys indicate that people without formal religious affiliations are more likely than church members to have such experiences.

These preliminary indications suggest that the world in which we live may indeed include identities without physical bodies who impinge upon us from time to time.

At the same time classical scholarship is showing signs of a greater appreciation of religious reality in the Graeco-Roman world. Robin Lane Fox paints a marvellous picture of a genuine struggle in the second through fourth centuries between two vital religions.[3] His study of the role of oracles in the ancient world and the traditional religions, and the Christian interpretation of these phenomena, is particularly well done. Christianity did not triumph because of a secular disbelief in the traditional gods, but because it displaced traditional religion with more potent religious reality.

Likewise scientism's disbelief in the spiritual world seems not to have diminished that world's vitality but rather to have robbed modern humanity of an ability to come to some measured judgement of what it experiences. Further, our age suffers from the lack of any but religious or imagic approaches to dealing with this level of reality.

Religious approaches of our own time include in the West traditional Christian understanding of these beings as agents of God or Satan on the one hand, and the ancient gnostic religion — reaching back at least to Pythagoras, with its concomitant teachings about humanity's divine origin, anti-matter, cycles of reincarnation and divination — on the other. At a level below these, animism and magic continue in various manifestations and revivals.

Imagic approaches — which depict reality in some parabolic form — range from Dante and Carolingian art of the Middle Ages, to contemporary artists such as Goethe and Rilke on the European continent and William Blake and C.S. Lewis in England. Humanistic Psychology — certainly the psychologies of Carl Jung and Fritz Perls — trades heavily in the religious world. Yet it is content to refrain from metaphysical claims. (Jung makes tantalizing flirtations with metaphysics, including his observation that there is no such thing as secular mental illness.)

Is it possible to construct a map of the world of religious personalities and their interactions with the world of people? Are there consistencies or patterns in this world's relation to the world of people? Can one, in other words, take the posture of an observer and advance the knowledge of the world in which we live? Is there a pool of knowledge here that can be made available to the community of discourse?

Someone like Antony of the Desert had his own collection of wisdom in dealing with the world of spirits. Demons are smaller than people. Angels are larger than people. If you hear your name called, say 'Who are you and where do you come from?'. If the being is from God it will identify itself. If it is not, it will flee.[4]

Is there also a pattern that leads to destruction? Is there a listening to voices from beyond that will rob one of prudence and the exercise of one's own power of reason? Is there mischief near the center of the universe?

Professor Smith describes this middle as a terrible muddle. I quite agree with him. Yet it may be possible to probe it, to make something of it that would both be useful to the general human community, and advance our understanding of this wild and wonderful world in which we live.

Notes

1. Huston Smith, *Beyond the Post-Modern Mind*, Theosophical Publishing House, Wheaton, 1982, p.74.

2. Andrew M. Greeley, *Death and Beyond*, Thomas More Press, Chicago, 1976.
3. Robin Lane Fox, *Pagans and Christians*, Harper & Row, New York, 1986.
4. Athanasius, *The Life of St Antony*, Newman Press, New York, 1960, Chapter 43.

CHAPTER 11

United Methodism in a World of Religious Diversity

Franklin Littell

This paper is based in part upon an address given in St Louis, Missouri, on 25 April, 1988. Huston Smith and I are both Methodist ministers, and our fathers before us. For fifty years we have walked parallel paths, appreciating our heritage and learning to appreciate persons of other faiths. F.H.L.

This study seminar, called in connection with the General Conference of the United Methodist Church, is intended to focus upon the future of our movement — and particularly upon what the Evangelical United Brethren component may contribute to the rest of us. We sometimes forget how much contemporary Wesleyanism, with its major background in the British Isles, owes to its German heritage. I was privileged to be present at the Uniting Conference of European Methodism, held in Copenhagen in July of 1939, and I am happy to participate in this transatlantic dialogue of 1988.

We are seeking to interpret what has happened to our church — especially during the nearly fifty intervening years. We want to understand as clearly as we can the time and the place within which we are presently called — the context within which we are to translate the Word of God into words and actions. To do so we must fix clearly in mind the place and contribution of Wesleyanism within the Christian movement, within Europe, and also on a world map that counts hundreds of millions of adherents of other religions and religion-substitutes.

Internally, one of the most important factors shaping Methodism has certainly been our church's continuance along the line of ecumenical association and church union. We have shared in this work which — as the comprehensive study by W. Richey Hogg demonstrated years ago (1952) — has been one of the most powerful spiritual forces in nineteenth and twentieth-century Christianity.

To the outsider, the picture of Christianity during this era — and especially of evangelical Protestantism — must seem profusely and bewilderingly varied. To the churchman, the story is one of growing rapprochement, cooperation, alliance and union. To the outsider, the some 1200 religious bodies in America — those the chaplains call 'Protestants and Others' — presented in Gordon Melton's two-volume *Encyclopedia of American Religion* (1987), paint a picture of endless fission and consequent dissipation of energy. To the church historian, the more significant story is built on the fact that in America eleven major denominations comprehend more than 80 percent of all Protestants.

Our own Wesleyan family, which at the time of the Civil War was the largest single denominational movement in the United States, has participated fully in this ecumenical and conciliar trend. And among the giants during the pre-World War II years of ecumenical formation, during the years when Huston Smith and I were in seminary and graduate school, were Methodists such as John L. Nuelsen, Ralph E. Diffendorfer, Ferdinand Sigg and John R. Mott — the latter the statesman who contributed more than any other single person to the creation of councils of churches in Europe and America, as well as in Asia and Africa. That we meet during these two days under the auspices of the Center for the Study of Evangelical United Brethren History reminds us that the impulse toward union has been intra-mural as well as inter-denominational.

Symbolic, too, is the fact that many of those who met to celebrate the unity of European Methodism in Copenhagen were also active in the First World Christian Youth Conference in Amsterdam.

Minority Identity and Counter-culture

Our sponsorship here in St Louis also reminds us that — at least in some sectors of the Methodist family — to make a Wesleyan affirmation of the Christian faith is to embrace a minority identity. Indeed, the post-World War II union of the *Bischoefliche Methodistenkirche* and the *Evangelische Gemeinschaft* brought together two small Free churches in a vast sea of established religion. Perhaps our American section of United Methodism, which has now for the most part embraced so wholeheartedly the role of 'mainline church', may learn something by studying more intently the life of those of our brethren who still find their identity expressed in a minority witness.

Certainly those sections of our church that carry on their work in Eastern Europe can nurse few illusions about their status. In fact, even spokesmen for the Protestant state churches — establishments that dominated some areas of Eastern Europe from the early sixteenth century to the rise of the Nazi Third Reich, and were accustomed to treat Jews, 'heretics' and 'sects' with triumphant contempt — are now forced to re-think their self-definition.

Three decades ago, during an intense conflict between Christianity and Marxist ideology symbolized by the forced choice between the church's confirmation and the state's youth dedication ceremony (*Jugendweihe*), a Lutheran superintendent from East Germany declared at a Special Synod of the Protestant state-church, (*Evangelische Kirche im Deutschland*):

> To alert minds, the situation of Christendom in contemporary Europe is defined by the fact that the end of the Constantinian era has arrived.
>
> The Theses of Barmen, in which all hyphenated Christianity is repudiated through proclamation that Jesus alone is Lord, remain significant as the documentation of the emancipation of the Biblical message from a Babylonian captivity.
>
> After the end of illusionism about the Constantinian era, and with return to the Early Christian witness, we no longer have the right to call upon the state to support the Gospel by privileges and monopoly.[1]

To what extent the churches under Marxist ideological establishment have been able to recover a genuinely pre-Constantinian and apostolic identity is a discussion in itself. According to the differing styles of different regimes, they may be licensed or incorporated or salaried — and in any case closely supervised — by state bureaucracies that at best tolerate their survival. In West Europe other accommodations are common. Two years ago the Italian Methodists joined with the Waldensians in accepting incorporation by the government. In West Germany the style of accommodation is older, displayed prominently by the practice of double membership (*Doppelmitgliedschaft*). Perhaps two-thirds of German Methodists continue to be listed as adherents of the state-church — to which church taxes are paid while they are members of a Free Church supported by voluntary contributions.

A bit later we shall consider some American types of accommodation. But at this point we must note that the extent of Free Church accommodation in our lifetime was most strikingly revealed during the Third Reich — when, for example, Paul Schmidt of the Baptists and Otto Melle of the Methodists allowed themselves to be used to undercut the witness of the Confessing Church (*Bekennende Kirche*) minority that had burst out of the establishment claims of the *landesherrliche Kirchenregiment* and in the Barmen Declaration (1934) had challenged the idolatry at the center of the *Fuehrerstaat*.

In sum, on the one hand our West German brethren are a far more significant Christian presence than the easy-going appraisal of the *Bundesrepublik* as a 'Christian nation' with huge and successful established churches would indicate. In Frankfurt am Main a typical parish of the established church may count 15,000 adherents paying church taxes, of whom perhaps 200 will come to church. A typical Free Church congregation may count 45 families in membership, with more than 200 persons participating in the Sunday services. On the other hand, they are caught in patterns of socialization and accommodation that weaken their testimony, sometimes giving it the shrunken form of an individualistic pietism. Europe — ravaged for a century and a half by powerful alternative systems of being (*Weltanschauungen, Ersatzreligionen*), of which Marxism and Nazism have been the most penetrating and devastating — badly needs a joyful Free Church alternative (*Corpus Christi*) to a disintegrating Christendom (*Corpus Christianum*).

Among Wesleyans in America the problems brought on by accommodation are in some respects not much different from those of Wesleyans in Western Europe. Here in America, with the abandonment of strict membership training and church discipline, we find ourselves paying the price of establishment — social, if not legal.[2] In Western Europe our brethren — now tolerated in so-called Christian nations that once persecuted them savagely but now permit their idiosyncrasies — have yet to articulate fully the message of a restored, apostolic, Christian counter-culture. And on both sides of the Atlantic what is needed most of all is a message accredited by islands of renewal in a polluted ocean, carried by cells of creativity that bring new life amidst an age that is passing away.

In each of the four major geographical areas of our work and witness, the battle against accommodation to the spirit of the dying age provides the context of our preaching, teaching, and dissonant style of life. Under the Marxist ideological establishment of Communist governments, the temptation is strong to accept governmental accreditation and concentrate upon individual and familial piety. Under tolerating governments with traditional Christian state-churches, the temptation is strong to accept the seductive myths and structures of 'Christendom' and accent a 'heartfelt religion' that avoids all politics except perhaps a vulgar anti-Communism. With the social acceptance and indigenization of 'mainline Protestantism' in America, scriptural separation has often yielded place to the affirmation of values and standards remarkably like those of high-thinking and service-motivated PTAs, Rotary Clubs, not to forget the League of Women Voters. Even in the fourth sector — the indigenous Younger Churches of Africa and Asia, which were once much closer to the Christian house-churches to which the Apostle Paul addressed his letters than they were to medieval Christendom or accommodated Western churches — the process of accommodation to national, racial, and social energies has in recent decades produced similar problems of internal indiscipline and dissolution.

Each of the four sectors has something to teach the others, I believe. And all of us have much to learn from each other as we confront the problem of Christian identity on a world map. Those of us who are Europeans or Americans will do well to think about the rapidly shifting center of the faith. According to the most thorough studies, the most rapidly growing Christian churches lie outside Europe and America — at the beginning of the century the lands popularly identified with 'Christendom'. One specialist has predicted that by the year 2000 the majority of the Christians of the world — in any case decade by decade a shrinking percentage of the total world population — will be found in Africa.

European Christendom in Dissolution
In 1910 the first of the modern ecumenical assemblies — the International Missionary Conference — was held in Edinburgh. In preparation for the event, at which the Methodist layman John R. Mott played a prominent role, six study volumes were issued. The Conference itself met at the hightide of the Great Century of Christian Missions, in which the conciliar movement had growing influence and the Free Churches were already the major carriers of world

Protestantism.

Looking across the map of the world, and then looking back across the centuries of church history, the church leaders at Edinburgh saw one great *caesura* of the past where a failure of theological and ecclesiastical leadership had cost the faith great losses. That was the time when a surging Islam had carried away the great centers of Christian civilization, the heartland of the Christendom of that era. They summarized their conclusions in this way:

> Meanwhile it remains tragically true that had the church of Syria been faithful to its Master the reproach of Islam [would have] never lain upon Christendom. The thought has somber consequences. It may be that in the Africa, the China and the India of today new religions are maturing which in like manner will be 'anti-Christian', and stand in future centuries as a barrier in the way of winning the world.[3]

Later ecumenical gatherings were to have increasing representations from the Younger Churches. But the men of Edinburgh, chiefly white westerners, portrayed the challenge of the hour within the parameters of their circumscribed concept of 'Christendom'. For them 'Christendom' was secure: the dangers lay on the borders and in the outposts of the faith.

Looking back today we can see that the anti-Christian 'new religions' did in fact emerge — but not among the new Christians on the distant fields that worried the fathers at Edinburgh. They emerged right in the heart of 'Christendom' itself.

Roland Allen, the great missiologist, later summarized a principle that has prevailed since the earliest days of the church, a principle of which the fathers at Edinburgh were apparently unaware:

> When the Christian Church was first spreading throughout the Roman Empire she certainly maintained a standard of doctrine, and that standard was not imperilled by the spontaneous activity of a multitude of Christians who were certainly not trained theologians. These unknown missionaries taught the doctrine which they had learned, and that teaching was so far adequate that the Bishops of the Church did not hesitate to consecrate new converts as Bishops for the new Churches without giving them any long or special training in theological colleges.
> The great heresies in the early Church were not from the rapid expansion resulting from the work of these unknown teachers, but in those churches which were longest established, and where the Christians were not so busily engaged in converting the heathen round them.[4]

Summarizing the review at Edinburgh, Robert Hume — later Professor of Missions at Union Theological Seminary — urged 'the value for the mission field today, both for courage and forewarning, of an understanding both of the New Testament and of the history of the early Church.'[5]

If we consider 'Christendom' a missionary field, which is the classical Free Church contention, the point was well made. To recover this vision today, we must break out of a narrow cultural and denominational indigenization, and also be cured of the white western astigmatism which kept even the wisest heads at Edinburgh from seeing the direction in which European 'Christendom' was floating.

There had been earlier warnings. In 1848, the year of the democratic revolutions across continental Europe that failed to break the reactionary control systems of the 'Holy Alliance', a German Free Church leader (Joules Koebner) spoke up for liberty and self-government. He understood the connection between Christian liberty of conscience and popular sovereignty.

> When Almighty God broke the chains of your civic servility, there was also cast aside that invention that had earlier bound your tongue. Today the defenders of your rights are rejoicing that they may speak political truth. And there is rejoicing also among those of your fellow citizens whose hearts beat even more warmly for God than for political freedom, that they may speak Christian truth, no longer crippled by a control system which limited the Word to a monopolizing churchianity alone — so that the truth was eternally hidden from you that Christianity and state-priesterdom are just as different from each other as Christ and Caiphas.

And when he declared the true nature of Religious Liberty, so different even today from toleration, Koebner put the matter plainly:

> We claim not only *our own* religious freedom. We urge it for *every* person who inhabits the earth of the Fatherland. We urge it to the same full degree for all, whether they are Christians, Jews, Mohammedans or something else. We not only say that it is a very un-Christian sin to lay the fist of violence upon any person's honoring of God: we also believe that any advantage to any party qualifies as an equal entitlement for all. If one or more than one remain in possession of special privileges, they will always be tempted to use the worldly apparatus left to them to lift themselves up and push others down.[6]

Koebner's message went unheeded. Jews, 'heretics' and 'sects' — including Methodists — continued to suffer the repressive measures of authoritarian rulers 'by divine right', rulers who considered authorized religion, large standing armies, a tightly controlled educational system, secret police networks, and efficient tax collectors the best tools to ensure civil peace.

In 1848, the year of *The Communist Manifesto*, a leader in the established Protestant churches (Johan Heinrich Wichern) issued a warning at the Leipzig *Kirchentag*. He said that unless the churches broke out of their enthralment to the alliance of Throne and Altar they would lose the people. The two most important elements in the emerging industrial civilization were being neglected: the working classes (*Proletariat*) and the educated professionals (*Intellektuellen*). His message went unheeded. The state churches continued to supply tax-paid clergy to hundreds of virtually deserted country and village chapels, while hundreds of thousands of people moved to the cities and factory towns and went unshepherded and virtually unschooled in the faith.

In spite of the popular picture of 'the Christian nations', the truth is that church attendance — a not unimportant measure of Christian adherence — declined steadily from the early nineteenth century through to the rise of Nazism and the creation of Hitler's European Empire. All the while the tax rolls showed the overwhelming percentage of the populations still formally 'Christian'. The truth is that the masses were seduced by anti-Christian systems of being. The truth is that the Third Reich — and its heathen programs, including the Holocaust and other genocides — was planned, supervised, rationalized and enabled by professors, PhDs and MDs, virtually all of them on the church rolls. What kind of Christianity was this?

The wholesale defection from central Christian beliefs and standards, which the resisting theologian Karl Barth equated with the rise of a 'New Islam', seduced workers and intellectuals in the 'New Germany' of the Thousand Years' Reich — and even to a considerable extent the same classes in occupied countries. The witness of heroic minorities like the Confessing Church in Germany, and elements of the Reformed Church of France, the Lutheran Church of Norway, the Hervormde Kerk of the Netherlands, the Orthodox Church of Bulgaria, should not blind our eyes to the overwhelming evidence that the Christendom that succumbed to Nazi ideology was in an advanced state of dissolution.

For that matter, the same malaise in Eastern Orthodoxy had already opened the door to the triumph of the Marxist ideology and establishment. The Russian Church, after the fall of Constantinople in 1453, the chief center of Orthodox Christianity, with Moscow 'the Third Rome' of its theologians and hierarchies, neglected to educate the masses and cultivated a privileged relationship to a viciously exploitative ruling class. And in the East as well as in the West, on those occasions when churchmen felt it useful to express a Christian identity, such identity was often accomplished by the exploitation of anti-semitic theological and cultural themes. It was the chief constitutional adviser to the Romanovs, Konstantin Pobedonostsev, a man who was also Presiding Officer over the Holy Synod of the Russian Orthodox Church, who justified persecution of 'heretics' and 'sects' and coined the brutal phrase covering treatment of the Jews: 'One third will be compelled to convert, one third will be driven into exile, and one third will be killed.'

Marxism came to the Russian masses as a morally and intellectually superior system of being and order, just as a millennium earlier Islam had come to the North African masses as a relief from the incessant doctrinal quarrellings and luxury-oriented Christian Church establishments of Asia Minor and North Africa.

Karl Holl, the great German theologian who defended the Lutheran state church so vigorously during the later Imperial and Weimar periods, openly depreciated what he called 'the sect-influenced Anglo-Saxon view of the Church' and attributed its origin to Thomas Muentzer, the sixteenth-century religious revolutionary. Accusing the Free Churches of mixing religion and politics, he never noticed how uncritically political his binding of the church to the world's princes and powers might be. More serious yet, his views are still cited with approval in both Germany and America, with few Free Church voices raised to protest his defense of a promiscuous policy of church 'membership' which threw the door wide open to the hyphenated churchmanship of the *Deutsche Christen*, and which even yet makes the established churches mirrors of the *Zeitgeist* rather than shapers of the world to come.[7]

Let me relate two personal experiences which ever since the summer of 1939 have symbolized for me the crisis of Christendom in dissolution.

Visiting a Methodist family in Nurenberg, I was invited by the young son to accompany him to a meeting that turned out to be a huge rally at the Stadium. Arriving late, we climbed the stairs to the high rim. Surrounding the assembly of nearly 100,000 were great spotlights, meeting high in the sky and creating the 'cathedral of lights' for which Speer later claimed credit. On the green field below a pageant, enhanced by colorful choreographed dance, terminated in the slaying of the Dragon by Siegfried. At this moment all lights went out.

After a moment lights came on — spotlights pointing at the podium. There he was! The entire crowd leapt to its feet, shrieking the unearthly antiphonal: 'Sieg Heil! Sieg Heil! Sieg Heil!' . . . talk about 'spirituality'! The person who thinks 'secular humanism' is the problem of the twentieth century has not been where the action is! The spiritual warfare of Europe at that time was summarized by Willem Visser't Hooft — then Executive Secretary of the World's Student Christian Federation, and later chief executive of the World Council of Churches — when in 1937 he published his *None Other Gods*:

> The main task of the Christian Community, and the greatest service it can render to the world, is . . . to be the Christian Community. For the real tragedy of our time is that we have on the one hand an incoherent mass of individual Christians and on the other hand powerful impulses towards new forms of community, but no Christian Community. Christians today do not form a true community, and the communities which shape the new world are not Christian.[8]

The second incident involves a meeting with Bishops John L. Nuelsen and Otto Melle during the same summer. Bishop Melle told us, a group of Methodist youth leaders from the States, what Adolf Hitler meant to German youth and their parents. He said that during the days of the Republic the youth had been smoking and drinking and dancing and otherwise dissipating. Now they had a great Leader, a man of God, who was giving them discipline and calling them to sacrifice for the *Volk*. He closed his message to us with a solemn affirmation: 'Hitler is God's man for Germany!'

I want to be understood clearly in my reference to Bishop Melle. We are much too inclined to think of such things in individualistic terms, to resolve structural and historical issues by blaming individuals. Otto Melle was a good man — a pastor, a patriot, President of the German Temperance Movement (*Blaue Kreuz*), personally devout. And yet, because his theology was defective — individualistic, lacking a sound doctrine of social sin and evil,

alienated *from* rather than linked *to* Israel's pilgrimage through history
— he simply failed to perceive the true meaning of Nazism and the
true crisis of the age.

He was not alone, of course. Emanuel Hirsch, a world-rank
theologian, never departed from the illusion that he expressed so
fervently in early summer of 1933 in response to Hitler's inaugural
speech:

> No other *Volk* in the world has a leading statesman such as ours, who
> takes Christianity so seriously. On 1 May when Adolf Hitler closed his
> great speech with a prayer, the whole world could sense the wonderful
> sincerity in that.[9]

But Hirsch was professor in a state-church theological faculty, while
Melle was head of a Free Church. Like those who live and work in the
atmosphere near a fertilizer plant or an oil refinery, they and most
other European church leaders of the first half of the twentieth
century no longer noticed the sour humors and poisonous miasmas
which emerged from a Christendom in decay.

What is the picture of that 'Christendom' today? Is it ripe for a
recovered and vigorous Free Church proclamation of the Gospel?
Although there is a present effort in several countries to perpetuate
the myth of Christian dominance through legislation against 'cults
and sects', as well as through a resurgence of anti-semitism, a quick
statistical review will give the picture of a needy mission field and
hopefully remove forever any illusions about the intactness of
European Christendom.

The almanacs and encyclopaedias — and not seldom the official
church statistics — tell the less important side of the story. For
example, Italy is said to be 99.2 percent Roman Catholic. The
church's own studies show only 11 percent of Italian men making one
confession and attending one mass a year, fulfilling the minimum set
at the Fourth Lateran Council (1215 CE) to avoid automatic
excommunication. A third will vote Communist in the next elections.
The Mayor of Rome himself is a Communist. In Spain, officially
Roman Catholic and until recently medieval RC as well, according to
a Spanish Jesuit study the figure of actual adherence is 17 percent. In
Hamburg province the Protestant figures are 84.5 percent church-tax
paying, and 4.5 percent in effective relationship. In Denmark the
Lutheran state-church figures are 96 percent and 3.4 percent. In
Sweden the statistics are 96.4 percent and 3.6 percent. A recent law
declaring all Swedes to be Lutheran who are not in the tiny minorities

of Roman Catholics and Jews hardly changes the true picture, which is — speaking bluntly — a fraud.

Statistics like these do not tell the whole story, of course. But they serve to reinforce the truth of the classical Free Church position: Europe is missionary territory, just like Africa and Asia and America. And the emergence of post-Christian systems of being, like Marxism and Nazism, underlines the need for a Christian proclamation that starts with the basic truth that the Constantinian era is gone, although some of its worst characteristics still haunt us. Of these, none has been worse than the anti-semitism that was expressed in the pogroms in tsarist 'Holy Russia' and the Nazi Holocaust of the years of Nazi domination of Europe, 1939-45.

The Free Churches, taking their stand for a restoration or restitution of apostolic Christianity, have frequently expressed their separation from the triumphalism and the violence of Christendom by dating a 'Fall of the Church' from the time when the witnessing and suffering Early Church was changed with the Emperor Constantine into part of the power system of a reconstructed 'Christian' Roman Empire. They have — when they remembered their true identity — stood for Religious Liberty against coercion of conscience, voluntary support of religion in place of government subventions, protection of 'sects' and 'cults' and Jews from *Gleichschaltung*, secular and limited government against the pretenses of sacral and authoritarian regimes.

Even the Free Churches, however, have seldom noticed how the same despotic regimes — with their vision of a monolithic and monochromatic Good Society — that persecuted 'heretics' and 'sects' have also made life unendurable for Jews. Jules Isaac, author of the classic *Jesus and Israel* (1959, 1971), pointed out the historical turning point in this way:

> ... after very deep historical research, I say and maintain that the fate of Israel did not take on a truly inhuman character until the 4th century A.D. with the coming of the Christian Empire.[10]

Even though neither Jewish nor Christian surveys of history have often noticed it, the same seasons of Christendom that have seen persecution of the Jews have also seen persecution of 'heretics' and dissenting Christians.

The generalization holds for the times of Constantine, Theodosius and Justinian, Innocent III, Ferdinand and Isabella, and into the modern period. Few historians of European civilization have noticed that the time of the Crusades, which brought death to so many thousands of Jews, were also marked by the slaughter of Waldensians, Albigensians and Bogomili. Every Jewish historian has pointed out Luther's malediction against the Jews, especially since eighteen editions of his 'Concerning the Jews and Their Lies' were issued during the Third Reich, but none has noticed that Luther justified the death penalty for Mennonites, Baptists, Schwenkfelder and other 'sects'. The brutality of the Black Legions in the tsarist pogroms from 1873 through 1905 is often mentioned by secular historians; few mention the simultaneous savagery against Old Believers, Stundists, Doukhabors . . .

How many students of our recent history — even specialists in the Holocaust — have noticed that the same Reinhard Heydrich who chaired the January, 1942, Wannsee Conference that mobilized the German bureaus to accomplish efficient slaughter of the Jews, had since 1936 been implementing an order to liquidate 'sects and cults' (Jehovah's Witnesses, Mormons, Seventh Day Adventists, Christian Scientists, Anthroposophists, and so on)?

For Free Church men who know their history — and also their Bible! — the case against Christendom includes both the denial of liberty of conscience and the perpetuation of an anti-semitism that ranged from the teaching of contempt to genocide. Three years ago the German Baptists, having reaffirmed their commitment to Religious Liberty after their lapse during the Hitler period, issued an official statement repenting of their failure during the Holocaust and calling for a reconstruction of their teaching and preaching vis-à-vis the Jewish people. Noting that the Presbyterian Church and the United Church of Christ have moved well ahead of us American Methodists on this frontier, let me say that on both sides of the Atlantic we Methodists have some distance to go before we catch up with the Synod of the Protestant Church of the Rhineland, which in January of 1980 achieved a new level of understanding of God's providence for the Jews and their place and presence in Christian history and teaching.[11]

Extricating ourselves from the decaying remains of state-church Christendom requires of us a genuine and total renewal of trust in God's purposes, including a radically different attitude and approach to persons of other faiths.

America Between Christendom and the
Younger Churches

Like other aspects of modern life, organized religion too is caught up in exponential rapid change. Sweden's parliament may vote every first-class citizen a Lutheran — but the largest congregation is the Philadelphia Church of Stockholm (Pentecostal). The encyclopaedia may repeat the claim that Brasil is the largest Roman Catholic nation in the world, with 80 million adherents — but on any given Sunday morning the largest total attendance will be in a Spiritualist Church based on the teachings of a Frenchman, Allan Kardec.

In America, too, rapid change is evident. During the last two decades conservative churches — including the pentecostals — have grown rapidly, while the liberal 'mainline' churches — including the United Methodist Church — have lost members steadily and sometimes dramatically. Even with some sectors making rapid growth, the overall place of Protestantism in American life has been radically reduced in the last half-century. In the meantime the Roman Catholic church has become the largest denomination, with *c.*60 million adherents, and the Jewish community (*c.*5.8 million) has grown to be the largest in the diaspora.

Many of our American ideas and understandings, however, are — like the Europeans' — still set in the circumstances of a vanished age. At the time of independence, out of 3.8 million inhabitants in the new republic, only about 20,000 were Roman Catholics and some 4,000 were Jews. With the termination of the colonial state-churches, then considered by European observers and many Americans to be a most dangerous innovation, church membership fell to *c.*7 percent of the population. The story of religion in America has been one of extraordinary success — not failure — from an institutional point of view. Those who walked out of the dismantled state-churches have been reclaimed on a voluntary basis, and tens of millions of newer immigrants have been drawn into voluntary membership, participation and support. Each of the major religious blocs developed distinctively American methods and institutions to match the challenge put by the separation of the powers and decision-making procedures of church and state.

The most characteristic innovations have been mass evangelism in Protestantism, parochial schools in Roman Catholicism, and intensely organized self-help and benevolence among the Jews. From some 7 percent in 1800, religious adherence moved to 15.5 percent in 1850, 37.5 percent in 1900, 49+ percent in 1926, and almost 70 percent in 1980. In striking contrast to the European situation, where almost universal official 'membership' is matched by widespread disinterest and disaffection, in America surveys show 96 percent claiming membership — a slippage of 26 percent between the affirmation of affiliation and listing on the record books.

The American situation is not post-Christendom; if anything, it is pre-Christian. Set in a pluralistic society, with as many as one million Muslims, with one state having a Buddhist plurality, even the statistics themselves show that our future lies with the minority model of the Younger Churches, rather than with the model of 'Christendom'.[12]

Voluntary support and attendance are greater in America than at any other place or time in church history. In sum, Religious Liberty — bracketing voluntary church membership and secular government — on the face of it has worked to the benefit of both religion and politics. The three great faiths for the first time in history confront each other in strength, not in weakness, and as joint beneficiaries of Religious Liberty. They have an opportunity to work out understanding and cooperative relationships that could never exist under even the most benevolent of tolerating regimes.

But there are soft spots in this scenario, especially in the Protestant sector, more especially in the 'mainline' churches of Free Church background, perhaps most especially in that section with churches like our own denomination that have most openly combined evangelicalism and Christian social concern. Forty years ago a leading Social Psychologist at the University of Michigan surveyed public attitudes to religion, and he came to the conclusion that people tend to be very critical of the church for neglecting social concerns; but when the church does become active in that area, they do not like it.

In any case, the swing to conservative piety has also affected the United Methodist Church, and we can detect a certain tiredness in the voices of Christian social concern today. It sometimes seems to me as though those Christians that I meet on the field who most enthusiastically wrestle with those themes that are traditionally Wesleyan — the priority of Scripture, the emphasis upon simplicity and evangelical piety, the willingness to risk present social opprobrium for the sake of the Kingdom to come, the disregard for bureaucratic rigmarole and pomp and circumstance — are liberal

Catholics who came alive with John XXIII and are hanging on by their fingernails under John Paul II, the most reactionary pope since Pio Nono (1846-78). I will even venture to suggest that if Roman Catholicism does take over America, as some predict, it will not be a solely biological triumph: it will also be a result of the attention of simple Catholic laymen, brothers, nuns and priests to openings that were once thought to be distinctively Protestant.

The Critical Issues

Out of our necessarily summary review of the basic historical factors that have conditioned European Christendom and Christianity in America, two critical issues may be lifted up. Both of them have fundamental implications for Christian theology, and on both of them hang the credibility of our proclamation of the Gospel. In both cases, where we have gone astray we have done so as a result of abandoning clear identity as a counter-culture for the pleasures and privileges of culture-religion.

Most serious, from a Wesleyan standpoint, has been our virtual abandonment of membership training and church discipline — a dereliction that weakens our impact on all fronts, and has often turned our joyful participation in inter-religious dialogue into an anxious and surly spiritual goal-tending.

Of the issues that challenge Evangelical Protestantism today, the first issue is our stand on Religious Liberty and the other is our preaching and teaching about other faiths — especially the survival and continuing religious contribution of the Jewish people.

The man who many consider America's greatest church historian, Philip Schaff, drew upon his vast knowledge and his experience as a transported European to affirm his conviction about America's place in Christian history:

> The glory of America is a free Christianity, independent of the secular government, and supported by the voluntary contributions of a free people. This is one of the greatest facts in modern history.[13]

The greatest Roman Catholic theologian of the nineteenth century, Ignaz von Doellinger, during the Infallibility controversy with the reactionary Pius IX, defined the issue of liberty of conscience in theological terms:

> It must be clearly understood how great the gulf is which divides the

holders of this principle [liberty of conscience] from those who reject it, both in faith and morals. He who is convinced that right and duty require him to coerce other people into a life of falsehood . . . belongs to an essentially different religion from one who recognizes in the inviolability of conscience a human right guaranteed by religion itself, and has different notions of God, of man's relation to God, and of man's obligation to his fellows . . .[14]

We do not have to look far in either Europe or America to see that tolerance is fragile and Religious Liberty is under attack. The Radical Right in American politics is vigorously pushing several measures that would basically change the direction in which under the First Amendment we have been moving for 200 years. We can be proud that in the present fight against government interference in religious affairs, as well as in exposing the cult-bashing racket, Methodist clergymen like Dean Kelly, G. Gordon Melton and Philip Wogaman have been prominent.

John Wesley was wont to say that he did what he did in imitation of the New Testament church. We need to declare with voices loud and clear: in the shadow of the record of the last century and a half of the European state churches, we renew our rejection of the concept and the practices of Constantinian Christendom; on the authority of the Scriptures, we affirm with renewed vigor our commitment to the model of the New Testament Church; as evangelical Christians, we continue to condemn all brands of civil religion and culture-religion — and all persecution conducted in their name; as Methodists, we call for a renewed commitment to a membership training and discipline that points us away from the spirit and customs of the dying age toward the Kingdom of God promised for all the world's peoples. We re-affirm our faith in God, our confidence in the way of life commanded us in the Scriptures, and our trust in Jesus Christ as the One through whom we gentiles are brought alive and grafted into holy history.

The second critical issue concerns our preaching and teaching about the people of God's first love. We can scarcely move effectively to relate to persons of distant faiths until we have achieved some measure of clarity and compassion toward those of a faith community closest to us in time and space. Since the rise of imperial Christianity and triumphalist theology the gentile church has been guilty in large measure of the sin against which the Apostle Paul entered one of his most pointed warnings: the cuttings of the wild olive tree have vaunted themselves against the natural tree, and the grafted branches have boasted a position superior to the root (Rom. 11:18, 24).

The theological establishment, including some fathers-in-God to whom we owe much that is true and good, has for centuries propagated a theory of the church's displacement of the Jewish people — a theory that has been un-Biblical in foundation and calamitous in its consequences. Christendom's cruel treatment of the Jews in the past has been without excuse, and in our own time its climax — the Holocaust — has confronted Christianity with the most serious credibility crisis in its history.

The fact that the persecution of the Jews has been paralleled in Christendom by persecution of 'heretics' and 'sects' in no way relieves those of us counted 'sectarians'. We too must turn away from anti-semitism in all its forms — theological, cultural and political — and call upon our seminaries, agencies and congregations to purge our preaching and teaching of its errors. We must reconstruct our theology of Christian/Jewish relations upon affinity and respect for the person and the people, rather than upon alienation and the teaching of contempt about a mythic abstraction: 'the Jew'.

We can rejoice that some of the greatest teachers to breast popular anti-semitism, to show fraternity to the Jews, and to demonstrate concern for Jewish survival, have been Methodists: William W. Blackstone, Josephus Daniels, William F. Albright, Inez Lowdermilk, Francis J. McConnell, A. Roy Eckardt . . . And we can take pride too in the fact that among the greatest teachers to reach out to persons of other faiths have been Methodists — none of them more significant as a writer, lecturer, and conference participant than Huston Smith.

I believe that we American Methodists, if we can divest ourselves of the illusion that improved PR will cure our problems, can turn around and give leadership comparable to that which we gave throughout the nineteenth century and into the first half of this century. I believe that we European Methodists, if we will abandon the role of pietist conventicles and fearlessly declare the Free Church message, can provide leadership that a post-Auschwitz 'Christendom' cries out for. I believe that we can, as a world church — with our brethren from Marxist areas and the Younger Churches — justify our invocation of the names of John Wesley and John R. Mott, to take a worthy position in our portion of the Christian heritage and to define our place for the twenty-first century among the religions of the world.

Notes

1. Guenter Jacob, 'Der Raum fuer das Evangelium in Ost und West' from *Bericht ueber die ausserordentliche Synode der evangelischen Kirchen in Deutschland: 1956*, Evangelischer Kirchenkanzlei, Hannover-Herrenhausen, 1956, pp.17-29.
2. See my essay on Methodism in Kyle Haselden and Martin E. Marty, eds. *What's Ahead for the Churches*, Sheed & Ward, New York, 1964, pp.74-93, portraying conditions which have not changed in a quarter of a century, and which (among other costs) have lost American Methodism over a million members in that period of time.
3. *The Missionary Message in Relation to Non-Christian Religions*, Fleming H. Revell Co., New York, 1910, chapter IV, p.244.
4. Roland Allen, *The Spontaneous Expansion of the Church*, World Dominion Press, London, 1949, p.64.
5. Edinburgh IV, 321.
6. Erich Geldbach, *Religioese Polemiken gegen 'neue Religionen' im Deutschland des 10. Jahrhunderts*, pp.193-4.
7. Karl Holl, 'Luther und die Schwaermer' from *Gesammelte Aufsaetze zur Kirchengeschichte*, J.C.B. Mohr, Tuebingen, 1932, chapter I, p.466; see my 'Church and Sect (with special reference to Germany)' in VI *The Ecumenical Review* (1954) 3:262-76, for abundant detail on the scurrilous traditional theological and legal definition of 'sects' (including Methodists).
8. Willem Visser't Hooft, *None Other Gods*, Harper & Bros, New York, 1937, p.70.
9. Robert P. Ericsen, *Theologians Under Hitler*, Yale University Press, New Haven, 1985, p.145. Ericsen's study of Hirsch, Althaus and Kittel — like Robert Jay Lifton's *The Nazi Doctors* (1986) — is a pioneer work in the review of professional ethics which the Holocaust requires of the modern university and its alumni.
10. Jules Isaac, *Has Anti-Semitism Roots in Christianity?*, National Conference of Christians and Jews, New York, 1961, p.45.
11. See the Synodical Declaration printed in translation in XVII *Journal of Ecumenical Studies* (1980), 1:211-12.
12. See my 'Amerika in vorchristlicher Zeitalter' from Peter Coulmas, ed., *Amerika deutet sich selbst*, Hoffman & Campe, Hamburg, 1965, pp.155-65.
13. Philip Schaff, *Germany: Its Universities, Theology, and Religion*, Lindsay & Blackiston/Sheldon, Blakeman & Co., Philadelphia & New York, 1857, p.105.
14. A.D. Lindsay, *The Essentials of Democracy*, Oxford University Press, London, 1935, 2nd edn, p.69.

CHAPTER 12

The Vocation of Man According to the Koran

Jean-Louis Michon

Introduction

Today we often hear questions such as 'Where do we come from?', or 'What, if any, is the meaning of life?'. Questioning of this kind is typical of Western Man, by which I mean people of modern Western societies, because Medieval Man, the Christians of the Middle Ages, did not ask themselves such things — any more than do contemporary believers, whether they be Christians, Jews, Muslims or, to go farther afield, Hindus, Buddhists or even animists.

All religions have, in fact, answered these fundamental questions in a peremptory way. Their responses have differed so greatly, some people would argue, that they have given rise to wars of religion. Moreover, under these conditions, how can we know what the truth is, or who is right?

This dilemma has not held any ambiguity for me for a very long time, ever since I grasped and tasted, beyond any difference in form and ritual, that which the present-day philosopher Frithjof Schuon has so justly called 'the transcendent unity of religions.'[1] In this paper, however, without taking a position on the subject, I will content myself with presenting, as clearly, accurately and objectively as possible, the point of view of Islam on the meaning of our destiny.

The following exposition will be based on facts drawn from the Koran and sometimes completed by quotations — *ḥadīth* — from the prophet Muḥammad. This is to say that it will never reflect personal opinions, but rather the doctrine of Islamic scholars and legal experts, as well as the belief of the ordinary faithful, both of which are founded

135

on adherence to two certainties: that the Koran is the Book of God, and that Muḥammad is the Messenger who was chosen to spread the Book's truth.

The Koran

It was in the year 610 of the Christian Era (the Era of the Hegira would not begin until twelve years later), that Muḥammad at age forty — the age of prophecy — received the first revelations of the Book of God, *Kitāb Allāh*, which is the most excellent reading and recitation: *al-Our'ān*.

Here, then, is the account of this important event that was the first descent of the Koran, a narration that was compiled from the earliest and most authentic sources by the British scholar Martin Lings, whose biography of Muḥammad I had the privilege of translating into French, and which was published at the beginning of 1986.

It must be remembered that Muḥammad, predisposed since childhood to an intense contemplative life, often withdrew to solitary places to pray and call upon the one true God (contrary to the great majority of Arabs of the time, who had little by little deviated from the cult of Abraham toward idolatry). One of his favorite places of meditation was the cave of Ḥirā, situated on the side of a mountain that juts out over Mecca. Here, then, is the account:

Ramaḍān was the month that was traditionally set aside as a time of retreat, and it was one night at the end of the month, during his fortieth year, when Muḥammad was alone in the cave, that an Angel came to him in the form of a man. 'Read!' the Angel commanded him; to which he replied, 'I cannot read!' Whereupon, as he himself related, 'The Angel seized me and grasped me tightly in his arms until I was unable to endure it any longer. Then he loosed his embrace and told me "Read!" "I cannot read," I answered again, and he grasped me once more until I could endure it no longer; thereupon he let go of me and said a third time, "Read!" and I repeated my answer, "I cannot read!" Once again he clasped me as before and then freed me and said:

> "Read: In the name of thy Lord who createth,
> Createth man from a clot.
> Read: And thy Lord is the Most Bounteous,
> Who teacheth by the pen,

Teacheth man that which he knew not".'　　　　　(XCVI, 1-5).[2]

The Angel left immediately, and Muḥammad recited the same words after he had gone. 'It was as if these words had been written on my heart,' he would later say; but he was afraid that what had taken place meant that he had to go back to the valley. When he was half-way down the slope he heard a voice above him that said, 'Oh Muḥammad, you are the Messenger of God, and I am Gabriel.' Lifting his eyes to the sky, he recognized his visitor, whose angelic nature at that moment manifested itself with unmistakable clarity, filling the horizon. The Angel again said, 'Oh Muḥammad, you are the Messenger of God, and I am Gabriel.' The Prophet watched the Angel without moving; then he turned away, but in whichever direction he looked, whether to the north, south, east or west, the Angel was there, blocking the horizon. Finally the Angel disappeared, and the Prophet descended the mountain and returned home.[3]

And it was thus that, little by little, over a period of twenty-two years — twelve of which were spent in Mecca and ten in Medina — from the year 1 of the Hegira (622 A.D.) until the death of the Prophet (632 A.D.), the entire Book was revealed to Muḥammad through Gabriel as intermediary, and was retained in the memory of men, transcribed at first on bones and skins in order later to be transmitted practically *ne varietur* in its original language, Arabic, across more than thirteen centuries.

The Creation
Read: In the name of thy Lord who createth,
Createth man from a clot　　　　　(XCVI,1-2).

These two verses, which were the first ones revealed in the Koran, set the tone of the Sacred Book. They immediately evoke the directing will of the Lord, creator of the world and man, who descends bringing a new message to his human creation.

But how is creation itself to be explained? Does it have a reason for being or a finality? These questions are answered in the Koran and in the prophetic tradition.

One verse of the Koran is particularly explicit. It says:

I created the jinn and humankind only that they might worship me. (LI, 56)

Ḥadīth are quotations from the Prophet that consist mostly of simple statements, words of advice, or narratives directly related by Muḥammad. However, the *ḥadīth qudsī* are veritable inspirations in which God Himself speaks through the tongue of his Prophet. One of the *ḥadīth qudsī*, which is very often quoted, particularly in mystical treatises, says:

> I was a hidden treasure, I wanted to be known and I created the creatures.

The will to be worshipped, to be known: these two 'desires' of God are at the center of our research at present, at the center of an interaction between God and man, and man and God, that explains and justifies our presence on earth, and, as we shall see, sheds light on many aspects of the human condition that at first seem obscure.

Let us return, then, to the previously cited verse on the creation, which says that God created djinn and men only that they might worship him. The last verb, 'to worship', is formed from the triliteral root *'abd*, as are the derivations *'ibāda* ('worship') and especially *'abd* ('servant'), and *'ābid* ('slave'); all are key words and are among the most frequently found in the Koran. Who, moreover, does not know the word *'abd*, which figures among such compound first names as Abdallah, Abdelkarim, Abdelkader, and so on. Abdallah is the most common of these names; it means 'the worshipper', 'the servant' or even 'the slave of God'; all of these meanings are equally valid. In the other compounds such as Abdelkader, Abdelkarim, etc., the name Allāh, that of the unqualified Divinity Himself, is replaced by one of His more than one hundred other names, which are those of His attributes, such as Severity or Forgiveness, Beauty or Majesty, attributes that deserve to be glorified and venerated by all creatures. It must be emphasized that the first name Abdallah, which is so widespread, is not only that of the Prophet Muḥammad himself, but is also that of each prophet. In the Koran, for example, the young Jesus, when speaking to the men who surround Mary, cries out, 'Lo! I am the slave of Allah (*'abd-Allāh*). He hath given me the Scripture and hath appointed me a Prophet' (XIX, 30).

Abdallah is, in fact, the true name of each human being. Thus the preacher who addresses the faithful from high up in his pulpit, before prayers every Friday, begins his sermon with the words, 'Oh servants of God! (*Yā 'ibād-All'a-h*)' (*'ibād* is the plural of *'abd*).

What then is meant or implied by the condition of being the servant of God, of having the status of servitude? There are two modes of servitude to be considered. On the one hand, there is a passive means, a state of existential worship that is submitted to, a total and absolute constraint that is exerted on all creatures; in this sense, the rocks themselves, the trees, and the animals are the servants and slaves of God. On the other hand, there is also an active means of servitude: it is conscious adoration, worship that is voluntarily offered by the being that recognizes its place in the universe and renders thanks to the Supreme Artisan. Only man is capable of this active mode of worship, and he is obligated to it by the very nature of his unique and privileged position.

Another notion that is very close to that of *'abd* is when a man is described as being *faqīr*, or 'poor'. This Koranic idea is expressed, *inter alia*, in the verse that declares 'Allāh is the Rich, and ye are the Poor' (XLVII, 38). Like the condition of servitude, the state of poverty, i.e. of extreme dependence on the Dispenser of all good, can either be passively submitted to or actively recognized and accepted, in which case man returns what he has to God and strips himself of all pretension to self-sufficiency. This attitude, according to the teachings of the Koran, is the supreme act of worship, which makes a man a true believer (*mu'min*) and a true Muslim (*muslim*): 'They are the (true) believers whose hearts feel fear when Allāh is mentioned, and when the revelations of Allāh are recited unto them they increase their faith, and who trust in their Lord' (VIII, 2).

Why is only man called to this conscious and active form of worship? One answer is that it is because he is the culmination, the completion of the creative work, because it is to him that the principle of *noblesse oblige* applies in its full right. 'Surely we have created man of the best stature', says a verse of the Koran (XCV, 4), and another adds: 'Allāh it is Who . . .fashioned you and perfected your shapes' (XL, 64). Finally, in the words of the Prophet, man has been created 'in the image of God' (*'alā ṣūrati-Allāh*). Let us now turn our attention to this form that is so beautiful that it resembles the divine.

Externally, man is endowed with five senses that give him the ability to:

see the blessings of God, His signs, and His reflection 'on the horizons' (according to a Koranic expression, XLI, 53);

hear the song of creation, for 'All that is in the heavens and the earth glorifieth Him' (LIX, 24 *et passim*);

smell the scent of flowers, symbol of the invisible presence of the Creator within his work;

taste the fruits of His generosity: the dates, pomegranates, figs and grapes that, even after the Fall, have retained the taste of Paradise;

touch, so that he may know her whom God has given him as a companion.

Man is also endowed with inner faculties, which permit him to enter into contact not only with visible things and beings, but also with the Invisible, with the hidden face of things. They are the memory, the imagination, the will, the reasoning mind and, above all, the spirit (*rūḥ*), which God has breathed into him. Spirit is also intellect (*'aql*), direct and intuitive intelligence that is able to grasp the deeper nature of things and beings without passing through the reasoning process.

Finally, man is endowed with the faculty of speech, which makes him fundamentally different from all other beings in the animal kingdom.

The exceptional nature of man, which is destined to be the very mirror of the divine, also explains the marked anthropocentrism of the Koranic message:

> He it is who created for you all that is on the earth. (II, 29)

> He it is who hath appointed for you the night that he should rest therein and the day giving sight. (X, 68)

> And after that [after the creation of the vault of heaven, *samk*] He spread the earth And produced therefrom the water thereof and the pasture thereof, And He made fast the hills, A provision for you and for your cattle. (LXXIX, 30-33)

Plants — grapevines, vegetables, olive and palm trees, gardens and various fruits — have been put on earth so that man can take his sustenance and create remedies from them (II, 2).

God has made subject to man:

> — the animals, so that he may drink their milk, ride them, use them for transporting his goods, make his clothes from them, eat them for his nourishment, and admire them in the morning when they go out to their pasture, or in the evening, when they come back from it (XVI, 6);
> — the stars, that he may use their paths to find direction at night and to measure time (VI, 97);
> — the earth, that it may be a stable dwelling-place (*qarār*) (XL, 64) and a restful bed (*firāch*) for him (II, 22);
> — the sea, 'that ye eat fresh meat from thence, and bring forth from thence ornaments which ye wear' (XVI, 14);

— ships, so that man may voyage on the sea (XIV, 32).

Man the Caliph

Placed at the center of creation, man has been designated by God to be his lieutenant, his 'caliph (*khalīfa*) on earth', in the terms of the Koran (II, 30). The office is a distinguished one, to the point of giving man a status superior to that of the angels, whose bodies are pure light and whose sole mission is to glorify the Lord by revolving around the divine throne. In order that he might exercise his earthly magistracy, God taught man the names of all things, names which man then passed on to the angels; afterwards He ordered the angels to prostrate themselves before Adam . . .

Was this primordial man going to remain faithful to the mission that had been entrusted to him? Alas, no: 'Everyone that is thereon [on earth] will pass away' (LV, 26). And since perfection only belongs to God, even an image of God can become tarnished . . .

It must be admitted that a certain risk of estrangement existed between the creature and its Originator, due to the fact that man had been made of water, clay, semen and blood, and that spirit had been breathed into coarse matter. From that moment on, a composite form existed, its hybrid nature (not yet beast and angel, as Pascal would say, but at least earth and angel) containing the potentiality for both destabilization and corruption.

This is why the Koran contains warnings such as: 'Man is made of haste' (XXI, 37); or again, that he has been created as 'weak' (IV, 28), 'anxious' (LXX, 19), 'in affliction' (XC, 4), and 'ever thankless (*kāfura*)' (XVII, 67).

There are, therefore, imperfections in the painting, and in spite of his deiform nature, man has degenerated. This is what is known as the Fall in biblical terms, and it is an event that is related in several passages of the Koran; for example:

> And when thy Lord said unto the angels: Lo! I am about to place a viceroy in the earth, they said: Wilt Thou place therein one who will do harm therein and will shed blood, while we, we hymn Thy praise and sanctify Thee? He said: Surely I know that which ye know not.
>
> And he taught Adam all the names, then showed them to the angels, saying: Inform me of the names of these, if he are truthful.
>
> They said: Be glorified! We have no knowledge saving that which Thou has taught us. Lo! Thou, only thou, art the Knower, the Wise.

He said: O Adam! Inform them of their names, and when he had informed them of their names, He said: Did I not tell you that I know the secret of the heavens and the earth? And I know that which ye disclose and which ye hide.

And when We said unto the angels: Prostrate yourselves before Adam, they fell prostrate, all save Iblīs. He demurred through pride, and so became a disbeliever.

And We said: O Adam! Dwell thou and thy wife in the Garden, and eat ye freely (of the fruits) thereof where ye will; but come not nigh this tree lest ye become wrongdoers.

But Satan caused them to deflect therefrom and expelled them from the (happy) state in which they were; and We said: Fall down, one of you a foe unto the other! There shall be for you on earth a habitation and provision for a time.

Then Adam received from his Lord words (of revelation), and He relented toward him. Lo! He is the Relenting, the Merciful.

We said: Go down, all of you, from hence; but verily there cometh unto you from Me a guidance; and whoso followeth My guidance, there shall no fear come upon them neither shall they grieve. (II, 30-38)

It will be noticed in this passage that Eve is not shown as having induced Adam into temptation; Satan, however, caused both of them to 'deflect'. The same thing occurs in another chapter of the Koran, in which the same event is related in a slightly different way and, in particular, the nature of the temptation is made more explicit:

And verily We made a covenant of old with Adam, but he forgot, and We found no constancy in him.

And when We said unto the angels: Fall prostrate before Adam, they fell prostrate (all) save Iblīs; he refused.

Therefore We said: O Adam! This is an enemy unto thee and thy wife, so let him not drive you both out of the Garden so that thou come to toil.

It is (vouchsafed) unto thee that thou hungerest not therein nor art naked.

And that thou thirsteth not therein nor art exposed to the sun's heat.

But the devil whispered to him, saying: O Adam! Shall I show thee the tree of immortality and power that wasteth not away?

Then they twain ate thereof, so that their shame became apparent unto them, and they began to hide by heaping on themselves some of the

142

leaves of the Garden. And Adam disobeyed his Lord, so went astray.

Then his Lord chose him, and relented toward him, and guided him. (XX, 115-122)

What is particularly important in this account is the existence of a pact (*'ahd*) that God had made with Adam and that the latter had forgotten. Such a pact was in fact concluded with all men even before they came into existence. It was the 'primordial' pact or Covenant that was made in pre-eternity when all souls were, as the Koran says, 'within the loins of Adam.' At that time God had asked them: 'Am I not your Lord?' They said: 'Yea, verily. We testify' (VII, 172).

In the primordial state, that is to say in conditions of existence like those in the Garden of Eden, man stayed faithful to his pact and worshipped without fault, overwhelmed with and grateful for the blessings of his Lord, whom he praised unceasingly. Various traditions call this time the Golden Age.

However, Adam's sin broke apart this primary state, and from that point on he was to be exposed to the constant seduction of evil: in other words, of his own soul, which whispers to him to devote himself to the illusory and ephemeral goods of the world as if they were destined to endure, and which wants him to give up what he already has in order to obtain uncertain benefits.

But God, who created man to be his regent on earth, pardoned and 'came back to' Adam and gave him 'a guidance', capable of abolishing fear and sadness for those who would follow it, for him to use among the greater hardships of his new earthly existence. From that time on, as humankind increased in number, spread over the earth's surface and split up into different races and tribes, God would send guides and messengers — angels, prophets, and saints — through whom he would renew His original pact with man. In the words of the Koran, 'And when We exacted a covenant from the Prophets, and from thee (O Muḥammad) and from Noah and Abraham and Moses and Jesus son of Mary. We took from them a solemn covenant (*miṭhāgan ghaliza*)'. (XXXIII, 7)

In many passages the Koran reminds us that in the course of human history there is not a single nation that has not received its alliance and its messenger. With the coming of the latest of these messages — the Koran — the earlier religions, especially those of the 'people of the Book' (Jews and Christians) were confirmed as being expressions of the one Truth, while at the same time a new union was proposed to mankind: Islam.

What makes a man a *muslim*?

He must believe in one God, who is all-powerful and is the creator of everything. This is the monotheistic credo, the doctrine of divine unity, the *tawḥīd*. He must also believe in the truth of the Koranic message brought by Muḥammad. These two articles of Muslim faith are summed up in the formula with which one bears witness to God (*shahāda*): 'There is no God but Allāh, and Muḥammad is his Messenger.'

Said with sincerity, the above formula re-establishes union with the divine and restores to fallen man his primordial status. It is the equivalent of baptism for the Christian. Thus, spoken at the moment of death, it erases previous sins and opens the doors of Paradise. Being at the same time an adherence of the spirit to the dogma of divine unity and a recognition of the authenticity of Muḥammad's mission, the *shahāda* implies a commitment to abide by the law proclaimed in the Koran. It is therefore considered to be the first pillar of Islam. The four other pillars are canonical prayer, said five times each day; the fast of Ramaḍān that requires each believer to go without food from sunrise to sunset for one month every year; the law of alms-giving, by which each well-to-do Muslim must give a sum to the public treasury in order to take care of the needy; and lastly, the pilgrimage which each Muslim must make to Mecca at least once in his life if he can afford it. These are the individual obligations that make up the fundamentals of the religion and that each Muslim must practice if he wishes to be right with the Lord. Beyond that, there is the set of rules of behavior and social conventions that makes up the code of personal morality and social ethics: measures governing marriage, inheritance, commercial transactions, the penal code, etc. Indeed, Islam, like Judaism and Christianity before it, although in a different form, bases itself strongly on community life in order to assure the individual salvation of the faithful.

The Muslim community, according to the Koran, was founded by God: 'We have appointed you a middle nation' (II, 143). This community has brought harmony to the hearts of its members: 'And hold fast, all of you together, to the cable of Allāh, and do not separate. And remember Allāh's favor unto you: how ye were enemies and He made friendship between your hearts so that ye became as brothers by His grace ...' (III, 103). 'Ye are the best community that hath been raised up for mankind. Ye enjoin right conduct and forbid indecency; and ye believe in Allāh' (III, 110).

Islam distrusts the recluse; it considers him to be overly exposed to the temptations of the devil and too weak to defend himself. While it is true that the Koran lauds the Christian anchorites, the monks of the desert, for their piety, it does not put forward their way of life as an example. 'No monasticism in Islam (*Lā rahbāniyyata fī al-Islām*)', advised Muḥammad. Indeed, marriage and the founding of the family are the norm, to the point that the Prophet also states that 'marriage is half of *dīn* (religion).'

Let us return, however, to the community, the *umma*, and to its merits, not the least of which is to have received, in the words of a Koranic verse cited above, the gift of the 'middle nation' (II, 143). It forms an organic whole of interdependent elements. In a *ḥadīth* that is often cited — without much of a lasting effect, unfortunately, judging by the dissensions within the Muslim world today — the Prophet said that, 'The believer is to another believer as are the parts of a building that give each other mutual support.' He also stated: 'You will see Muslims in their kindness, their affections, and their reciprocal feelings, form a body which, when one of its members suffers, sees all the other parts share its sleeplessness and fever in emulation.' Finally, Muḥammad gave assurance that 'My community will never agree together on an error': a statement that was to have considerable repercussions in the formation of law through the principle of the consensus of the believers (*ijmāʻ*). This solidarity, in Muslim law, was expressed by a statute of collective obligation called the duty of sufficiency (*farḍ kifāya*), which frees the individual believer from a compulsory prescription whenever a sufficient number of the faithful join together to fulfil it. This obligation applies, for example, to prayers for the dead, holy war (*jihād*), and to the carrying out of duties that require a detailed knowledge of religious science.

It goes without saying that man, through his conduct, commits only himself, and that it is he alone who will appear before the Supreme Judge to answer for his actions. However, his ties with the social body are so strong that, in order to find his salvation, he depends in large measure upon those around him and upon whether or not his surroundings provide conditions that are favorable for the fulfilment of the Revealed Law. As the Koran says: 'Lo! man is in a state of loss, Save those who believe and do good works, and exhort one another to truth and exhort one another to endurance' (CIII,

145

2-3). These verses underline the importance of mutual encouragement for the fundamental virtues. The goal that is assigned to the community, to the Islamic Holy City, is to achieve the most complete harmony possible between, on the one hand, the search for individual salvation and, on the other, the functioning of the social body that is the guardian of the Divine Message, of institutional wisdom, and of the example of the just.

It is a question then, as has recently written Professor S.H. Nasr, author of numerous works on Islamic spirituality and science, of an 'egalitarian theocracy' or, to use another expression, of a 'normocracy' (the latter term emphasizes the sovereign domination of the Revealed Law).[4]

Let us examine the principal functions incumbent upon the community of believers.

First of all, there is the *executive power*. In the image of the community that Muḥammad founded in Medina and that was ordered to 'obey Allāh and His messenger' (VIII, 1), for 'Whoso obeyeth the messenger obeyeth Allāh' (IV, 80), the supreme head of the Muslim nation is the caliph, or 'commander of the believers', who is the successor to the Prophet and who unites all the duties associated with spiritual authority and temporal power.

The main concern of the Umayyad Caliphate, quite soon after the death of the Prophet, was to strengthen its political power, and the later Abbasid Caliphs transformed the caliphate into a royal autocracy. Thus a split arose between political and administrative duties on the one hand, and juridical and religious ones on the other; this split has become more accentuated with the division of the Muslim world into a multitude of autonomous entities. It was not, however, until the formation of nation-states along the Western model and the abolition of the Ottoman Caliphate in 1924 that the break between the executive and the religious functions became complete in most of *dār al-islām*, the Muslim world.

It seems understandably surprising that today, in what is called the Muslim world, so many peoples are subjected to governments that are quite obviously not impelled by any concerns of a religious nature.

Without entering here into a discussion that would necessitate large numbers of examples, it could nevertheless be stated that if there exists a certain passivity or resignation towards the lack of government interest in religion, it is because the Muslim conscience is thoroughly impregnated with the idea, expressed in the Koran, that 'Allāh's is the whole command' (XIII, 31). God therefore can carry out his government as and through whomever he wishes. He commands the faithful to 'Obey Allāh, and obey the messenger and those of you who are in authority' (IV, 59), so that they must recognize constituted authority, at least as long as those in power do not overtly contravene the precepts of the Revealed Law.

The second function of the Holy City of Islam is to provide justice. The idea of justice is fundamental to Islam, for the Islamic world itself, *dār al-islām*, is also called the world of justice, *dār al-'adl*, since the Law that prevails over it is that of God, the Just (*ad-'adl*). All the obligations and prohibitions stipulated in the *sharī'a*, the body of Koranic law, as well as the virtues that are for the believer the corollary and consequence of his submission to the Will and Wisdom of the Divine Legislator, have the same end result: 'Give the right to each who has the right,' or, more explicitly, 'Respect the rights of God and the rights of men.'

Thus, all the functions of the Holy City are organized around contractual relations. The first of these relations is the original pact through which God suggested that man be his lieutenant on earth and to which man subscribed by his acceptance. Next, there is for those in authority the duty of protection, and its inverse, that of obedience for those who are ruled over. Finally, there are the contracts that regulate the acts of social life and private law by which men pledge themselves to each other without ever losing sight of the sovereign prerogatives of Him who, before any human intervention, had already fixed the order of all things.

The affinity between the above conception and the Platonic vision of a just society is immediately evident. Moreover, when Farabi, in the tenth century A.D., described an ideal of the city of virtue (*madīna fāḍila*), it was both as a Muslim and as a disciple of Platonism that he specified the ends and the means: 'To make men enjoy as much as possible, during this life and on this earth, the happiness and delights of the life to come by making use of community institutions based on justice and solidarity.'

On the level of the Holy City, the exercise of judicial power is left to the judge, the *qāḍī*, who receives his office from the caliph or head of the executive branch of government. Enthroned in the mosque where he will often be called to preach the Friday sermon, his domain is that of the law, the *sharī'a*, and includes all the Koranic prohibitions, which he ensures are applied to specific cases. He pronounces marriages and divorces, attends to the execution of wills, cares for the upbringing of orphans and the handicapped, and, in particular, decides the disputes that are submitted to him and, in the case of a public or private transgression, applies the penalties provided for by the Koran.

The *teaching of religion* must also, of course, occupy an important position in the Community.

Government legal officials are of necessity chosen from among the *ulemā'*, or Doctors of Law, and the important role that is assigned to them explains why the formation of the *ulemā'* was established as one of the Community's 'duties of sufficiency'. Indeed, there is no higher distinction for the Muslim than that which is conferred by learning (*al-'ilm*), that is, knowledge of the Revealed Law. 'He to whom God wishes well,' said the Prophet, 'is made learned in matters of religion.' He also stated that, 'One single Doctor of Law has more strength against Satan than a thousand men who devote themselves to worship.' This does not mean that the learned man can dispense with worship, but that religious practices, when combined with the intelligent knowledge of their significance, acquire an almost invincible power against temptation, error, and excesses of passion.

The duty of calling the believers to their religion and of preaching good conduct does not belong solely to the learned judges or imams of the Community. The upholding of high moral standards and the encouragement to do good are duties that are incumbent upon each citizen. 'And there may spring from you a nation who invite to goodness, and enjoin right conduct and forbid indecency,' declares the Koran (III, 104). Thus, each Muslim is expected (within the conditions defined by jurisprudence, and which, except for circumstances beyond one's control, exclude the shedding of blood) to criticize and denounce public or private acts which are contrary to the 'limits' (*ḥudūd*) set by God. If it is within his power, he is also expected to reform the transgressors, so that order may be re-established in the Community, which suffers as does a body when one of its members becomes diseased, and the wholeness of which is an almost indispensable condition for the salvation of its constituents.

Not even a detailed enumeration of the precepts and rules of religious law would be able to exhaust the contents of Muslim life. Transformations and syntheses take place inside of the institutional framework within which the believers live; they constitute a veritable spiritual alchemy that, although entirely inspired by the Koranic message, nevertheless transcends its normative aspects.

The Mystical Path

The Revealed Message has two dimensions or faces: one is external and superficial; the other is internal and profound. The first is the Law of which we have just spoken: it is imposed upon all responsible men, must be accepted in terms of reason, and governs their faculties of sensation and action. Followed to the letter, it institutes and assures a sacred order that aims to restore created beings to their original status, and to make them able to attain the promised happiness of the Hereafter. The second dimension is that of the truth (*ḥaqīqa*): it is concerned with the essential realities hidden behind appearances and is only perceived by *'the eye of the heart'* that is open to contemplation. It is a kind of advance vision that God grants to those close to Him in this world. Access to this interior vision, of opening the eye of the heart to the penetration of the divine light, is by the mystical way (*ṭarīqa*), which is like a tree that rises toward the sky while its roots thrust down into the common way, the *sharī-a*.

I spoke at length several years ago of the mystical way and of the practices that are associated with it. I will not, therefore, repeat myself, but will simply bring to mind again its essential element: the *dhikr*, the remembrance or recollection of God.

The word *dhikr* can be interpreted on various levels because it in fact refers to every act and every thought that brings one closer to God. Thus the whole Koran is *dhikr-Allāh*, or 'remembrance of God', and its verses are *ayat*, 'signs', that recall the existence of the Creator. *Dhikr-Allāh* is also one of the over 200 names of the Prophet Muḥammad, which are used in the litanies and praises that the faithful address to him. 'Remind them, for thou art but a remembrancer,' Muḥammad is told in the Koran (LXXXVIII, 21), and in fact for all believers, the imitation of the customs of the Prophet (*sunna*) is the means of remembering God.

The *dhikr*, in the language of the Muslim mystics known as the Sufis, refers in particular to the mention of the Divine Name, or of one of the ninety-nine ritual Names of the Divinity, such as the Beneficent, the Merciful, the Generous, etc. Its repetition, under conditions and in forms that can vary from one school of mystics to another, is always and everywhere the supreme sacrament. Many verses of the Koran recommend the practice of the *dhikr*. Here are several of them:

Cry unto Allāh, or cry unto the Beneficent [al-Raḥmān], unto whichsoever ye cry (it is the same). His are the most beautiful names. (XVII, 110)

Therefore remember Me, I will remember you. (II, 152)

O ye who believe! Remember Allāh with much remembrance. And glorify Him early and late. He it is who blesseth you, and His angels (bless you), that He may bring you forth from darkness unto light . . . (XXXIII, 41-43)

(This lamp is found) in houses which Allāh hath allowed to be exalted and that His name shall be remembered therein. Therein do offer praise to Him at morn and evening men whom neither merchandise nor sale beguileth from remembrance of Allāh and constancy in prayer and paying their due . . . (XXIV, 36-37)

Verily in the messenger of Allāh ye have a good example for him who looketh unto Allāh and the Last Day, and remembereth Allāh much. (XXXIII, 21)

The spiritual advice given by Muḥammad to his disciples is in the same vein:

Men never gather to call upon Allāh without being surrounded by angels and covered with Divine Favor, without peace (sakīna) descending upon them and Allāh remembering them.

There is but one means of polishing all things, that removes rust; and that which polishes the heart is the invocation of God.

'Shall I point out to you the best of your acts? The purest in intent toward your King, that which raises you the highest in degree, the accomplishment of which is more beneficial than distributing gold and silver (as alms)? Or than meeting your enemy and hitting him on the back of the neck, or being hit upon the back of the neck?' His companions said, 'Tell us what it is.' The Prophet replied, 'It is the invocation of God Most High.'

Among the most commonly used formulas for the *dhikr*, there is the repetition of the first part of the testimony of faith: '*Lā ilāha il-Allāh.*' The special effectiveness of this formula comes from its evocation of two phases of spiritual realization: a first phase of negotiation of all 'divinity', that is, of all secondary 'reality', of that which does not have sufficient reason in itself; and a second phase that is the affirmation of the sole reality of the Absolute Being. In other words, it represents phases of the obliteration of the created being and of the return to the Creator; or the annihilation of separative consciousness, followed by reunification in God.

However, the highest invocation is that of the name *Allāh*, the name of the Unqualified Divinity, 'the Supreme Name', 'the Unique Name', 'the Name of Majesty'. Within its two syllables and four letters, the symbolism of which has been often commented on, this name concentrates all of the redemptive effectiveness of the divine word. 'God is present in His Name,' say the sufis. Indeed, through the conjunction of this Presence and serious concentration on the part of he who invokes Him, the worshipper finds himself practically obliterated, reabsorbed into the Invoked, the *dhikr* becoming that of God alone, in which the invocation, the invoked, and the invoker are one with the One that has no second.

Doubtlessly this state of perfect concentration is not attained automatically by practicing the *dhikr*. The initiate needs a master to instruct and educate him; he must learn to know himself, for, according to one of the sayings of Muḥammad, 'Whoever knows himself, knows his Lord.' In short, the initiate must travel over a difficult itinerary, the steps of which have often been described by mystics of diverse traditions, sometimes in symbolic form, sometimes with great psychological realism. In Islam in particular, there exists a tradition of examining the conscience which was specifically illustrated by a sufi who lived in Baghdad in the third century of the Hegira (ninth century A.D.), and who was given, while he was living, the title *Muḥāsibī*, that is, 'Master of Introspection'.

In order to describe the way of the sufis, I will make use of a teaching that, in its written form, dates back to another great master, a contemporary of Muḥāsibī, and who, like him, lived in Baghdad, where he was buried. His name was Junayd, 'the Master of the Circle (*shaykh al-ṭā'ifa*)', a name that he received because the first mystical fraternities, the *ṭurûq* (plural of *ṭarīqa*, 'the way'), were formed around him. Moreover, this particular teaching has been handed down without interruption ever since that time, and I personally found it in a treatise written at the beginning of the last century by the Moroccan sufi Ahmed Ibn'Ajiba, who died in 1809.

The mystical journey, Junayd explains, consists of three stages. The first is the realization of the *unity of actions (tawḥīd al-ad'al)*, which is the understanding that none of our actions belongs to us, but that God is actually the only Agent. This is what God, speaking through the Prophet, expressed in the famous *ḥadīth qudsī* that says:

> My servant never ceases to approach me through pious devotions until
> I become the mouth through which he speaks, the eye through which

he sees, the ear through which he hears, the hand with which he grasps, and the foot with which he walks.

The second stage is that of the *unity of qualities (tawḥīd al-ṣifāt)*. This unity, for the human being, lies in the realization that his own attributes, powers, gifts and abilities come from the Lord of the Worlds, are only reflections of divine qualities, and do not in any way belong to him. 'The most beautiful names are of God; call Him by them!' the Koran often advises; and the recitation of the Divine Names is one of the means used to attain this second stage of the mystical way, in which the *faqīr il-Allāh*, the 'poor man within God', having renounced granting himself some merit or qualification, sees his own deficiencies replaced by the riches of the Most Generous.

The last level of the way is the *unity of the Essence (tawḥīd adh-dhāt)*. At this point, the human subject completely dissolves into the Infinite Being; the drop enters the ocean. Subject and object become one, and even if he remains among his fellows, without any apparent change, the person who has extinguished himself within the Divine Essence, who is one with it, is no longer the same. Having achieved the way of return through its final stage, the subject from that time on enters the category of the 'intimates of God' (*awlīyā'Allāh*), those saints of whom the Koran repeatedly says that 'they will not know either fear, nor affliction' (X, 62ff.).

Such is, finally, the vocation of man, for, again according to the Koran, 'Lo! we are Allāh's, and lo! unto Him we are returning' (II, 156).

Notes

1. Title of a work by Frithjof Schuon, *The Transcendent Unity of Religions*, Gallimard, Paris, 1946, Collection 'Tradition'. It was subsequently republished several times, both in the original French and in English translation.
2. All Koranic quotations are from *The Meaning of the Glorious Koran: An Explanatory Translation*, trans. Marmaduke Pickthall, George Allen & Unwin, London, 1948, 2nd edn.
3. M. Lings, *Le Prophète Muhammad*, Seuil, Paris, 1986, pp.57-8. Originally published as *Muhammad, His Life Based on the Earliest Sources*, Islamic Texts Society/Allen & Unwin, London, 1983.
4. Seyyed Hossein Nasr, *Ideals and Realities of Islam*, Allen & Unwin, London, 1966, Chapter IV. Published in France as *Islam — perspectives et réalités*, Buchet/Chastel, Paris, 1975.

CHAPTER 13

Islamic Studies in America

Seyyed Hossein Nasr

The name of Islam appears in the news nearly every day and several million Muslims constitute an element of American society which can no longer be ignored. The thought of Islamic philosophers and the contribution of Islamic scientists is embedded in one way or another in the background of the philosophy and science being cultivated in the Western world, including America; and words of Arabic and Persian origin are used in American English more than are Japanese, Chinese or Hindi words. The adobe architecture of the American southwest reflects clearly its Islamic influence through both its forms and its building techniques, as well as the word 'adobe' itself; and the poetry and music of the Islamic peoples is read and heard to an ever greater degree in this land. Yet, despite all these and many other similar facts, the state of Islamic studies in America is far from satisfactory.

In this essay, which is confined to Islamic studies in American colleges and universities, we wish to consider some of the factors which prevent Islamic studies from occupying the position one would expect for a field which embraces the culture and history of a billion people stretching across the Afro-Asian land mass, with important extensions into Europe and now to an ever greater degree the Americas. One must ask why it is that whole areas of the Islamic world such as Southeast Asia fail even to be considered in most centers of Islamic studies; and why, despite so many universities where Islamic studies is taught, America has produced so few outstanding scholars in this field who can be compared to such European Islamicists as Louis Massignon, Sir Hamilton Gibb or Henry Corbin. One must, of course, also ask why much of the fruit of scholarship in Islamic studies in America is so strongly opposed by Muslims, despite the attempt by a number of American scholars to cultivate a more sympathetic view of Islam than that which was developed by classical European orientalism.[1]

Some of the causes for the existing state of affairs are related to the history of the development of Islamic studies as a discipline in this country. The early American scholars of Islam were mostly missionaries with an often open and vocal opposition to Islam. A number of the early scholars, however, came from the background of Rabbinical studies, and since they belonged to the era preceding the partition of Palestine in 1948, did not feel the need to produce the polarized and 'motivated' scholarship associated with Zionism which has affected Islamic studies so greatly since the decade of the 1950s. There appeared among them, therefore, some outstanding figures who contributed greatly to Islamic studies, such scholars as Harry A. Wolfson, who although primarily a scholar of Jewish thought, made notable contributions to the history of Islamic theology (*Kalām*) and philosophy. Among the pioneers of Islamic studies there were also a number of Maronites like Philip Hitti, who while being outstanding scholars of Arabic were not Muslims, although they were seen by many in America as authentic voices of Islamic scholarship, since most people almost naturally equated Muslim and Arab. Many of these early scholars, however, had little love for the specifically Islamic dimension of the subject which they were studying, although they helped to advance the cause of Arabic studies.

Despite the appearance of a number of scholars of distinction, there existed from the beginning a trait in Islamic studies in America which distinguished it from, let us say, Chinese, Japanese or Indian studies, this trait being an opposition to or even disdain for Islam and its culture among many scholars in this field. Usually when an American went into the field of Far Eastern studies — a few missionaries being the exception — he was attracted by some aspect of that civilization or religion which he loved and defended, as can be seen by the attitude of Langdon Warner of Harvard University, who played such an important role in saving Kyoto from being bombed during the Second World War. This attitude of love and empathy has manifested itself much less frequently in Islamic studies, not that of course it was or is totally absent.

After the Second World War, with America entering the international scene in an active way, a new phase opened in the history of Islamic studies which caused the field to expand, but at the expense of depth and concern for the historical and religious dimension. Centers of regional studies began to be developed in many universities throughout the country from Harvard to UCLA, usually under the name of Middle Eastern, but also occasionally Near Eastern, Studies. Oriented mostly toward the present-day period and based upon the social sciences rather than theology, religion or the humanities, these centers taught many subjects concerning the Islamic world, but with the minimum of reference to Islam itself. A whole generation of scholars was trained, some of whom became decision makers in America who affected the history of the Islamic world itself, usually in an adverse manner, while the majority became experts and scholars of the central regions of the Islamic world. With a number of notable exceptions, however, few of these scholars made any outstanding contributions to Islamic studies or could predict any of the major transformations which came about in the region of their specialization, transformations such as the revival of Islam in various forms in the decade of the 1970s. It is only the events of the past ten years in the Islamic world that have forced many of these centers to pay more attention to Islam in the Middle East.

Even to this day, however, in many of the major centers of Middle Eastern studies everything is taught seriously except Islam itself. One sees often in such centers numerous courses on history, anthropology, languages, sociology, political science, and similar subjects pertaining to the Islamic world, but little in-depth study of Islam as the religion which forms the heart and arteries of the body of the society and civilization being considered.

There are, in fact, in America only a handful of institutions of higher learning, like the University of Chicago and Temple University, where Islam is studied seriously in the religion department as religion and not as something else. Moreover, despite the rapid expansion of religious studies in this continent during the past four decades to include 'non-Western' religions, and the establishment of centers for the study of religion on a worldwide scale such as those at Harvard, Colgate and Claremont, Islam has not at all fared as well as Hinduism, Buddhism or the Chinese religions. The discipline of comparative religion, in fact, has produced very few Islamicists of note.[2] Besides the historical opposition to Islam in the Christian West, going back to the Crusades and the Reconquest in Spain, which affects almost unconsciously the attitude of many modern Westerners, including those who do not even consider themselves to be Christian, there is the question of the way religious studies have evolved.

During the nineteenth century, there developed in the field of 'the science of religions', or *Religionswissenschaft*, the idea of the evolution of religion from so-called 'primitive' to higher forms, reaching its peak with Christianity. Such a conception of religious history, which continued into this century, obviously had great difficulty coming to terms with such a major postscript as Islam. As a reaction to this historicism, there developed the school of phenomenology which had its most influential representative in America in the person of M. Eliade, who himself made major contributions to nearly every field of religious studies except Islam. With its emphasis upon myths and symbols, this school was much more attracted to such traditions as Hinduism, whose truths are for the most part expressed in mythological language, than to Islam, whose metaphysical and theological teachings are couched mostly in an 'abstract' language,[3] and whose teachings include a Sacred Law which is central to the understanding of the religion.

To these factors were added the age-old distortions of Islam as the 'religion of the sword', or the 'dry' religion of the desert, whose blindingly clear spirituality was supposedly somehow borrowed from foreign sources and grafted upon the body of Islam. As a result, while in the case of Hinduism usually such sublime texts as the *Bhagavad-Gita* were taught and not laws of inheritance in various castes and sub-castes, and Hindu art rather than social and commercial conflicts, in the case of Islam only the most external aspects of the religion came to be taught along with a distorted history of a religion seen in constant conflict and war.

The result of all these factors has been that Islamic studies has not fared well as religious studies, even when compared to Hindu, Buddhist or Chinese religious studies, despite — or perhaps because of — the fact that Islam is theologically much closer to Judaism and Christianity and has shared so much more common history with the Christian West than have the Indian and Far Eastern religions. It is interesting to note that the incredible synthesis created in Muslim Spain, and the culture in which under Muslim rule Muslims, Jews and Christians lived at peace for several centuries, contributing to a glittering civilization in which they all played a role, is passed over more or less in silence. Almost no-one refers to the Judaeo-Christian-

Islamic tradition, but on the contrary in forgetfulness of the reality of Abrahamic monotheism and to abet the cause of passing political goals, most scholars juxtapose the Judaeo-Christian heritage to the Islamic.

Not only has Islamic studies fared by and large poorly in the field of religion, it has been also more or less neglected in the field of the humanities. Whether it be in philosophy or history, literature or the arts, Islamic studies in America has not succeeded in flowering in any notable manner in comparison with, let us say, Japanese studies. Not only in medieval European universities did the Islamic humanities play a greater role than they do today in America, but even during the Romantic movement in England and Germany there was greater interest at least in the literature of the Islamic peoples than one finds today.

It is only in the field of the social sciences that Islamic studies, or rather subjects related to the Islamic world, have been treated fairly extensively in America. Here, however, there stands the major question of whether Western models apply to the Islamic world. Is it possible to study Islamic society on the basis of the theories of Durkheim, or to carry out an anthropological study of a part of the Islamic world on the basis of the theories of Lévi-Strauss? These are major questions which are now being debated, and one hopes that as a result more serious contributions will be made to Islamic studies in those fields which in the West are called the social sciences. Until that is done, however, even in this domain where so much effort is being spent, the results will usually not have much to do with the social and religious reality of the Islamic world.

As for law, which plays such an important role in Islam, it is only during the past decade that certain American law schools have begun to teach Islamic Law, and that mostly for practical reasons. The teaching of the Divine Law, or *Shari'ah*, however, has not become part and parcel of Islamic studies, and few American scholars have made notable contributions to this field.

At the heart of Islamic studies stands not only the religion of Islam, but also the languages involved with the study of that religion and the civilization it brought into being. Arabic is the most important of Islamic languages and has been taught in America since the eighteenth century. In recent decades, however, despite the appearance of several eminent Arabists who either themselves or their families migrated from the Islamic world, such as George Makdisi and Irfan Shahid, and the appearance of a number of fine American Arabists such as James Bellamy, William Brenner, Victor Danner, Richard Frank and Nicholas Heer, the teaching of Arabic has still suffered as far as Islamic studies is concerned. The main reason has been the emphasis upon 'modern' Arabic at the expense of the classical language. Until recently in most centers of Arabic studies, Quranic Arabic was made subservient to the prose of al-Ahram and little attention was paid to the fact that among literate Arabs themselves, the Quran is read and understood first, and only later is modern literary Arabic mastered. During the past decade some changes have been made in the direction of classical Arabic, and more students are now being trained who can read classical texts. Still, the training is far from complete because too few students even with advanced degrees are actually able to read classical Arabic texts with full in-depth comprehension of their meaning.

The situation of the second major Islamic language, Persian, is much more deplorable. First of all, even the name of the language is now used incorrectly; it is frequently called *Farsī*, as if in English one called French *français* or German *Deutsch*. Secondly, it is usually forgotten that not only is Persian (by whatever name it is called) still the spoken and written language of Iran, Afghanistan and Tajikistan, as well as that of many people in Iraq, the Persian Gulf and Pakistan, but that for a thousand years it was the *lingua franca* of Asia. Quranic commentaries in China were written in Persian while even after the Second World War, just before Albania became Communist, Persian books continued to be printed in this Western outpost of the Islamic world. Without knowledge of Persian, the Muslim culture of India and most of its medieval history, both Hindu and Muslim, is a closed book, and later Islamic thought as it developed in the eastern lands of Islam a forbidden territory. The remarkable indifference to the teaching of Persian in many American universities has done much to weaken Islamic studies and to prevent well-rounded students from being trained. Persian is essential not only for the study of eastern history, literature and the arts, but also for Islamic studies itself where some of the most important figures, such as Ghazzali, wrote in both Arabic and Persian.

The other major Islamic languages such as Turkish, Urdu, Bengali and Malay are taught here and there, but rarely as an integral part of Islamic studies. This is partly due to an unfortunate classification of religions which is detrimental to Islamic studies, the division in question being the one between Eastern religions and Western religions. In many universities Islam is taught as a Western religion despite being 'non-Western'. This is correct to the extent that Islam is an integral part of Abrahamic monotheism of which Judaism and Christianity are the other two branches. But whereas these branches were to grow primarily in the West, Islam was destined to spread as much in the East as the West. There are more Muslims in Southeast Asia today than in the whole of the Arab world. The religious life and culture of several hundred million Muslims in South Asia, Bangladesh, Indonesia, Malaysia and China is hardly ever mentioned in general courses on Islam, and not even known to any appreciable degree by advanced students in the field.

Likewise, African Islam is rarely treated as part of Islamic studies. General courses on Islam and its history deal only accidentally and tangentially with Africa south of the Sahara, and courses on Africa rarely relate the advent and history of Islam in Africa to the rest of the Islamic world. It is possible to attain the highest degree in Islamic studies and not know anything about either the great Islamic empires of Mali nor of the millions of Muslims living in Xinjiang (Sinkiang). A work such as the *Venture of Islam* by Marshall Hodgson, who was one of the most gifted American scholars of Islam, covers the whole of the Islamic world in time as well as geographically, in a manner that is quite exceptional, and far from the usual treatment that is given to the subject.

The criticism made of Islamic studies in America does not mean to detract from the achievements made in this domain by a number of American scholars in so many fields such as Islamic history, anthropology, sociology, the history of art and archaeology, music, literature, philosophy, the history of science and several aspects of the religion of Islam itself. But considering the importance of the subject, the existing distortions and the high price in terms of practical matters which the Islamic world itself, as well as America, have paid and continue to pay as a result of the misunderstanding of Islam and the Islamic world in America, it is necessary to investigate means whereby the situation can be improved. It must, therefore, be asked what can be done to improve the condition of Islamic studies while benefiting from the achievements of the past few decades and learning from its mistakes. This question must, however, be asked in light of the fact that Islamic studies in America involves to an even greater degree the Islamic world itself, as a result of the presence of a large number of

Muslim students in America as well as a number of Muslim scholars and teachers whose works have an extensive influence, not only upon these students but also within Islamic countries.

The first and most important step which must be taken in Islamic studies is to study this field within the framework of religion rather than a discipline, which no matter how significant in itself, is not concerned with religion as such. As already mentioned, in the vast majority of institutions of learning in America Islam is studied as history, language, culture, a political system and the like, but not as a religion. The heart of Islamic studies must be moved from all these other disciplines or regional centers and placed in religion departments where the central, religious significance of all things Islamic can be brought out. In the Islamic world not only theology and ethics, but also law, economics and politics, not to mention the arts and sciences, possess a much greater religious significance than their counterparts in post-medieval European civilization. There is no greater source of distortion than applying the secularist perspective of the past few centuries in the West to a religion and civilization where it does not apply. The activity in the bazaar of a Muslim city is economic activity, but it is not just economic activity. It possesses a religious dimension which is crucial to its understanding and without which any study of it will be superficial, to say the least.

In stating that Islamic studies should be placed in religion departments, however, it is not meant that the contemporary Western religious categories should be applied blindly to Islam. For example, in Christianity theology is much more central than law, whereas in Islam law is more central. In Christianity mysticism was never organized into orders independent of the authority of the Church, whereas in Islam Sufi orders have always been independent of the exoteric *ulama*. In fact, the whole question of religious authority is posed in a different way in the two traditions. There is need to make use of a theology and metaphysics of comparative religion which is able to deal with Islam in a manner that does justice to the nature of that tradition, and yet is comprehensible to the Western worldview. The prejudices which have marred the study of Islam in the West since the time of Peter the Venerable, when the Quran was first rendered into Latin and even before that important event, must finally be overcome if understanding in depth is to be achieved. Unfortunately, despite so much claim to objectivity, much of Western scholarship concerning Islam remains distorted as a result of many old prejudices, to which have been added new ones resulting from the Arab-Israeli conflict and the rise of so-called fundamentalism.

Despite this fact, however, Islam must be first and foremost studied as a religion and not simply a social force or historical event. This task is made easier by the appearance of a number of works in European languages during the past few decades which speak with both sympathy and authority about Islam. Most of these works have been written by Westerners who have developed an understanding of the Islamic tradition, or who speak from within that tradition. But also a number of books in this category of writings have been written by Muslims themselves, but in European languages, primarily English and French. Although some of these works do not address the Western mind and the questions usually posed by a Westerner in quest of understanding Islam, others do succeed in creating a bridge between the Islamic world and the West.[4] In any case, the in-depth, thorough and sympathetic yet objective study of the Islamic religion, and the placing of this study at the heart of Islamic studies, is a necessary task which is already facilitated by the research, study and writings of those Western and Muslim scholars who speak with the voice of authority in such a manner that they are accepted by Muslims themselves, and at the same time comprehensible to the Western audience.

There is under present circumstances, in any case, no excuse for the large number of Middle Eastern, Near Eastern or Islamic studies programs in which Islam is relegated to a single introductory course, and in which everything else Islamic, whether it be history, art, sociology or economics is taught in almost complete detachment from the Islamic tradition, which in reality is the lifeblood of all those other domains. Nor is there any excuse for the remarkably weak representation of Islam in so many comparative religious studies programs throughout the country, where there are often several professors in Hindu, Buddhist and Far Eastern religious studies but hardly anyone in Islam. Of all the major religions of the world, Islam fares worst in most religious studies programs in America. Until that weakness is solved, there is little hope for a serious improvement in the situation of Islamic studies.

Once Islamic studies is constituted in such a manner that at its heart stands the religion and its study, then it is possible and even necessary to relate this central concern to a number of fields such as sociology, economics, international relations, political science, as well as the humanities for those students who wish to have such an interdisciplinary education. This is particularly true of Muslim students coming to America for advanced education. To an ever greater degree such students are interested in studying not only economics, sociology, anthropology, or for that matter the history of art or the history of science. They are primarily interested in Islam in relation to those fields. In light of the present-day interest within the Islamic world in the process that has become known as 'the Islamicization of knowledge', this type of interdisciplinary approach could become one of the most fruitful developments in Islamic studies in America, with far-reaching consequences for the Islamic world itself. But the condition of success in this program remains a carefully prepared core Islamic studies program grounded in religious studies.

The second important consideration in improving Islamic studies is the proper teaching of Islamic languages. As far as Arabic is concerned, fortunately much attention is being paid to the subject but still not enough to classical Arabic. As already stated, emphasis should be placed upon classical Arabic which must serve as the basis for modern Arabic, and not vice versa. Also, greater attention should be paid to the reading of classical texts and being able to interpret these texts according to the traditional methods of hermeneutics. Earlier orientalism, despite its numerous prejudices, rendered much service to Islamic studies by editing critically many important texts. Even this art, however, is being lost especially in America, where so many young scholars prefer to write about texts without being able to read them carefully, not to speak of editing them. The fault in this matter lies most of all in the manner in which Arabic is taught.

As for Persian, the whole philosophy of teaching it must be changed. Persian must first of all be recognized for what it is, namely the *lingua franca* of what Toynbee called the Iranic zone of Islamic civilization stretching from Iraq to China. After Arabic, Persian is the most important Islamic language and the only language other than Arabic which became global within Islamic civilization. No program of Islamic studies can be serious without the teaching of Persian. Semitic philology is one thing, and Islamic studies another. Arabic is of course very important for Semitic linguistic studies, where it is studied along with Hebrew, Aramaic, Syriac and other Semitic languages. But this relationship has little to do with the relationship of Arabic to Persian, and through Persian to other major Islamic languages such as Turkish and Urdu. Islamic studies, in contrast to Semitic studies, must emphasize this latter relationship and teach both Arabic and Persian to students seriously interested in Islamic studies, especially as far as Islamic thought is concerned.

As for the other Islamic languages, they must also be offered in major centers, while a number of centers will naturally specialize in a particular region of the Islamic world, such as North Africa, South or Southeast Asia, in which case Berber, the Indian language, or Malay must be taught. But the role of such languages and even such a major language as Turkish is that of a vernacular language, while Arabic and Persian constitute the classical and universal languages of the Islamic world. These languages, because of their immense richness and long history, must be mastered in depth and on the basis of a program which would enable at least a small number of students to gain full mastery of them. American institutions of learning have not until now been as successful in this endeavor as the amount of effort spent would lead one to expect. There has, however, been more success in the field of Arabic than Persian, where there are very few American scholars who possess complete mastery over the classical literature. But the flowering of Islamic studies requires a deepening of language teaching in such a manner that at least a number of young scholars are trained every year who can read and translate with precision the texts with which Islamic studies is concerned.

As for different aspects of Islamic studies, the situation varies from one field to another. In history a number of gifted young scholars have been trained, but there is a shortage of competent scholars in the field, to the extent that many of the works written around the turn of the century continue to be reprinted and taught despite many important new discoveries which have been made since they were written. It is necessary to encourage a greater number of students with a real flair for history to turn to the subject of Islamic history by emphasizing not only the significance of the field itself, but also its relation to other major fields of history such as medieval European history, Indian history and the like.

In the field of philosophy, Islamic studies in America suffers particularly from the fact that the prevalent philosophical trend in America since the Second World War is particularly opposed to the religious and metaphysical concerns of Islamic philosophy. This fact, added to the lack of attention paid to the study of philosophy in secondary schools, has prevented Islamic philosophy from attracting as many gifted students as one finds in Europe. There are very few centers in America, even major ones, where Islamic philosophy is taught seriously; and where it is, rarely is it related to the Islamic tradition to which it is inalienably linked.[5]

The situation of Islamic science is not much better. There are a small number of fine scholars in the field teaching in several centers, but in most cases the study of Islamic science is cut off from the rest of Islamic studies and taught more as a chapter in the history of Western science. Rarely, in fact, are the Islamic sciences seen as the fruit of the tree of Islamic civilization, nurtured and developed within a worldview which has its roots in the Islamic tradition.

The field of Islamic art, however, has come into its own during the past decade and there is a greater degree of interest in both Islamic art and architecture than ever before. The Aga Khan program in Islamic art and architecture at Harvard and MIT has been in its own way a catalyst in this domain, and has caused a number of young Muslim architects, urban designers and the like to come to America to pursue their studies in Islamic art and architecture. This very active domain of Islamic studies can be further developed by strengthening its link with the study of Islam itself, and not losing sight of the nexus between Islamic art and the religion which made the creation of this art possible.

The non-plastic arts, however, have not fared as well. The literature of the Islamic peoples has attracted a number of scholars and a few like Herbert Mason have created literary works based on Islamic themes. But the situation is very far from that of Persian literature in Victorian and Edwardian England. There is need of studying anew the great masterpieces of Islamic literature, particularly Sufi poetry. Classical Persian Sufi poetry remains to this day a subject which attracts many who are drawn to mystical and spiritual subjects. Much more needs to be done along the lines of works by A.M. Schimmel, William Chittick, Omar Pound and others, to make this poetry as well as the literary masterpieces of Arabic, Turkish, Urdu and other Islamic languages known and made part and parcel of Islamic studies.

As for the social sciences in relation to Islam, the works of American scholars are numerous and American centers remain very active in various social sciences, such as sociology, anthropology, political science and more recently economics. In some fields such as anthropology, American scholars such as Clifford Geertz have

164

produced works of great influence. But by and large these fields suffer from the imposition of alien models upon the Islamic world, with often catastrophic results, as witnessed by the predictions made by so many American political scientists concerning the Islamic world during the past few decades. These disciplines need to sink their roots more in the Islamic religion, its theology and philosophy, its Sacred Law and the politico-social and economic teachings which issue from it and the history and culture of the Islamic peoples. Today in most American centers of Islamic studies, Western social, economic or political models are used for the study of the Islamic world and there is little interaction between the social sciences and Islamic studies. The walls drawn around each discipline are so high and thick that it is difficult to either mount them or pierce through them. If Islamic studies is to be strengthened in this domain, there is no choice but to remove some of these obstacles; otherwise studies whose results are usually contradicted by events will remain the order of the day.

It must be added that in order for Islamic studies to flourish in America to the benefit of both America and the Islamic world, it should also be taught as part and parcel of the general education and liberal arts programs in American universities. The experience of Muslim Spain, where Christians and Jews lived in harmony with Muslims and where all the communities interacted and collaborated with each other to create one of the most glorious episodes of human history, must be recalled and studied carefully rather than purposefully forgotten because of current political or ideological interests. The Western humanities must be taught as related both historically and morphologically to those of Islam. It is not sufficient to simply mention the 'Arab philosophers' in an intermediate chapter linking late antiquity to the scholastics in the history of philosophy. The Muslim philosophers must be taught fully not only as one of the pillars of the foundation of medieval Western thought, but also as philosophers who, while sharing the same Graeco-Hellenistic intellectual heritage and Abrahamic religious background as Western philosophers, developed their thought in a direction different from that of the post-medieval West. Islamic philosophy must be seen as not only a chapter in the history of Western thought, but also an independent school of philosophy close to, yet different from, Western philosophy and having its own history which continues to the present day. Islamic philosophy, moreover, should be taught in philosophy departments as philosophy, and not only in Middle East departments where neither the teachers nor the students are necessarily trained to understand philosophical discourse.

The same could be said for other disciplines. Islamic literature should be taught not only to students specializing in Islamic studies, but to all students of world literature who should see Arabic literature in relation to Provençal poetry, to the *Divine Comedy* of Dante, to the treatises of Raymond Lull, to the introduction of rhyme into European poetry, to the *Fables* of La Fontaine. They should read Persian poetry along with their study of Goethe and Ruckert, or English romantic poetry, or the American Transcendentalists, and come to understand something of the significance of the influence of the literature of these languages upon the European literary tradition. They should also study the literature of the Islamic peoples as literature.

In music the origin of many European instruments should be made clear, as should the interaction between Spanish and Arabic music. The introduction of the Turkish military bands, not to mention works of Mozart and Haydn with purported Turkish themes, should be combined with familiarity with some Turkish music, and even in modern times the study of Bartok and Kodály should be accompanied by some acquaintance with Arabic and other forms of music of the Muslim peoples in which they were so interested.

As for art, rarely is the history of Western art taught with reference to the significance of the Cordova mosque for medieval Gothic arching, or Arabic illuminations for the art of illumination, or, for that matter, the Persian miniature for certain aspects of the art of Matisse. Without denying the very different nature of European art from Islamic art, various forms of Islamic art which over the centuries have fecundated or influenced European or American art, can be taught as a part of those subjects in the same way that Greek or Roman influences, which were of course influential on a much wider scale, are studied. Although Islam was not simply the foundation of Western civilization as was Rome once Christianized, it was one of the elements which played a great role in the formative period of Western civilization. Islamic studies should therefore be taught in the light of that role as well as independently of Western studies.

Finally, it must be mentioned that every intellectual endeavor flowers and develops through the quality of thought of those who lead, and not through the quantity of those who happen to study in the particular field in question. Islamic studies is no exception. In

American centers until now there has not been in general enough emphasis upon the hierarchical concept of a program which would begin with many students and end with very few; a few who would, however, be highly qualified. There is a tendency to offer too many courses which move in a parallel and horizontal direction rather than a vertical one. Too much emphasis is placed upon the quantity of teachers and students, as if the greatest Islamicists that the West has produced were not products of universities where one or two outstanding scholars trained a very small number of gifted students over the years, in a manner which did not simply widen their horizon but also deepened their scholarship and enabled them to penetrate more profoundly into the subject with which they were dealing. No excellence in Islamic studies, or for that matter practically any other field of intellectual endeavor, is possible without emphasis upon quality and hierarchy in the sense of building an ever higher intellectual edifice on a firm and broad foundation, and not only expanding the foundation horizontally.

The future of Islamic studies in America is not only a matter of theoretical or academic concern. Upon the knowledge or ignorance of the Islamic world in America depends the future of both the Islamic world and America. The incredible distortions of the image of Islam in the American mass media complements the lack of in-depth understanding of many facets of Islam by the 'experts' upon whose views depend the decisions which affect the life of millions of human beings. The Islamic world is too large and Islam too strong a force to be relegated to the status it possesses in the West, and especially in America today. The development of Islamic studies upon a more solid foundation, with greater depth and on the basis of more vigorous scholarship and intellectual honesty cannot but be of the greatest benefit to both America and the Islamic world. The destinies of the Islamic world and the West are intertwined in such a way that ignorance of one world by the other cannot but result in calamitous results for both worlds. It is hoped that the bitter fruits of the past decade will help usher in a period in which Islamic studies can both provide a greater understanding of that world, and enrich to the extent possible the religious, cultural, artistic and educational life of America itself.

Notes

1. A number of scholars have written on the meaning of 'Islamic studies' in the present-day context of academic studies and also from a more theoretical point of view in its relation to religious studies as a whole. See for example Ch. Adams, 'The History of Religions and the Study of Islam' from J. Kitagawa, M. Eliade and Ch. Long, eds., *The History of Religions: Essays on the Problem of Understanding*, Chicago, 1967, pp.177-93; also R. Martin, ed., *Approaches to Islam in Religious Studies*, Tucson, 1985; and J.J. Waardenburg, *L'Islam dans le miroir de l'occident*, Paris, 1963. W.C. Smith, although a Canadian, must also be mentioned both because of the influence of his numerous studies on the relation between Islamic studies and religious studies, and because of his influence as a teacher at Harvard University for over two decades.

2. See the essay of Y.Y. Haddad, 'Muslim in America: A Select Bibliography' from *Muslim World* Vol. LXXVI, No.2, April 1986, pp.93-122, containing many entries relevant to Islamic studies in America. This fact has been noted by Ch. Adams of the McGill Institute of Islamic Studies among others, in the study cited above and elsewhere.

3. This does not, of course, mean that Islam does not use the symbolic mode of expression. The Quran is replete with symbolism and itself states that God uses symbols (*amthal*) in order to convey the truth to mankind.

4. Such an attempt has already been made in academic circles by H. Smith (the noble scholar to whom this volume is dedicated) and W.C. Smith, while a completely adequate framework for the comparing of religions has been provided by F. Schuon in many of his works, especially *The Transcendent Unity of Religions*, trans. P. Townsend, London, 1984; and *Christianity/Islam — Essays on Esoteric Ecumenicism*, trans. G. Polit, Indiana, 1985.

5. For reference to some of these works see the bibliography at the end of each chapter of our *Ideals and Realities of Islam*, London, 1986.

CHAPTER 14

The Religious Tradition of the Australian Aborigines

Kenneth Oldmeadow

Preface

Professor Seyyed Hossein Nasr has written of:

> ... those whose vocation it is to provide the keys with which the treasury of wisdom of other traditions can be unlocked, revealing to those who are destined to receive this wisdom the essential unity and universality and at the same time the formal diversity of tradition and revelation.[1]

Such a vocation dignified the work of René Guénon, Ananda Coomaraswamy, Titus Burckhardt and Marco Pallis, as it does, at the present time, the work of Frithjof Schuon, Whitall Perry, Martin Lings and Professor Nasr himself. Although, to my knowledge, none of these representatives of the traditional outlook has been familiar with the religious beliefs and practices of the Australian Aborigines, they have all been indefatigable champions of everything which deserves the name traditional. I shall not apologize for my subject: the Aboriginal tradition can stand, I think, next to those several integral traditions to which Dr Coomaraswamy, for example, devoted such prodigious scholarship. As Frithjof Schuon has reminded us, 'In all epochs and in all countries there have been revelations, religions, wisdoms: tradition is a part of mankind, just as man is part of tradition.'[2] However, I must say at the outset that I do not speak as an expert on Aboriginal religion but rather as a sympathetic observer who feels that the religious and spiritual heritage of the Aborigines is one which, so far, has received too little attention from the traditional point of view exemplified in the work of those distinguished writers whom I have already mentioned. On the other hand it *has* received a great deal of attention from those least qualified to understand it, which is to say from scholars whose inquiries are cramped and distorted by a materialistic and quasi-scientific outlook, which immediately disqualifies them from reaching the heart of the matter. In my remarks here I would like to address three general questions: What factors have governed the European perceptions of Aboriginal culture and the religious tradition which underpinned it? What were some of the central features of the Aboriginal tradition? What might be some of the lessons which we can derive from a study of this culture? It is these last two questions which will command most of our attention. I turn now to the first of our questions.

European-Aboriginal Relations and Perceptions of Aboriginal 'Religion'

Since the first contact between the Europeans and the Australian continent's earliest occupants the Aborigines have been the subject of feelings ranging from a sentimental and euphoric romanticism to profound contempt. They have been cast in various roles: the 'Noble Savage'; a figure of fun; a harmless and infantile creature; an embodiment of all that is morally repugnant in man's nature; an anthropological relic of the Stone Age; a biological curio; a victim of the Creator's displeasure with humankind; a social misfit incapable of living a responsible and productive life; a parasite on the social welfare system.[3] The stereotypes have changed under the pressure of new circumstances and the shifting ideological presuppositions of the observers, but throughout them all runs the persistent European failure to understand Aboriginal culture, in particular that complex network of interrelated beliefs, values, attitudes, relationships and patterned behaviors which we can loosely assemble under the canopy of Aboriginal 'religion'. We do not have time here to rehearse the melancholy story of how one negative European stereotype has replaced another over the last 200 years. Nor would I presume to try to tell the story from the Aboriginal viewpoint. Rather I would like simply to remark briefly on a few of the more conspicuous factors which have governed European attitudes to Aboriginal culture generally, and more particularly to Aboriginal religion. Unhappily they are precisely those factors which have been responsible for the ongoing cultural vandalism of modern, industrial societies against indigenous traditional cultures across the globe. Whether we turn to the nineteenth-century destruction of the culture of the American Plains Indians or of the Australian Aborigines or of the South African Bushmen, or to the brutal attempt by the Chinese to extirpate the Buddhist heritage of Tibet, or to the current rape of the Amazonian forests and the communities which live in them, we find the same sorts of factors at work. Here we shall focus on only four of these factors: ignorance about the culture in question; ideas about the cultural superiority of modern, industrial, European civilization; evolutionism of both a biological and social stamp; and the claims of an aggressive, evangelical Christianity operating as an accomplice to European colonialism in the destruction of Aboriginal culture. We shall look particularly at how these factors influenced and shaped the intellectual disciplines most closely concerned with investigating Aboriginal culture, namely ethnology and anthropology.

The attitude of most early observers and scholars to the subject of Aboriginal religion was, as one commentator has recently written, 'a melancholy mixture of neglect, condescension and misunderstanding.'[4] From the outset of European settlement there has been a persistent and, in some cases, a wilful refusal to acknowledge that the Aborigines had any religious culture at all. In 1798 an early observer wrote:

> It has been asserted by an eminent divine, that no country has yet been discovered where some trace of religion was not to be found. From every observation and inquiry that I could make among these people, from the first to the last of my acquaintance with them, I can safely pronounce them an exception to this opinion.[5]

Such a view is echoed in the words of an otherwise sympathetic missionary, writing in the mid-nineteenth century:

> The Aborigines of New Holland, in this part of the Colony, have no priesthood, no altar, no sacrifice, nor any religious service, strictly so-called; their superstitious observances can scarcely be designated as divine rites, being only mysterious works of darkness, revellings and suchlike.[6]

One is reminded of nineteenth-century European reactions to much sacred art of the East, reactions which, being ignorant of the iconographic vocabularies concerned, could perceive only 'many-armed monsters' and 'improper' statues of one kind and another.[7] It was a cardinal part of Coomaraswamy's achievement to initiate a process of education which gave Europeans access to these inexhaustible treasures.

The European blindness to Aboriginal religion served covert political purposes. As Professor W.E.H. Stanner has observed:

> It allowed European moral standards to atrophy by tacitly exempting from canons of right, law and justice acts of dispossession, neglect and violence at Aboriginal expense.[8]

The European recognition that the Aborigines did have a rich and complex spiritual life and an ongoing tradition came slowly, and never represented more than a partial understanding. This was because such scholarship as there was concerning Aboriginal religion often rested on rotten foundations, namely those vague but potent Victorian prejudices and cultural valuations which assumed the biological and cultural superiority of the white man, the belief that mid-Victorian British institutions marked the apotheosis of civilization, and the notion that the extinction of the indigenous peoples of Australia was inevitable and divinely appointed.[9]

The profound ignorance which I have been discussing would matter less if it were not accompanied by the assumption of European cultural superiority, one which was buttressed by social Darwinism in the nineteenth century. Notions of cultural superiority had a long and sordid pedigree in Europe, but here we shall only focus on one particular set of ideas which exercised a particularly baleful influence: I refer to evolutionism in both its scientific and sociological guises. A writer in a late nineteenth-century Australian newspaper articulated a very widespread notion when he wrote the following:

> It seems a law of nature where two races whose stages of progression differ greatly are brought into contact, the inferior race is doomed to disappear. . . . The process seems to be in accordance with a natural law which . . . is clearly beneficial to mankind at large by providing for the survival of the fittest. Human progress has all been achieved by the spread of the progressive race and the squeezing out of the inferior ones. . . . It may be doubted that the Australian aborigine would ever have advanced much beyond the status of the neolithic races . . . we need not therefore lament his disappearance.[10]

One of the most eminent Australian ethnologists of the last century, Baldwin Spencer, felt no apparent qualms in making the following comparison:

Australia is the present home and refuge of creatures, often crude and
quaint, that have elsewhere passed away and given way to higher
forms. This applies equally to the Aboriginal as to the platypus and the
kangaroo.[11]

Indeed, the global decline of the darker races was a theme which
enjoyed widespread currency.[12] Biological Darwinism was paralleled
by an evolutionist cultural theory, elaborated by men such as E.B.
Tylor and Herbert Spencer. It was Tylor who articulated another
typical mid-Victorian prejudice which had been clothed in the
raiments of evolutionary 'science' when he wrote:

If there have remained anywhere up to modern times, men whose
condition has changed little since the Early Stone Age, the Tasmanians
seem to be such a people. They stand before us . . . illustrating man
near his lowest known level of culture.[13]

Evangelical Christianity, fired with a crusading zeal and frequently
invoking the name of the Deity, provided one of the most
fundamental impulses behind the dismantling of the early Romantic
images which had been derived, in large part, from the writings of
Rousseau. With widespread missionizing activity in Australia and the
Pacific came a reaction against romantic primitivism: to churchmen
of evangelical persuasion it was less than proper that 'pagan savages'
should be idealized as either noble or innocent. All manner of
pseudo-Biblical rationales for the white treatment of the Aborigines
were offered up. John Dunmore Lang, a prominent colonial cleric,
for example, had this to say in 1856:

The white man had indeed only carried out the intentions of the
Creator in coming and settling down in the territories of the natives.
God's first command to man was 'Be fruitful and multiply and
replenish the earth.' Now that the Aborigines had not done, and
therefore it was no fault in taking the land of which they were
previously the possessors.[14]

This claim also flags the persistent European failure to understand the
Aboriginal perception of and relationship to the land, one which is
absolutely fundamental to the whole culture. The theme of the
Aborigines' moral abasement also enjoyed widespread currency in
the second quarter of the nineteenth century. Some clerical
commentators suggested that the moral degradation of the
Aborigines was a sure sign of the visitation of the Supreme Author's
wrath. In short, God's name was invoked to legitimate the racialist

prejudices of the Victorian Age and the often self-interested motives of European settlers in Australia.[15] At this point it must be emphasized that what is in question here is not Christianity in any of its integral and traditional forms, but an alliance between European colonialism and certain forms of anti-traditional Protestantism.

Twentieth-century anthropologists have certainly abandoned many of the crudest racist assumptions of their predecessors, but all too often have succeeded only in replacing Victorian prejudices with those more characteristic of our own age while still retaining a childish faith in the capacity of a rationalistic and materialistic science to grasp the mysteries of a complex and rich spiritual tradition. Nothing more dramatically betokens the failure of Durkheimian anthropology in the face of Aboriginal religion than its continuing insistence that Aboriginal 'religion' is, essentially, a system for 'sanctifying' certain social functions and relationships. It is not for nothing that Mircea Eliade has written of the 'religious illiteracy' of so many of the writers on so-called 'primitive' religious traditions.[16] It must be said that while intellectual fashions amongst ethnologists and anthropologists have changed over the last two hundred years, the one constant factor has been a kind of reductionism which refuses to treat Aboriginal religion on its own terms, or in terms appropriate to any religious tradition. The theories of Freud, Durkheim and Levy-Bruhl, for instance, all massively influential in anthropological circles, are all variations on the reductionist theme.[17] As Whitall Perry once observed:

> . . . the scientific pursuit of religion puts the saddle on the wrong horse, since it is the domain of religion to evaluate science, and not vice versa.[18]

One must, in fairness, concede that anthropology has produced some imaginative, sensitive and sympathetic scholars who have alerted us to the many misdemeanors of their predecessors, and who have helped to foster a more respectful approach which tries to understand Aboriginal religion on its own terms: the late Professor W.E.H. Stanner is pre-eminent amongst such scholars.[19] Stanner was insistent that Aboriginal religion must be studied '*as* religion and not as the mirror of something else', and strenuously refuted the fallacy that 'the social order is primary and in some sense causal, and the religious order secondary and in some sense consequential.'[20]

The ethnological data collected over the last two hundred years has often been misinterpreted; of that there can be no doubt. Nevertheless it is, in part, on the basis of that data that a more appropriate understanding of Aboriginal religion must be constructed. The reason for this is both sad and simple: the European desecration of the Aboriginal tradition has left us, through most of the continent, with little more than fragmentary remnants which can provide only partial clues to what was once a magnificent and vibrant tradition. In this context we must be grateful for the incisive if rather fragmentary work of the great comparative religionist, Mircea Eliade, who, in his book *Australian Religions*, was able to re-interpret some of the anthropological data, to liberate it, so to speak, from the conceptual straitjackets of anthropology. There has been some recent scholarship which is receptive to the Aboriginal understanding of their own tradition. Nevertheless, in the domain of academic scholarship it is a great pity that the study of Aboriginal religion has been largely the preserve of the anthropologists, rather than the comparative religionists who would have been much better situated to understand it. Aboriginal religion still awaits the work of a scholar who can carry out the kind of work done by Joseph Epes Brown in respect of the North American Indians.[21] That is to say, there is still an urgent need for someone fully cognizant of the traditional outlook as exemplified by men like Coomaraswamy, René Guénon, Frithjof Schuon and Titus Burckhardt, to bring the right perspective to bear on the study of Aboriginal religion.[22] To put the matter plainly, no other conceptual framework is adequate to the task. As the traditionalists have so often remarked, nothing so characterizes the mentality of modernism as the naive belief that the greater can be contained in the lesser, which is precisely the impossibility attempted when a profane scholarship, immune to anything of a spiritual order, tries to force a living spiritual tradition into the sterile categories of a quasi-scientific reductionism — no matter whether the reductionism in question be Durkheimian, Freudian or Marxist! Furthermore, from a traditionalist viewpoint we cannot too often remind ourselves that:

> It is the spiritual, not the temporal, which culturally, socially and politically is the criterion of all other values.[23]

Before we turn to the second of our questions a few observations about the ways in which Aboriginal culture was destroyed by the Europeans might be in order. From the earliest days of the colony the legal fiction of *terra nullis* was used to rationalize and legitimate the dispossession of the Aborigines' land. The central plank in the *terra nullis* convention is that Australia was a continent without owners at the time of European arrival. From the start some colonists could see through the moral hypocrisy of the *terra nullis* argument, one which is still accorded some credibility by Australian courts. Writing in 1838 a Reverend J. Saunders argued that:

> It is not just to say that the natives have no notions of property, and therefore we could not rob them of what they did not possess; for accurate information shows that each tribe had its distinct locality . . . from these their hunting grounds they have been individually and collectively dispossessed.[24]

However, *terra nullis* was only one amongst many stratagems used to justify the unjustifiable. The story of how the Europeans made the Aborigines exiles in their own land is a profoundly melancholy one. The introduction of European diseases such as tuberculosis, influenza and syphilis, the appropriation of Aboriginal hunting grounds, the spreading of culturally destructive influences such as alcohol and gunpowder, the sexual exploitation of Aboriginal women, brutal physical violence which escalated into a program of genocidal extermination in parts of the continent,[25] institutionalized racial discrimination which ranged from a well-intentioned paternalism to programs of vicious repression, and governmental policies of assimilation and integration all played a significant role in this tragic story.[26] Perhaps more crucial than any of these depredations has been the desecration of sacred sites without which the ceremonial life cannot survive. Greed, racial pride, a sense of cultural superiority, a smug confidence that 'science' validated the disappearance of the Aboriginal peoples, and Christian exclusivism all compounded a lethal, and to some extent wilful ignorance about the real nature of Aboriginal culture, whereby the Europeans were, at the least, guilty of a radical failure to understand what it was that they were destroying. Although it is not part of our present purpose to canvas the possible directions in which some remedy for past and present ills might lie, it might usefully be remarked that a well-known Australian author reflected the view of many thoughtful non-Aboriginal Australians today when he wrote:

> Until we give back to the black man just a bit of the land that was his, and give it back without strings to snatch it back, without anything but

generosity of spirit in concession for the evil we have done to him — until we do that we shall remain what we have always been, a people without integrity, not a nation, but a community of thieves.[27]

Some Central Characteristics of the Aboriginal Tradition

The technical simplicity of traditional Aboriginal culture contrasts with the richness, complexity and profundity of their spiritual culture. One might say that here we are dealing with a technologically simple but spiritually dense culture, whereas modernism provides us everywhere with the spectacle of a dazzling technological sophistication accompanied by spiritual sterility.[28] We might also note in passing that the technical simplicity of Aboriginal culture depended on the most sophisticated level of environmental knowledge. Before we turn to a discussion of some of the central characteristics of Aboriginal culture, it might be as well to establish several cautionary points. The first, as R.M. Berndt has reminded us, is that:

> . . . traditionally, Aboriginal culture was not the same throughout the continent. Nor was there any central or federal authority. The picture was one of relatively independent socio-cultural constellations that interacted only within a certain regional range — it was not strictly possible to speak of one Aboriginal religion. There were, rather, many Aboriginal religions. [However] We can identify basic similarities . . .[29]

The second is that to speak of Aboriginal 'religion' as somehow distinct from the rest of Aboriginal culture is merely a theoretical expedient: in reality no such separation could be made, the whole culture being pervaded by a sense of the sacred and contoured by the imperatives of the spiritual tradition. Thirdly, it should perhaps be said that the use of the word 'religion' in reference to the Aborigines constitutes some looseness of expression. This word properly implies the presence of certain formal elements which are not present in this case, for which reason it is more strictly correct to speak of a mythologically based tradition. In the present context we shall use the terms more or less interchangeably. Finally, it should be acknowledged that the very word 'Aboriginal' is out of favor with some of the people so designated who prefer the term 'Koori' to describe the peoples indigenous to the Australian continent.[30] It should also be noted that the very concept of 'Aboriginality' is a European construct and one which still has no relevance or validity for some of the peoples to whom it is applied.[31]

Generally Aboriginal culture can be described as primal, a term to which we will return presently; in terms of its socio-economic organization and lifestyle it can be described, over most of the continent, as a hunter-gatherer society in which tribal members were highly mobile within clearly understood geographical boundaries, and one in which the social dynamics were governed by complex kinship and totemic systems, and by principles of reciprocity and exchange; the constellation of beliefs and practices which might be labelled 'religious' is best described as mythologically based, spatially rather than temporally oriented, and embedded in a ritual-ceremonial complex centering on a sacramental relationship with the land itself. I hope to show later that this culture also deserves the term, if it be understood aright, 'traditional'. By way of contrast we could say that the dominant cultures in the contemporary world are shaped by an aggressive and acquisitive individualism, a profane science with its attendant technology of exploitation, and by a *Zeitgeist* dominated by time rather than space.

I have suggested that generally Aboriginal religion or culture can be described as 'primal', which is to say that it is primordial, or prehistoric, in origin, mythologically based, pre-literate, tribal, and one in which the distinction between 'religion' and 'culture' at large has no meaning.[32] The qualities which one recent scholar has identified as characteristic of primal cultures generally apply specifically to Aboriginal society: such cultures are ethnocentric, non-universal, non-missionizing; they are intimately related to the natural world by a perceived spiritual kinship; they emphasize the existence of supernatural powers which are accessible to the human world; and they experience the world as saturated with spiritual power; the conception of the universe is thus sacramental.[33] We might add that such cultures are also governed by sacred mythic accounts which leave them indifferent to the linear and chronological conception of history as it is understood in the West,[34] and by a sacred geography which constitutes an ordered and meaningful world and, indeed, which situates both the community and individual in relation to the whole universe.[35] In this context we are using the word 'myth' not in its pejorative modern sense of meaningless fabrication, but rather in its perennial sense as a narrative account carrying metaphysical and spiritual messages.

Rather than trying to describe Aboriginal religion as a whole, which would be to paint on a canvas altogether too large for our present purposes, let us turn our attention momentarily to several highly significant and suggestive manifestations of their spiritual heritage, namely the central religious conception of the Dreaming, beliefs about transcendental powers and the soul, and the sacred geography which characterizes all Aboriginal religions.We shall then illustrate some general points through reference to Aboriginal ritual life and to their sacred art.

Central to all branches of the Aboriginal religious tradition is the Dreaming, expressed in various terms, amongst the best-known of which are *altjiranga, wongar* and *bugari*.[36] The Dreaming is a 'plurivocal' term with a number of distinct though connected meanings:

> First, it is a narrative mythical account of the foundation and shaping of the entire world by the ancestor heroes who are uncreated and eternal. Second, 'The Dreaming' refers to the embodiment of the spiritual power of the ancestor heroes in the land in certain sites, and in species of fauna and flora, so that this power is available to people today. Indeed, one might say that for the Aboriginal his land is a kind of religious icon, since it both represents the power of the Dreamtime beings and also effects and transmits that power. Third, 'The Dreaming' denotes the general way of life or 'Law' — moral and social precepts, ritual and ceremonial practices, etc. — based upon these mythical foundations. Fourth, 'The Dreaming' may refer to the personal 'way' or vocation that an individual Aboriginal might have by virtue of his membership of a clan, or by virtue of his spirit conception relating him to particular sites.[37]

(One might note in passing that, in some limited senses, the multi-layered meanings of the Dreaming are analogous to the central conception of 'dharma' in the Buddhist tradition.) The Dreaming is an ever-present reality, not only 'a long-past period in a time when life filled the void. It is rather the ever-present, unseen, ground of being — of existence'. Or, as Elkin has also said:

> The concept is not of a 'horizontal' line extending back chronologically through a series of pasts, but rather a 'vertical' line in which the past underlies and is within the present.[38]

The landscape as a whole, particular sites, objects, myths and rituals, and human groups and individuals are all inter-related within the Dreaming. The Aranda phrase *altjiranga ngambakala* is highly suggestive in its English translation — 'having originated out of one's own eternity' — suggesting as it does notions of immortality and the 'uncreated'. (Mircea Eliade has noted that the Aboriginal conception of an indestructible human spirit can be compared to post-Vedic conceptions of *atman* within the Hindu tradition.[39] He has also emphasized how the ritual life of the Aborigines was based on the reiteration of paradigmatic acts first performed in the Dreamtime. We shall return to this subject shortly.)

> The Dreaming is then the most real and concrete and fundamental aspect of Aboriginal life and has nothing to do with the Western concept of dreaming as an imaginary, fantastic and illusory state of consciousness.[40]

All of the most cardinal features of Aboriginal society are derived from the Dreaming:

> The most momentous communication is the plan of life itself, the all-encompassing scope of which is shown in the shapes of the landscape, the events narrated in myth, the acts performed in rites, the codes observed in conduct, and the habits and characteristics of other forms of life.[41]

We find here a feature characteristic of all religions — the notion of a Revelation of supra-human origins which lays down the 'will of heaven', so to speak, and which invites but does not compel conformity to its dictates. As a recent anthropologist has noted:

> The way in which the plan was 'passed on' to humans as the powers withdrew above or below the earth is left obscure . . . but at least it is certain that men are not constrained to fidelity by their nature. The Aborigines know that they can fall away from what their traditional culture requires . . .[42]

— which is to say that they were no strangers to that fundamental freedom which constitutes the human estate, its dignity and its most terrible responsibility; for this and many other reasons the Aboriginal conception of the human can be described, in the deepest and most fundamental sense, as 'religious' (although it should be acknowledged that the traditional religious valuation of man was sometimes qualified and vitiated by secular considerations and by the low status given to the very young, the very old, and to women[43]). From a traditionalist point of view we can say that the Dreaming constitutes a revealed mythology whilst the ongoing ritual and ceremonial life of the Aborigines can be seen as the chain which joins their society to its origins. Indeed, as Lord Northbourne so rightly observed, 'Tradition, in the rightful sense of the word, is the chain that joins civilization to Revelation.'[44] In this context we might also recall Marco Pallis's definition of tradition as 'an effective communication of principles of more-than-human origin ... through use of forms that will have arisen by applying those principles to contingent needs.'[45] Tradition might also usefully be thought of as 'the mediator between time and eternity'. Each and all of these definitions are quite apposite in reference to the Aborigines' mythological-ceremonial heritage.

The early ethnologists, especially those of an evolutionist bent, were unable to grasp the possibility of any religious conception amongst the Australian Aborigines which might be comparable to the belief in a supreme, benevolent and ethical Deity such as was to be found in the great monotheisms: it ran counter to their assumptions about the intellectual and spiritual inferiority of the Aborigines.[46] Nevertheless, as Eliade has remarked:

> There is no doubt that the belief in such a celestial Supreme Being belongs among the most archaic and genuine traditions of the southeastern Aborigines.[47]

The ethnologists likewise had difficulty in coming to terms with Aboriginal notions about the pre-existent and eternal soul in which most tribes believed: again, Eliade has emphasized that 'the indestructibility of the human spirit seems to be a fundamental and pan-Australian conception.'[48] Furthermore, it is hardly too much to say that the whole Aboriginal conception of what it is to be human is profoundly spiritual.

> To begin with, the essence of man or woman is purely spiritual. After birth ... it takes on a materialistic form: but it never loses its sacred quality. Woman possesses this sacredness almost without any effort ... but for man the accent is on ritual, and organized ceremony. For both, sacredness increases with advancing age; and at death they become, again, completely spiritual.[49]

The transcendental, world-creative power of the South-Eastern tribes is known under a variety of names — *Baiame, Bunjil, Daramulan, Nurelli* — and is anthropomorphic, masculine, creative, sky-dwelling, ethical, and paternally related to all of humankind, perhaps best translated in English as the 'All-Father'; this Deity is unchanging and eternal, existing before all things. Indeed, the belief in the divinity who created both man and the world and then ascended into heaven after bestowing on humankind the rudiments of culture, 'is attested in many other archaic cultures.'[50] The same kind of transcendent, world-creative power is portrayed in some tribes, particularly those of Northern Australia, as feminine — the 'All-Mother'.[51]

Between the supreme being and more localized and so-called 'totemic' spirits and powers are supernatural beings with whom much of the mythology is concerned — the Rainbow Serpent is one of the most widespread of such figures.[52] Then there are also totemic powers which are more parochial in character. The so-called 'totemism' of the Aborigines is a subject fraught with hazards of all kinds which we do not have time to negotiate here: too often it has been a destructive instrument of a tendentious anthropological agenda. No-one has written more intelligently on this subject than Stanner: here let us simply remember his claim that:

> Students with the patience to look beyond the symbol to the symbolized will find that the end of Aboriginal religion was in Confucian terms 'to unite hearts and establish order'. Understood in that way, a 'totemic' system shows itself as a link between cosmogony, cosmology and ontology; between Aboriginal intuitions of the beginnings of things, the resulting relevances for men's individual and social being, and a continuously meaningful life.[53]

As to the Aboriginal relationship with the natural world, what Joseph Epes Brown has said of the American Indians is also, in large measure, true of the Australian Aborigines:

> . . . the world of nature was their temple, and within this sanctuary they showed great respect to every form, function and power. That the Indians held as sacred all the natural forms around them is not unique . . . But what is almost unique in the Indians' attitude is that their reverence for life and nature is *central* to their religion: each form in the world around them bears such a host of precise values and meanings that taken altogether they constitute what one would call their 'doctrine'.[54]

In the case of the Aborigines we have already seen how a mythic and sacred geography is derived from the Dreaming itself. Indeed, 'in the end, the land is no more than a bridge between [them] and the sacred realm of the Dreaming.'[55] Much of the sacred art of the Aborigines was directed towards the preservation of the tribal knowledge of that mythic geography. (We might here note in passing a certain affinity with Taoist perceptions of the landscape, indeed of the whole of nature, as a manifestation of the ineffable and immutable Tao.)

The Aborigines' simple technology and semi-nomadic lifestyle ensured that they remained in touch with, indeed immersed in, the world of nature. It is as well to remember that such a relationship with nature, of itself, confers spiritual gifts. As Frithjof Schuon has so eloquently put it:

Wild Nature is at one with holy poverty and also with spiritual childlikeness: she is an open book containing an inexhaustible teaching of truth and beauty. It is in the midst of his own artifices that man most easily becomes corrupted, it is they who make him covetous and impious; close to virgin Nature, who knows neither agitation nor falsehood, he had the hope of remaining contemplative like Nature herself.[56]

The mythical time of the Dreaming is sacred:

because it was sanctified by the real presence and activity of the Supernatural Beings. But like all other species of 'sacred time', although infinitely remote, it is not inaccessible. It can be reactualized through ritual.[57]

Through ritual life the members of the tribe not only recuperated sacred time but by reiterating the paradigmatic acts of the supernatural powers they helped to regenerate life by 'recreating the world'.[58] To neglect these awesome responsibilities would be to allow the world to regress into darkness and chaos. (Indeed here we have one of the keys to the demoralization of those survivors who must live in a world made meaningless by their separation from their land and the consequent annihilation of their ritual life. They are no longer able to communicate with the Dreamtime, nor to fulfil those ritual obligations which gave life dignity and purpose. The substitutes and palliatives the modern white world offers are, of course, tawdry and trivial in comparison, whether they be sinister, as in the case of alcohol, or comparatively benevolent and well-intentioned — a Western 'education', for instance.)

Another proof of the spiritual integrity of the Aboriginal tradition is that it produced 'medicine men' or shamans, or, as Elkin has called them, 'men of high degree' — individuals whose role it was to cure the sick, defend the community against black magic, perform important functions in the tribal ceremonial life, especially in initiation rituals, and to serve as cultural and spiritual exemplars by way of their access to arcane powers. These men were viaducts, so to speak, between the supernatural and mundane worlds.[59] The initiation ceremonies (always involving some kind of death and rebirth experience), the central role of visions and other ecstatic experiences, and the healing functions of the men of high degree, are reminiscent of shamanic practices in Tibet, Siberia and amongst the Indians of both North and South America.[60] Nevertheless, the Aboriginal tradition developed its own esoteric spiritual practices and metaphysical wisdom to which the medicine men conformed themselves, and by which they were sanctified.[61]

It is perhaps appropriate that I should say a few words about the art of the Australian Aborigines. Here we find an art that conforms to Frithjof Schuon's claim that:

> Traditional art derives from a creativity which combines heavenly inspiration with ethnic genius, and which does so in the manner of a science endowed with rules and not by way of individual inspiration.[62]

The symbolic vocabularies of religious iconographies was, of course, one of Coomaraswamy's abiding interests. Aboriginal art assumed many different forms: sand sculptures, rock wall art, body painting and decoration, ritual objects, and, in more recent times, bark paintings. Many of these incorporated pictorial designs and all were fundamentally symbolic, not in the superficial modern sense whereby a symbol is a more or less arbitrary representative of something else, but in the traditional sense that the symbol and the symbolized shared some kind of fundamental affinity which, in turn, conferred the power of the symbolized reality onto the symbol itself. The symbols were also 'layered and multi-referential'. As a recent Aboriginal commentator has suggested, they are to be read more in the manner of poetry than prose.[63] This should not be taken to imply that there is anything either arbitrary or subjective about the symbolic vocabulary of Aboriginal art: it was informed by a language which rested on the analogies between spiritual realities and transitory material phenomena which, by way of this relationship, carried qualitative significances.[64] To put it another way, we can say that Aboriginal art rested on an understanding of symbolism which informed traditional sacred art everywhere: a symbol may be defined as a reality or phenomenon of a lower order which participates analogically in the reality of a higher order. A properly constituted symbolism rests on the inherent and objective qualities of material phenomena and their relationship to spiritual realities. This was a principle on which Coomaraswamy insisted again and again in his writings.[65] In this context it is also worth remembering a point frequently articulated by Eliade: for *homo religiosus* (who is also *homo symbolicus*) everything in nature is capable of revealing itself as a 'cosmic sacrality', as a hierophany, in contrast to the profane outlook of modern man, an outlook which makes the universe 'opaque, inert, mute'.[66] To put the same point differently, an ordered and profoundly meaningful *cosmos* becomes no more than a swirling chaos of dead matter, a *universe*.

A word or two about the indifference of Aboriginal art to the claim of naturalism. As Coomaraswamy and Schuon have repeatedly emphasized, the attempt to 'imitate' nature, to accurately reproduce the surfaces and appearances of the material world, is not the purpose of traditional art. Aboriginal art is no exception. Artistic naturalism proceeds from an exteriorizing mentality which could not be normative in a traditional civilization.[67] The deepest and most significant meanings of sacred art were accessible only to those of appropriate ritual standing, which is to say those initiated into the wisdom whereby such meanings could properly be understood. The meanings which have been disclosed to us are only those which can be communicated to the uninitiated. Nevertheless, it is clear that in its depth, complexity, and spiritual resonance, Aboriginal art is comparable to the artistic manifestations of the great Occidental and Oriental traditions. It conveyed transcendental values and meta-physical truths to the social collectivity. Bypassing the pitfalls of abstract and merely ratiocinative thought, it was accessible to all mentalities and through its symbolism addressed the whole person rather than the mind only, and thereby helped to actualize the teachings of tradition.[68] The contrast with our own modern art could hardly be more dramatic, confronted as we so often are by an 'art' which is flagrantly, indeed boastfully anti-traditional, governed by a rampant individualism and an insatiable appetite for novelty (mistaken for 'originality'), preoccupied with an aestheticism attuned to the fashions of the day, directed towards little more than the stimulation of the senses, and quite indifferent to the spiritual functions of art, an art characterized by stylistic excesses veering from a pedantic naturalism on one side to the grotesqueries of an inhuman surrealism on the other. Aboriginal art which retains even some of its traditional character is so fresh, so clean, so direct in comparison.

Like all properly constituted traditions Aboriginal culture exhibited those four characteristics which exalt all sacred traditions.

Firstly, *a divine source of tradition*: as we have seen, the origins of the Aboriginal tradition are primordial, stretching back into time immemorial.We cannot anchor its origins in historical time nor tie it to any place, person or book. Nevertheless, we can affirm that this sacred mythological-ritual complex was not and could not have been of merely human provenance, though doubtless its vocabulary and its spiritual economy reflected the psychic and spiritual receptivities of the Aboriginal peoples. In this sense the Aboriginal tradition is directly comparable to the profound mythological traditions which we find amongst primal cultures the world over — the Plains Indians of North America furnish perhaps the most obvious parallel.

Secondly, the Aboriginal tradition enshrined *a doctrine* about the nature of the Absolute and the Relative, and the relationship of the Real and the relatively or provisionally real: in the case of the Aborigines the doctrines were not cast in the mould of a book or a collection of canonical writings, nor were they formulated in abstract dogmatic language, but rather inhered in the relationship of the Aboriginal and the land, or better, the Aboriginal and the whole cosmos; the doctrine is implicit in the mythology, in the ritual life, and in the sacred art of traditional Aboriginal culture, each of these dimensions of Aboriginal culture hinging, so to speak, on a sacramental relationship with the land itself. It is appropriate at this point, perhaps, to recall Ananda Coomaraswamy's words about myth:

> The myth is the penultimate truth, of which all experience is the temporal reflection. The mythical narrative is of timeless and placeless validity, true nowhere and everywhere . . . Myth embodies the nearest approach to absolute truth that can be stated in words.[69]

It is also worth pointing out that the Aboriginal sense of the sacred expresses itself most readily in 'spatial' rather than 'temporal' terms. As Frithjof Schuon reminds us, traditions of prehistoric origin are:

> . . . symbolically speaking, made for 'space' and not for 'time'; that is to say, they saw the light in a primordial epoch when time was but still a rhythm in a spatial and static beatitude, and when space or simultaneity still predominated over the experience of duration and change.[70]

A failure to understand this principle has been one of the factors explaining the apparent incomprehension of the anthropologists in the face of the central conception of the Dreaming, a category of the sacred which escapes completely the grip of all profane and linear notions of time, not to say of 'history'.

A further point which cannot be too heavily accented is that metaphysical doctrines do not of necessity find their expression only in verbal forms. Metaphysics can be expressed visually and ritually: Far Eastern forms of Buddhism and Taoism furnish signal examples of this possibility. As Schuon has remarked:

> . . . the criterion of metaphysical truth or of its depth lies not in the complexity or difficulty of its expression, but in the quality and effectiveness of its symbolism, having regard to a particular capacity of understanding or style of thinking. Wisdom does not lie in any complication of words but in the profundity of the intention . . .[71]

The third characteristic mark of any integral tradition is a *spiritual methodology* which enables its practitioners to cleave to the Absolute and the Real, to conform their being to the demands of eternity: this can be found primarily in the rich ritual life which characterized Aboriginal society all over the continent. Contrary to whatever extraordinary claims have been made by the anthropologists about the social 'functions' of these rituals, it is clear to those with eyes to see and ears to hear that the fundamental purpose of most of these rituals was to put both the tribe and the individual into right relationship with the Divine, and more specifically with the natural world which was, in a sense, the material vestment in which the Eternal was clothed.[72]

And fourthly, we find the *formal embodiment of tradition* in the sacred arts and sciences which determine the character of a civilization and which give it its own spiritual 'personality', if one might so express it. Here we need look no further than Aboriginal art: far from being the 'childish scratchings' of 'ignorant savages' this art constitutes a rich symbolic vocabulary, always rooted in the world of nature and of human experience, but comprising the vehicle for the most complex metaphysical ideas and the most resonant spiritual messages. It is true that in recent years Aboriginal art has been afforded a new respect and a rather fashionable 'status' within both the Australian and the international art establishment.Unhappily this new attitude is often informed by altogether anti-traditional values whereby Aboriginal art is seen primarily in terms of aesthetically pleasing craft objects which are expressions of the material culture of the Aborigines. A sacred art resonant with symbolic and spiritual messages is thus wrenched out of its ceremonial context, is culturally appropriated and eventually becomes an art commodity on which the art market can fix a monetary value. This parallels, or at least follows, a similar process of cultural appropriation of North American Indian art.[73] We turn now to the last of our central questions: what lessons might be derived from a study of Aboriginal culture?

The Lessons of Aboriginal Tradition

The Aboriginal tradition enshrined *a sense of proportion and an ordered scheme of values and priorities* which gave precedence to the demands of the divine, which stamped everyday life with a sense of the imperishable, and which afforded humankind an ontological dignity all but impossible to recover in a world which is prepared to countenance talk of man as a 'naked ape'. In our own culture, cemented into all the childish prejudices of the age, intoxicated with the drugs of modernity, and dedicated to the pursuit of a selfish and barbarous 'progress', Aboriginal culture can stand as a reminder of those human possibilities, both individual and collective, on which we have so often turned out backs. It can remind us anew that we live, in the fullest sense, only in relation to the Absolute.

> In traditional worlds, to be situated in space and time is to be situated in a cosmology and an eschatology respectively; time has no meaning save in relation to the perfection of the origin and the maintenance of that perfection, and in view of the final breaking up that casts us almost without transition at the feet of God.[74]

In an age and culture, tyrannized by time and imprisoned in historicism, the Aboriginal indifference to profane history can provide us with another perspective on our human condition and on our earthly existence. The messages implicit in Aboriginal culture can, of course, have no meaning for those whose materialistic worldview leaves them utterly impervious to anything and everything of a spiritual order. As Eliade has remarked, many students of archaic religions ultimately 'take refuge in a materialism or behaviorism impervious to every spiritual shock'.[75] One can only be saddened by the kind of ignorant condescension betrayed by this kind of formulation from a contemporary, well-respected, widely published and doubtless well-intentioned Australian anthropologist, writing about Aboriginal religion:

An encounter with Aboriginal religion may leave the outsider ultimately unpersuaded, but it will certainly enlarge his sense of the scope and possibilities of human imagination.[76]

... as if we are here dealing with nothing more than curious and colorful 'imaginings'!

Anyone not in the grip of prejudices of this kind cannot study Aboriginal religion without being continually reawakened to *a sense of the sacred*. If we are to ask what precisely constitutes the 'sacred' we can do no better than turn again to the words of Frithjof Schuon, the most profound and sublime metaphysician of our times. That is sacred, he writes:

> which in the first place is attached to the transcendent order, secondly possesses the character of absolute certainty, and thirdly, eludes the comprehension and power of investigation of the ordinary human mind ... The sacred introduces a quality of the absolute into relativities and confers on perishable things a texture of eternity.[77]

To reanimate such a sense is one of the most invaluable services which cultures such as those of the Australian Aborigines might perform for the modern world. Without a sense of the sacred we are lost in the world of accidental contingencies. As Schuon again reminds us:

> When people talk about 'civilization' they generally attribute a qualitative meaning to the term, but really civilization only represents a value provided it is supra-human in origin and implies for the civilized man a sense of the sacred ... A sense of the sacred is fundamental for every civilization because fundamental for man: the sacred — that which is immutable, inviolable and so infinitely majestic — is in the very substance of our spirit and of our existence.[78]

It is not without some irony that it is the so-called 'primitive' who recalls us to this sense of the sacred. At the same time we can say that Aboriginal religion was life-affirming in the most down-to-earth fashion, or, to put it another way, for the Aboriginal outlook the sacred was always materially incarnated in the world of nature. Indeed, one scholar has identified the 'magnification of life' as a central characteristic of Aboriginal culture, and has emphasized the:

> preoccupation with the signs, symbols, means, portents, tokens and evidences of vitality. The whole religious corpus vibrated with an expressed aspiration for life. ...[79]

189

Aboriginal society was one in harmony with the world of nature rather than one intent on 'conquest' and plunder; the 50,000 years or more during which time the Aborigines lived alone on the continent left it in a more or less primordial state of 'Edenic innocence', if one might so express it. The Aborigines found in the world about them not only beauty and harmony but signs of *divine intent* to which men could and should conform themselves.[80] This lies at the heart of their relationship to the land. One of the many lessons we can learn is that a properly constituted ecological awareness can only be built on the foundations of what is ultimately a *spiritual recognition* of the sacredness of the world around us: furthermore, this sacredness is conferred by the immaterial and spiritual realities which the world of nature reflects. No amount of fashionable concern about the evils of pollution, no amount of 'socially responsible' science, or of the idolization of 'Nature' can in any way substitute for this spiritual intuition which lies at the heart of many primal cultures. The sacredness of the world is necessarily inaccessible to a view which sees the planet as nothing more than a configuration of physical properties and energies and 'knowledge' as a quantitative accumulation of data about these material phenomena. As René Guénon reminded us, such a scientistic outlook has nothing to do with true knowledge:

> Never until the present epoch had the study of the sensible world been regarded as self-sufficient; never would the science of this ephemeral and changing multiplicity have been judged truly worthy of the name of knowledge . . .[81]

Aboriginal man also offers us *an exemplum of spiritual responsibility and authenticity*. As Mircea Eliade has observed:

> . . . it would be wrong to believe that the religious man of primitive and archaic societies refuses to assume the responsibility for a genuine existence. On the contrary . . . he courageously assumes immense responsibilities — for example, that of collaborating in the creation of the cosmos, or of creating his own world, or of ensuring the life of plants and animals, and so on. But it is a different kind of responsibility from those that, to us moderns, appear to be the only genuine and valid responsibilities. It is a responsibility on the cosmic plane, in contradistinction to the moral, social or historical responsibilities that are alone regarded as valid in modern civilizations. From the point of view of profane existence, man feels no responsibility except to himself and to society . . .[82]

190

A study of the Aboriginal tradition can also act as a salutary reminder of the dismal inadequacy of most of the mental categories and explanatory frameworks with which modern man has approached primal cultures, and through which the academic and anthropological study of Aboriginal religion has been pursued. As Professor Stanner has observed:

> It is preposterous that something like a century of study, because of rationalism, positivism and materialism, should have produced two options: that Aboriginal religion is either (to follow Durkheim) what someone called 'the mirage of society' or (to follow Freud) the neurosis of society.[83]

Such a situation should alert us to the dangers of the presumptions and impostures of modernism in its many different 'scholarly' guises.

In his magisterial study of the crisis of modern civilization, *The Reign of Quantity*, René Guénon refers to:

> . . . the darkest enigmas of the modern world, enigmas which the world itself denies because it is incapable of perceiving them although it carries them within itself, and because this denial is an indispensable condition for the maintenance of the special mentality whereby it exists.[84]

Those enigmas can only be unravelled by recourse to the wisdom which existed within the cadre of all integral traditions: I hope I have said enough about the Aboriginal tradition to allow you to recognize the place it deserves amongst such traditions. It might also serve to remind us that no people anywhere has been bereft of tradition. The ultimately important lessons of any traditional culture do not invite any kind of 'imitation', which would be quite fruitless, but a return to the sources of the perennial wisdom which can always be found within our own cultures if only we have the will to look.[85]

Notes

1. Seyyed Hossein Nasr, *Sufi Essays*, Allen & Unwin, London, 1972, p.126.
2. Frithjof Schuon, *Light on the Ancient Worlds*, Perennial, London, 1965, p.35 (hereafter F. Schuon: *LAW*). This quote should not be understood as

implying that each and every tradition is, from a metaphysical point of view, equally inclusive or integral. In any case no doctrine, no mythology, no form can comprise an exhaustive account of Reality: we are always dealing with an ensemble of elements and dispositions which together make up a particular spiritual economy which, in the traditional world, is adequate to its purpose but never metaphysically exhaustive.

3. Kenneth Oldmeadow, *The Science of Man: Scientific Opinion on the Australian Aborigines in the Late 19th Century*, BA History Hons. Thesis, Australian National University, 1969, pp.11-16 (hereafter referred to as K.S. Oldmeadow: *SM*).

4. Max Charlesworth, 'Introduction' to *Religion in Aboriginal Australia*, University of Queensland Press, St Lucia, 1984; edited by M. Charlesworth, H. Morphy, D. Bell and K. Maddock, p.1 (hereafter referred to as *RAA*).

5. David Collins, *An Account of the English Colony in New South Wales*, 1798; quoted in W.E.H. Stanner, 'Religion, totemism and symbolism' from *RAA*, p.138.

6. L.E. Threlkeld, quoted in M. Charlesworth, *op.cit.*, p.2.

7. See Kenneth Oldmeadow, *Frithjof Schuon, the Perennial Philosophy and the Meaning of Tradition*, MA Hons. Religious Studies Thesis, Sydney University, 1982 (hereafter referred to as K.S. Oldmeadow: *FSPP*); pp.48ff.

8. W.E.H. Stanner, *op.cit.*, p.140.

9. See K.S. Oldmeadow, *SM*, pp.17ff. See also the excellent historical survey in Tony Swain, *Interpreting Aboriginal Religion*, AASR, Adelaide, 1985.

10. *The Age*, 11.1.1889; quoted in Henry Reynolds, *Dispossession: Black Australians and White Invaders*, Allen & Unwin, Sydney, 1989, p.9.

11. From *The Arvanta*, quoted in M. Charlesworth, *op.cit.* p.1.

12. See, for instance, L. Fison and A.W. Howitt, *Kamilroi and Murnai*, Geo Robertson, Melbourne, 1880, pp.181-82.

13. E.B. Tylor, 'Preface' to Roth, H.L., *The Aborigines of Tasmania*, Halifax, 1899, p.v. See also 'On the Tasmanians as Representatives of Palaeolithic Man' from *Journal of the Royal Anthropological Institute*, XXII, 1893-1894, pp.147-48. For a detailed analysis of the appalling effects of evolutionary theory on attitudes to the Aborigines see K.S. Oldmeadow, *SM*, especially chapters 3 and 4.

14. *Moreton Bay Courier* 19.1.1856, quoted in H. Reynolds, *op.cit*, p.5.

15. The role of Christian missionaries and their impact on Aboriginal culture is an extremely complex one which has been vastly oversimplified by apologists on both sides of the fence. It would certainly be misleading to suggest that the role of the missionaries was entirely negative and destructive. In some areas — the Lutherans at Hermansburg, for instance — the missionaries were instrumental in providing a refuge in which Aboriginal people were able to survive physically and in which at least

some remnants of traditional culture were preserved.

16. Mircea Eliade, *Australian Religions*, Cornell University Press, Ithaca, 1971, pp.xiii-xiv (hereafter referred to as Eliade: *AR*).

17. See E.E. Evans-Pritchard, *Theories of Primitive Religion*, Clarendon Press, Oxford, 1965; and Eliade, *AR*, p.xvii.

18. W. Perry, Review of Ninian Smart's 'The Phenomena of Religion' from *Studies in Comparative Religion* VII.ii, 1973, p.127.

19. As well as the source already cited, see W.E.H. Stanner, *White Man Got No Dreaming — Essays 1938-1973*, Australian National University Press, Canberra, 1979. (This anthology includes the seminal essay to which we have referred previously as part of *RAA*.)

20. *On Aboriginal Religion*, Oceania Monograph No.11, Sydney, 1963, quoted in Eliade, *AR*, pp.196-97.

21. See Joseph Epes Brown, *The Spiritual Legacy of the American Indians*, Crossroad, New York, 1972.

22. For one of the more immediately accessible expositions of the traditionalist outlook see Huston Smith, *Forgotten Truth: The Primordial Tradition*, Harper & Row, New York, 1977. The only work in the field of Aboriginal religion which has been done from a traditionalist point of view is by James Cowan; see 'Wild Stones — Spiritual Discipline and Psychic Power Among Aboriginal Clever Men' from *Studies in Comparative Religion* XVII, i and ii, pp.33-44; and 'The Dream Journey — Ritual Renewal Among Australian Aborigines' from *Tenemos* VII, pp.158-83.

23. Frithjof Schuon, 'Usurpations of Religious Feeling' from *Studies in Comparative Religion* II,ii, 1968, p.66.

24. *The Colonist* 19.10.1838, quoted in H. Reynolds, *op.cit.* p.76.

25. At least 20,000 Aborigines had been killed by whites by the time of Federation. H. Reynolds, *op.cit.*, p.22. As late as 1902, white commentators were still justifying the deliberate killing of Aborigines in terms such as these: 'The substitution of more than a million of industrious and peaceful people for a roaming, fighting contingent of six thousand cannot be said to be dearly purchased even at the cost of the violent deaths of a fraction of the most aggressive among them.' H.A. Turner, *A History of the Colony of Victoria* V.i., London, 1902, p.239, per H. Reynolds, p.9.

26. As well as the work by Reynolds already cited, see H. Reynolds, *The Other Side of the Frontier*, Penguin, 1982; and C.D. Rowley, *The Destruction of Aboriginal Society*, Penguin, 1972.

27. Xavier Herbert in S. Harris and J. Wright, eds., *We Call for a Treaty*, 1985, p.xiii, quoted in H. Reynolds, *Dispossession* . . . , p.66.

28. See M. Eliade, *AR*, pp.xvi-xvii, and M. Charlesworth, *op.cit.*, p.5.

29. R.M. Berndt, quoted in M. Charlesworth, *op.cit.*, p.7. Berndt concludes this sentence with these words: '. . . notably in the organization of activities associated with ritual expressions . . . .' The 'basic similarities', in fact, go much deeper than such a formulation would suggest, as will become clear presently.

30. The term 'Koori' is also problematic, being an Aboriginal word which had no currency outside New South Wales, and which is consequently rejected by many outside this area.
31. See Bob Reece, 'Inventing Aborigines' from *Aboriginal History* XI, 1987, pp.14-23.
32. See M. Charlesworth, pp.13-14.
33. See Hilton Deakin, 'Some thoughts on transcendence in tribal societies' in *Ways of Transcendence*, AASR, Adelaide, 1982, ed. E. Dowdy.
34. M. Eliade, *AR*, pp.xvff.
35. On this general subject see M. Eliade, *The Sacred and the Profane*, Harcourt Brace Jovanovich, New York, 1959.
36. These terms come, respectively, from the Aranda tribe of Central Australia, the Karadjiri people of the Kimberley region of the North-West, and the Murngin tribe of the Western Desert.
37. M. Charlesworth, *op.cit.*, p.10. These multiple and very dynamic meanings are better signalled by the term 'Dreaming' which has, at least in the anthropological literature, replaced the more static and misleading 'Dreamtime'.
38. A.P. Elkin quoted in Charlesworth, p.10.
39. M. Eliade, *AR*, p.172.
40. M. Charlesworth, *op.cit.*, p.11. This claim should not be taken to imply that one avenue of access to the Dreaming could not be dreaming, in the normal sense of the word. See also Eliade, *AR*, pp.1-3.
41. K. Maddock, 'The World Creative Powers' in M. Charlesworth et al., *op.cit.*, pp.86-87.
42. *Ibid*.
43. W.E.H. Stanner in M. Charlesworth et al, *op.cit.*, p.149. Stanner observes that 'the valuation of women was low in respect of their personal as distinct from their functional worth'. (This claim would not be accepted by all scholars today.) The part played by Aboriginal women in spiritual and ceremonial life has, until recently, been a much neglected field. However, following the pioneering work of P. Carberry, scholars such as Diane Bell are now illuminating this subject. See, for instance, D. Bell, *Daughters of the Dreaming*, McPhee Gribble, Melbourne, 1983.
44. Lord Northbourne, *Religion in the Modern World*, J.M. Dent, London, 1963 (perennial reprint, no date given), p.34.
45. Marco Pallis, *The Way and the Mountain*, Peter Owen, London, 1960, p.203.
46. M. Eliade, *AR*, p.14.
47. *Ibid*, p.7.
48. *Ibid*, p.172.
49. R.M. & C.H. Berndt quoted in M. Eliade, *AR*, pp.64-5.
50. M. Eliade, *AR*, p.7.
51. K. Maddock, *op.cit.*, pp.88-92.

52. M. Eliade, *AR*, pp.79ff.

53. W.E.H. Stanner, 'Religion, totemism and symbolism', p.172.

54. J.E. Brown, *op.cit.*, p.37.

55. J. Cowan, 'The Dream Journey', p.181.

56. Frithjof Schuon, *LAW*, p.84.

57. M. Eliade, *AR*, p.43.

58. *Ibid*, p.61. (It is important not to oversimplify the purposes of 'renewal' rituals: again, the article by Cowan offers a useful counterbalance to Eliade's possible over-emphasis on the reiterative nature of such rituals.)

59. *Ibid*, pp.128f and 1156ff; and A.P. Elkin, *Aboriginal Men of High Degree*, University of Queensland Press, St Lucia, 1977.

60. See M. Eliade, *Shamanism: Archaic Techniques of Ecstasy*, Bollingen Series LXXVI, Princeton, 1964; and *AR*, pp.128-64; and A.P. Elkin, *op.cit.*, pp.575-58, 60-64.

61. See James Cowan, 'Wild Stones', passim. See also his article 'The Dream Journey', p.1771.

62. Frithjof Schuon, 'The Degrees of Art' from *Studies in Comparative Religion* X, iv, 1976, p.194.

63. W. Caruana, ed., *Windows on the Dreaming*, Australian National Gallery, Canberra, 1989, p.10.

64. See K.S. Oldmeadow, *FSPP*, Chapter 9.

65. See, for instance, A.K. Coomaraswamy, 'The Nature of Buddhist Art' from *Selected Papers* Vol.1, pp.174-5.

66. M. Eliade, *The Sacred and the Profane*, pp.12, 178.

67. See Frithjof Schuon, 'The Degrees of Art' (already cited, note 62 above); *The Language of the Self*, Ganesh, Madras, 1959; and *Spiritual Perspectives and Human Facts*, Perennial, London, 1959, Part II. Also A.K. Coomaraswamy, 'The Medieval Theory of Beauty', 'Imitation and Expression', and 'Figures of Speech or Figures of Thought', all from *Selected Papers* Vol.1; *Traditional Art and Symbolism*, Bollingen, Princeton University Press, 1977, ed. R. Lipsey, pp.189-228, 276-85, 20-25.

68. See K.S. Oldmeadow, *FSPP*, pp.142-43.

69. A.K. Coomaraswamy, *Hinduism and Buddhism*, quoted in J.E. Brown, *op.cit.*, p.84.

70. Frithjof Schuon, *LAW*, p.14.

71. Frithjof Schuon, *Understanding Islam*, p.11.

72. M. Charlesworth, *op.cit.*, p.4. In this context we might again remind ourselves that the persistent anthropological insistence on seeing Aboriginal 'religion' as a function or epiphenomenon of Aboriginal 'society' inverts the real relationship.

73. See J.E. Brown, *op.cit.*, p.134. As one commentator has recently observed, 'Australian art remains the last great non-European cultural form available to the voracious appetite of the European art machine.' T. Smith,

'Black Art — Its Genius Explained' from *The Independent Monthly*, September 1989, p.18.

74. Frithjof Schuon, *LAW*, p.10.

75. M. Eliade, *The Quest — Meaning and History in Religion*, University of Chicago Press, 1969, p.62. See also p.36.

76. K. Maddock, *op.cit.*, p.27.

77. F. Schuon, *Understanding Islam*, Allen & Unwin, London, 1976, p.48.

78. *Ibid*, p.33.

79. W.E.H. Stanner, 'Religion, totemism and symbolism', p.149.

80. *Ibid*, pp.146-8.

81. René Guénon, quoted in Gai Eaton, *The Richest Vein*, Faber & Faber, London, 1949, p.196.

82. M. Eliade, *The Sacred and the Profane*, p.93.

83. W.E.H. Stanner, 'Religion, totemism and symbolism', p.155.

84. René Guénon, *The Reign of Quantity*, Penguin, 1972, p.1. 1985. This paper was originally delivered as the inaugural A.K. Coomaraswamy lecture at the Sri Lanka Institute of Traditional Studies.

Principal Sources Cited

On Tradition

Brown, Joseph Epes, *The Spiritual Legacy of the American Indian*, Crossroad, New York, 1972.

Coomaraswamy, A.K. *Selected Papers*, Vol.I *Traditional Art and Symbolism*; Vol.II. *Metaphysics*, ed. R. Lipsey, Bollingen Series, Princeton University Press, 1977.

Guénon, René, *The Reign of Quantity*, Penguin, 1972.

Northbourne, Lord. *Religion in the Modern World*, J.M. Dent, London, 1963.

Oldmeadow, Kenneth S. *Frithjof Schuon, The Perennial Philosophy and the Meaning of Tradition*, MA Hons. Thesis, Sydney University, 1982.

Pallis, Marco. *The Way and the Mountain*, Peter Owen, London, 1960.

Schuon, Frithjof. *Light on the Ancient Worlds*, Perennial, London, 1965. — *Understanding Islam*, Allen & Unwin, London, 1976. — *In The Tracks of Buddhism*, Allen & Unwin, London, 1968. — *Spiritual Facts and Human Perspectives*, Perennial, London, 1969. — *Language of the Self*, Ganesh, Madras, 1959.

Smith, Huston. *Forgotten Truth: The Primordial Tradition*, Harper & Row, New York, 1977.

On Primal Cultures and the Aboriginal Tradition

Baker, Richard. 'Land is Life: Continuity through change for the Yanyuwa from the Northern Territory of Australia', PhD. Thesis in Geography, University of Adelaide, 1989.

Caruana, Wally, ed. *Windows on the Dreaming*, Australian National Gallery, Canberra, 1989.

Charlesworth, M., ed. *Religion in Aboriginal Australia*, University of Queensland Press, St Lucia, 1986.

Cowan, James. 'Wild Stones — Spiritual Discipline and Psychic Power among Aboriginal Clever Men' from *Studies in Comparative Religion*, Vol.17, No. i&ii (no date). — 'The Dream Journey — Ritual Renewal among Australian Aborigines' from *Tenemos*, Vol.7.

Deakin, Hilton. 'Some Thoughts on Transcendence in Tribal Societies' from E. Dowdy (ed.) *Ways of Transcendence*, Australian Association for the Study of Religion, Adelaide, 1982.

Eliade, Mircea. *Australian Religions*, Cornell University Press, Ithaca, 1971. — *The Sacred and the Profane*, Harcourt Brace Jovanovich, New York, 1959. — *Shamanism: Archaic Techniques of Ecstasy*, Bollingen Series LXXVI, Princeton, 1964.

Elkin, A.P. *Aboriginal Men of High Degree*, University of Queensland Press, St Lucia, 1977.

Evans-Pritchard, E.E. *Theories of Primitive Religion*, Clarendon Press, Oxford, 1965.

Oldmeadow, Kenneth S. 'The Science of Man: Scientific Opinion on the Australian Aborigines in the late 19th Century — The Impact of Evolutionary Theory and Racial Myth', History Hons. Thesis, Australia National University, 1969.

Reynolds, Henry, ed. *Dispossession: Black Australians and White Invaders*, Allen & Unwin, Sydney, 1989.

Stanner, W.E.H. 'Religion, totemism and symbolism' from M. Charlesworth, *Religion in Aboriginal Australia*, University of Queensland Press, St Lucia, 1986. — *White Man Got No Dreaming — Essays 1938-1973*, Australia National University Press, Canberra, 1979.

Swain, Tony. *Interpreting Aboriginal Religion*, Australian Association for the Study of Religion, Adelaide, 1985.

CHAPTER 15

The Underlying Order: Nature and the Imagination

Kathleen Raine

This paper was originally written for the 1985 Conference of the Centre for Spiritual Studies, whose theme was The Underlying Unity.

It is heartening to see that at last the long unquestioned assumptions of naive materialism that have dominated the modern Western world are beginning to seem less certain, less self-evident than they were even a few years ago. When I was a student — more than fifty years ago — I was torn between two possible choices. I intended to be a poet — that was certain — and it seemed therefore obvious to those who advised me that I should read English literature at university. But to me this was by no means obvious — why need to be taught how to read the literature of one's own language when books were available in libraries? I felt I had no need to seek the opinions of others on my fellow-writers, and I have had no reason to regret my decision to read instead natural sciences. For that was the other alternative. Always, from infancy — and in this I was perhaps no different from every child born into this marvellous world — nature had been my passion, and I thought I could best learn to contemplate and know its inexhaustible order and meaning by becoming a botanist or a marine biologist. But my love of nature was really a poet's love for meaning and beauty, rather than for fact or for manipulations and applications of scientific knowledge for practical ends. I found great delight in my studies of nature at that time, in contemplating that order and beauty that is to be found throughout the whole structure of the world, whether as it appears to the eye, or in

198

those minute worlds revealed by microscope or beyond the visible altogether. But my love of these things was a poet's love first and last. When a year or two ago one of my grand-daughters showed me one of her examination papers in botany and asked me which questions I could answer, I had to say that once I could have answered question 4 but that at no time any of the others! For science, knowledge is ever changing; what is 'knowledge' when we are young is no longer so when we are old.

But poetry and the other arts relate to the everlasting. One might say that all art is contemporaneous, the cave-paintings of Lascaux with those of Ajanta and Ellora; Greek classical sculpture with that of Chartres; the music of Monteverdi is not superseded by that of Mozart or of Wagner; Murasaki is as close to us as Marcel, the people of Shakespeare, with Homer's Hector and Achilles, with Rama and Arjuna, and all these are ourselves.

Orthodoxy, in our world, means scientific orthodoxy, and although the conclusions of science in some particular area may be open to question, the premises of the materialist ideology are not. To question these is to invite exclusion from any discussion whatsoever. As I understand it, science as we know it presumes a universe which consists of something called 'matter', which, whatever else may be said about it, is measurable, quantifiable, and constitutes an ordered and autonomous system, coherent and unified in all its parts and as a whole, the space-time continuum of the universe. Newton — and psychologically do we not still live in the Newtonian era? — conceived the material universe to be a mechanism functioning autonomously by the so-called 'laws of nature' which are the Ten Commandments, so to speak, of science. Within this great self-coherent order, value-judgements are superfluous. It is 'unscientific' to attribute to 'nature' any purposes, or qualities; any of those invisible and immeasurable human qualities such as joy and sorrow and love, or meaning of whatever kind. The human mind, according to Locke (the philosopher of the Newtonian system) thus becomes 'passive before a mechanized nature'. These words are Yeats's, who was a disciple of Blake, the sole lonely prophet to call in question, at the end of the eighteenth century, this whole structure of thought.

Thus the materialist hypothesis — for it is no more — attributes order and reality to the outer world, leaving mind itself, consciousness itself, as the mere mirror or receptacle of impressions. All knowledge comes from without, the mind of an infant is a blank page on which these impressions can be written. Even now the *reductio ad absurdum* of this theory — behaviourism — keeps its hold on transatlantic thought. At this point human beings are themselves conceived as mechanisms activated by so-called reflexes — mindless parts of a mindless material order, with consciousness itself degraded to a mere attribute of matter. Paradoxically — and no wonder — transatlantic mythology shows a marked tendency to treat machines as if these possessed human qualities, computers as if they possessed 'knowledge', even as the brain is treated as a short-lived computer. Such assumptions, consciously or unconsciously held, continue in a large measure to determine the kind and quality of the world we live in — the products of the machines, and all the advertising that goes with the age of the multinationals, all the direct or indirect propaganda for material values. Yet we are in reality living in a world whose assumptions and values rest on the no-longer tenable hypothesis that 'nature' operates in independence of the perceiving mind, and is itself the source and the object of all knowledge. The great regions of consciousness itself are deemed unreal because immeasurable. The mind is popularly identified with the brain; knowledge is stored away in right or left lobes as it is in a computer; you can tell that people are meditating or dreaming by affixing electrical apparatus to their heads, but what does that tell us of *what* is thought, or of the dream itself, or of the *experience* of meditation? Nothing at all. The human kingdom — the kingdom of consciousness — is excluded by definitions which see the real as identical with the measurable. It is not our conclusions but our premises that are false. We might even reverse them and say that reality is what we experience, and that all experience is immeasurable.

According to another view — and we must remember that this is the view the Eastern world, in various forms, has held over millennia — 'nature' is a system of appearances whose ground is consciousness itself. Science measures the phenomena which we perceive, and which Indian philosophical systems call *maya*. *Maya* has sometimes been termed illusion, but it is, more exactly, appearances. Blake used the word 'visions': this world, he wrote, 'is one continued vision of fancy or imagination'. But if the materialist premises are reversed, then 'reality' is not material fact but meaning itself. And it follows that in those civilizations grounded on this premise — our own included, up to the Renaissance — the arts, as expressions of the value-systems of a culture, have been held in high regard as expressions of knowledge of the highest order. Is not our human kingdom in its very nature a universe of meanings and values? For these are inherent in life itself, as such, the Vedantic *sat-chit-ananda*, being-consciousness-bliss: being *is* consciousness, and the third term *ananda* (bliss) is the ultimate value of being and consciousness. We are made for beatitude, as the theologians would say; Freud, indeed, said something not dissimilar when he spoke of the fundamental nature of 'the pleasure principle' as the goal all seek. Plotinus wrote of 'felicity' as the goal and natural term of all life, and attributed it not only to man and animals but to plants also. Beatitude — felicity — is not an accident of being and consciousness: it is our very nature to seek, and to attain, joy; and it is for the arts to hold before us images of our eternal nature, through which we may awaken to, and grow towards, that reality which is our humanity itself.

This view of reality Blake defended in its darkest hour, at the end of the rationalist eighteenth century and the beginning of the materialist nineteenth. Few heeded him or understood him when he said, 'all that I see is vision' and 'to me this world is one continued vision of imagination'. That is the sort of thing unpractical poets and painters do say! But Blake was in earnest and spoke as a metaphysician sure of his ground when he wrote of the living sun:

> 'What', it will be Questioned, 'When the Sun rises, do you not see
> A round disk of fire somewhat like a Guinea?' O no, no, I see an
> Innumerable company of the Heavenly host crying 'Holy, Holy, Holy
> Is the Lord God Almighty'. I question not my Corporeal or
> Vegetative Eye any more than I would Question a Window concerning
> A Sight. I look thro' it and not with it.[1]

Plato had used the same words about looking 'through not with' the eye. And what else, after all, could that innumerable multitude of beings proclaim, being themselves not objects in a lifeless mechanism, but an epiphany of life which not only has, but is, being, consciousness and bliss? The real, therefore, is ultimately — and this again has been understood by all traditions — not an object but a Person. A 'Person' in this sense not by a human act of personification of something in its innate reality neither living nor conscious; but rather human 'persons' are a manifestation in multitude of the single Person of Being itself, from which consciousness and meaning are inseparable, these being innate qualities of life itself, as such. Not 'life' as a property of matter, but life as experienced. 'Everything that lives is holy' summarizes Blake's total vision of reality — not holy because we choose to think it so, but intrinsically so. The 'holy' is, again, a reality that cannot be defined but can be experienced as the ultimate knowledge of consciousness. It cannot be measured, but neither can it be denied, if by knowledge we mean what is experienced. Within the scope of human experience there are degrees of knowledge and value, self-authenticating, of which those who have reached the farthest regions tell us, the vision of the holy, and the beatitude of that vision is the highest term. And therefore Blake's stars and grains of sand can say no other than 'Holy, Holy, Holy'.

> To see a World in a Grain of Sand
> And a Heaven in a Wild Flower,
> Hold Infinity in the palm of your hand
> And Eternity in an hour.[2]

That is not poetic fancy: it is profoundest knowledge.

How deeply we are all immersed in the world of duality is clear in the bewilderment we must all share through our Western conditioning in the matter of 'inner' and 'outer'. Blake was very clear in his understanding that the externalization of nature is a tragic consequence of what he called the 'wrenching apart' of the apparently external world from the unity of the wholeness of being. This has created an unhealed wound in the soul of modern Western man, leaving nature soulless and lifeless, and the inner world abstracted from the natural universe, its proper home. In the *unus mundus* the very terms 'inner' and 'outer' are not applicable at all. Both soul and nature have suffered; nature by being banished, in Blake's words, 'outside existence' in 'a soul-shuddering vacuum', natural space. At the same time the soul can no longer inhabit nature, and the 'after-life' is situated — again in Blake's words — 'in an allegoric abode where existence has never come'. But, for the universal spiritual teaching, mind is not in space, but space in mind. 'Nothing', as it is said in the *Hermetica*, 'is more capacious than the incorporeal.'

It is hard to reverse the more or less unconscious assumptions of a culture, and to turn our heads, like the prisoners in Plato's Cave who had taken the shadows of things for realities and were at first dazzled and bewildered by the light. But such a reversal — and more and more leading scientists are themselves coming to think so — the times demand, not of a learned few but of the world as a whole. Science itself has come full circle to this confrontation with the observing mind as an element in the phenomena observed. Many can see clearly, and many more obscurely feel, that some essential thing is lacking in our ways of life and thought. We have reached this confrontation; and I believe a change of the premises of our civilization is about to take place, that naive realism is already an obsolete hypothesis and — again the words are Yeats's — 'wisdom and poetry return'. Nothing in history is static and we are moved by invisible powers, call these what we will.

What is only now dawning on the Western mind was already plain to William Blake, when he wrote:

> . . . in your own bosom you bear your heaven
> And Earth and all you behold.
> Tho' it appears Without it is Within,
> In your Imagination, of which this World of Mortality is but a Shadow.[3]

A shadow, an image in a mirror; 'for now we see in a glass, darkly, but there face to face.'

'Matter' is in any case — and this the scientists themselves have taught us — such a mysterious and insubstantial thing, if it exists, as such, at all. That stone Dr Johnson kicked seemed to him real and solid enough when he said with such naive assurance (referring to Berkeley, who held the same view as Blake and the Neoplatonists and the *Hermetica*), 'thus I refute him'. All those spinning fields of force the scientists tell us of seem far from Dr Johnson's stone, and much nearer to 'matter' as Plotinus understood it, as a shadowy *non-ens* which, the more we pursue, the more it recedes into its 'labyrinths' of mystery. No-one knows what matter is in its ultimate nature. Stones were quite solid for Berkeley also, and tulips quite real, but for different reasons: because he saw them. And we too have to realize, in Yeats's words (referring to Berkeley) that:

> This preposterous, pragmatical pig of a world, its farrow that so solid seem
> Would vanish on the instant, did the mind but change its theme.[4]

— the mind that is, in the words of Laurens van der Post's bushmen, 'a dream dreaming us'.

You may ask if it really matters whether we believe nature to be a mechanism outside mind and consciousness, or hold the opposite view, that it is an ever-changing panorama passing through our minds, a *maya*. Do we not all see the same world, whatever we may think about it? I suggest that though the sense-impressions may be the same, the experiences are different. The difference is between the factual observation and a living encounter. To the materialist the natural world is other, it is mindless, lifeless, meaningless. With the advent of materialism, consciousness itself changes, as Blake understood when he wrote 'They behold/What is within now seen without', and this externalized nature becomes 'far remote, in a little and dark land', where all is diminished and emptied of meaning and value. But once the ground is removed from the observed object to the observing mind, that 'wrenching apart' of outer and inner of which Blake spoke is healed. The universe is then not alien to us; in Martin Buber's words, it is no longer an 'I-it' but an 'I-thou' relationship. The universe is one with us not merely in the sense in which the matter of our bodies is continuous with the entire material system, but in quite another sense nature lives with our lives, it 'comes alive', it has meaning, qualities, and a kinship with us. Nothing in nature is alien to our moods and thoughts, our aspirations and sorrows, our delights and laughter; all find in nature their language. We can love our world, we experience everything as a kind of unending dialogue, and not with sentient beings only but with sun and mountains and trees and stones. They tell us those things which constitute our wisdom in a way far deeper than the mere measurement of scientific experiment. We are one with nature not merely as insignificant parts in a vast mechanism, or as detached observers of its phenomena: nature itself becomes a region of our humanity. It becomes, in other words, human. It is our world, created for us, with us, by us, and it lives with our life.

Of course consciousness cannot be transformed by a mere change of opinion; rather it involves a change of our whole receptivity, an opening of the heart, the senses and the imagination. Consciousness is in the Vedantic writings described as synonymous with being, and being with bliss: *sat-chit-ananda*. Bliss is a word Blake also used, and he too associated it with the principle of life itself:

> And trees and birds and beasts and men behold their eternal joy.
> Arise, you little glancing wings, and sing your infant joy!
> Arise, and drink your bliss, for every thing that lives is holy![5]

Plotinus writes of 'felicity' as proper to all living beings, animals and plants no less than humanity, when these attain the fullness of their development, as a plant expands in the sun. Consciousness and nature are not two separate orders, but one and indivisible; to know this, to experience this, is to heal the divided consciousness, in modern jargon the 'schizophrenia' of modern secular thought, which since the Renaissance has grown ever deeper. It is to restore a lost wholeness, the *unus mundus*, that unity of inner and outer, nature and the soul, sought by the alchemists. It is the secret that can transform crude matter into the gold of the 'philosopher's stone', into something of infinite value.

Is it not, besides, an experience very familiar to us, for in childhood did we not know instinctively the values and meanings of all we saw? Can we not all remember a time when not only did we talk to animals and birds and plants and stones and stars and sun and moon, but they to us? C.S. Lewis in his Narnia children's books writes of 'talking animals', who communicate meaning, not perhaps in words, but none the less clearly and unmistakably. One of the disastrous consequences, as Blake saw it, of the materialist philosophy is that we could no longer communicate with the things of nature:

> . . . a Rock, a Cloud, a Mountain
> Were now not Vocal as in Climes of Happy Eternity
> Where the lamb replies to the infant voice, and the lion to the man of years
> Giving them sweet instructions; where the Cloud, the River and the Field
> Talk with the husbandman and shepherd.[6]

The natural world 'wanders away' into the 'far remote', and the animals 'build a habitation separate from man'. 'The stars flee remote . . . and all the mountains and hills shrink up like a withering gourd.' These are not changes in the object but in the consciousness of the perceiver.

Blake addresses one of the four sections of his last great prophetic book, *Jerusalem*, 'To the Jews' and appeals to the Jewish esoteric tradition of the primordial man, Adam Kadmon, when he writes:

> You have a tradition that Man anciently contain'd in his mighty limbs all things in Heaven and Earth: this you received from the Druids. 'But now the Starry Heavens are fled from the mighty limbs of Albion.'[7]

— the Giant Albion, who is the English national being: we are Albion.

To those unaccustomed to the symbolic language in which alone it is possible to speak of invisible realities this may seem remote from anything that can concern us today. In fact this is by no means so, and the esoteric teaching that 'Man anciently contain'd in his mighty limbs all things in Heaven and Earth' is perhaps only now becoming comprehensible in terms other than mythological. Blake, here as throughout his writings, is taking issue with the materialist philosophy that separates all things in heaven and earth from the 'body' of man.

Let us examine what he is in reality saying. The human 'body' as Blake uses the term is much more than the physical frame, to which indeed Blake always refers as 'the garment not the man'. In this respect he is following Swedenborg, his earliest master, who is himself drawing on that primordial tradition to which Blake refers. Plato wrote that 'the true man' is intellect; Blake changed the term to 'imagination', which he called 'the true man'. Under either term the meaning is that man is not merely his physical but his mental and spiritual being. According to Swedenborg this human 'body' is neither large nor small, not being in space at all; it is a spiritual and mental body which is not contained in the material universe. Mind is not in space, but space in mind, which contains the entire universe that we see, hear, touch and know. This 'body' Swedenborg called the 'Divine Humanity', a phrase most of us associate rather with Blake, who borrowed it, and identified the term (as did Swedenborg) with the Eternal Christ, Blake's 'Jesus, the Imagination'. 'This world of Imagination is the world of Eternity', Blake writes, 'All Things are comprehended in their Eternal Forms in the divine body of the Saviour, the True Vine of Eternity, the Human Imagination'.[8] 'I am the true vine', Jesus says, 'I am the vine and ye are the branches'; and so the mystics have ever understood his words. All humanity is incorporated within this great spiritual organism; not a mechanism but being, living and conscious, a 'person', whom Swedenborg described as 'the Grand Man of the Heavens', the collective spiritual being of all humanity.

Some of you may here recall Plato's parable of the first human beings, who were spherical. And it seems that this was more than a joke by Aristophanes at the banquet; for is not the universe of the scientists said to be spherical because of the curvature of the path of light? And is not each of us, in this sense, the centre of a spherical universe which 'contains all things in heaven and earth?' And as all see the same sun, so from our myriad centres we each contain not a part of the universe but the whole. It is this tradition — the primordial tradition of that first religion of all humanity that Blake attributes, rightly or wrongly, to 'the Druids', that Blake in his address 'To the Jews' recalls. In symbolic terms the Jewish Adam Kadmon, humanity as first created 'in the image of God', is the same as Blake's and Swedenborg's 'Divine Humanity', and the Christian's mystical body of Christ present in and to every created human individual. Man in reality still contains in his mighty limbs all things in heaven and earth but through the 'wrenching apart' of inner and outer worlds, the 'mortal worm', the 'worm of sixty winters' has lost his spiritual body and his universe is all outside him. It is through the materialist philosophy that modern man has come to this pass, summed up in Blake's line:

> But now the starry heavens have fled from the mighty limbs of Albion.[9]

Albion is the English nation, and it is in England that Bacon, Newton and Locke (whom Blake holds responsible for the 'wrenching apart') elaborated the materialist system which has since overspread the whole world. (There was of course also Descartes, but Blake was an Englishman.) The 'starry heavens' are Newton's especial domain; and by, as Blake understood the matter, separating the stars from the mountains, the mountains from man, and postulating a space-time universe outside mind itself, man becomes only 'a little grovelling root outside of himself', and the physical body, which is in reality only a 'form and organ' of boundless life, seems all. How differently the world appears when the rift between man and his universe is healed, Blake has sought to express in the poem *Milton*, whose theme is the world of Imagination. Answering Newton, for whom space is an external system, Blake writes of the same universe seen as within the human imagination. 'The Sky is an Immortal Tent', he wrote:

> And every Space that a Man views around his dwelling-place
> Standing on his own roof or in his garden on a mount
> Of twenty-five cubits in height, such space is his Universe:
> And on its verge the sun rises and sets, the Clouds bow
> To meet the flat Earth and the Sea in such an order'd Space:
> The Starry heavens reach on further, but here bend and set
> On all sides, and the two Poles turn on their valves of gold:
> And if he move his dwelling-place, his heavens also move
> Where'er he goes, and all his neighbourhood bewail his loss.
> Such are the Spaces called Earth and such its dimension.[10]

Spaces are, according to Blake, 'visionary', and time and space come into being by the creative power of the imagination, measured out 'to mortal man every morning'. For him it is all so very simple, not at all because he took issue with Newton on the 'facts' or arguments of his system (which within its own terms is not to be faulted) but because his premises were quite other.

Teilhard de Chardin has made an attempt to situate the theory of evolution within a spiritual rather than a materialist context; the divine humanity (to use Blake's term) is implicit in the alpha, to emerge as the omega of creation by the One who says 'I am alpha and omega, the first and the last'. Naive materialism must deem man an accident in a blind mechanism. Somehow the less can produce the greater by the laws of chance. Was it Bertrand Russell who calculated the chances of a thousand monkeys at a thousand typewriters producing the plays of Shakespeare? Absurd as the notion is, it is a calculation that has to be made by those who deny spiritual cause. It seems self-evident that a mechanism cannot produce spirit; but spirit can embody itself. The greater can produce the less, but the less cannot produce the greater, nor can the laws of chance write the plays of Shakespeare, who could write, on this very subject, 'What a piece of work is man! How noble in reason! How infinite in faculty! In form, in moving, how express and admirable! In action how like an angel! In apprehension, how like a god! the beauty of the world! the paragon of animals! And yet, to me, what is this quintessence of dust!' Can dust of itself produce such a quintessence? The materialist would have it so; and Blake, with his genius for going to the heart of things, saw no third alternative: 'Man is either the ark of God or a phantom of the earth and of the water.' If the naive materialist supposes that 'nature' can produce man, that man is a product of nature, sacred tradition sees, on the contrary, 'nature' as the domain of man.

Blake insisted continually on the 'human' character of the natural world, in its whole and in its parts; for 'nature' *is* the human imagination when understood not as a mechanism but as a 'vision', a reflection of the one living and indivisible universe.

> . . . Each grain of sand,
> Every stone on the Land,
> Each rock and each hill,
> Each fountain and rill,
> Each herb and each tree,

Mountain, hill, earth and sea,
Cloud, Meteor and Star
Are Men Seen Afar.[11]

'All is Human, Mighty, Divine,' he wrote; not in an excess of emotion but with the certitude of a profound understanding.

Swedenborg — who as we have seen was in the eighteenth century the principal defender of this mode of thought — elaborated his famous theory of 'correspondences'. If every creature is seen as the 'correspondence' of its inner nature — for such is Swedenborg's teaching — we find in the outer world continually and everywhere, in beasts and birds down to the minutest insects, the expression of 'spirits of different orders and capacities' whose outer forms bear the imprint of their living natures. Swedenborg was by profession a scientist (he was Assessor of Minerals to the Swedish Government) and his pages on the rich variety of living creatures, understood as 'correspondences' of states of being, certainly inspired Blake, who in his battle against materialism does not fail to make use of this view of nature as an expression of the living Imagination. He too presents the creatures not as objects but as forms of life:

> Does the whale worship at thy footsteps as the hungry dog;
> Or does he scent the mountain prey because his nostrils wide
> Draw in the ocean? does his eye discern the flying cloud
> As the raven's eye? or does he measure the expanse like the vulture?
> Does the still spider view the cliffs where eagles hide their young;
> Or does the fly rejoice because the harvest is brought in?
> Does not the eagle scorn the earth and despise the treasures beneath?
> But the mole knoweth what is there, and the worm shall tell it thee.
> Does not the worm erect a pillar in the mouldering church yard
> And a palace of eternity in the jaws of the hungry grave?[12]

Everything in nature has its inner no less than its outer being. The 'mortal worm' is 'translucent all within' and of 'the little winged fly smaller than a grain of sand', Blake writes:

> It has a heart like thee, a brain open to heaven and hell,
> With inside wondrous and expansive; its gates are not clos'd:
> I hope thine are not: hence it clothes itself in rich array:
> Hence thou art cloth'd with human beauty, O thou mortal man.[13]

Yet another version of the figure of the Universal Man who contains in himself all things — Blake's Divine Humanity, the Imagination, is the One distributed in the Many, like the Egyptian God Osiris, scattered throughout the universe, whose 'body' is reassembled by the devotion of his wife Isis:

> So man looks out in tree and herb and fish and bird and beast
> Collecting up the scatter'd portions of his immortal body
> Into the Elemental forms of every thing that grows. . . .
>
> In pain he sighs, in pain he labours in his universe,
> Screaming in birds over the deep, and howling in the wolf
> Over the slain, and moaning in the cattle, and in the winds . . .
>
> . . . his voice
> Is heard throughout the Universe: wherever a grass grows
> Or a leaf buds, The Eternal Man is seen, is heard, is felt,
> And all his sorrows, till he reassumes his ancient bliss.[14]

Blake is following the Swedenborgian doctrine of 'correspondences' which is, of course, a continuation of the earlier Alchemical and Astrological doctrine of 'signatures'. Everything in nature, according to this prematerialist view, bears in its outer form the 'signature' of its qualities. Plants, animals, minerals are classified according to their qualities by an elaborate system of 'signatures' from planets and the houses of the Zodiac, themselves deemed to be under the guidance of heavenly influences. Albeit modern thought has discarded the literal interpretation of these influences as coming from 'the stars' or planets in a physical sense, nevertheless this older cosmology can be understood as a projection of the Imagination into the natural universe, a model of the *unus mundus* which affirms the intrinsic qualities and order of the visible world. Applied to human nature astrological correspondences similarly describe and affirm the unity of inner and outer, man the microcosm within the macrocosm of the universe. Or, as Blake and Swedenborg would have it, the outer universe is within man. Dismissed as an inexact and rudimentary science, are we not now obliged to re-examine alchemy, astrology and the rest — as C.G. Jung has done — as pertaining rather to our inner universe, and to the indivisibility of inner and outer? As the alchemists, and before them the Neoplatonists understood, 'nature' is a mirror, a looking-glass in which we see reflected everything that is, and everything we are. We are once more in a living universe, a universe moreover whose life is not alien to us but indistinguishable, inseparable, part and parcel of what we ourselves are. This, it seems to me, is the point at which we, at this time, are; where human knowledge has brought us. I suggest that we are not in a phase of further development of materialist science in directions already foreseeable, but at the moment of a reversal of premises, a change of direction. Not, indeed, that anything of the scientific observation of the natural phenomena will be denied or invalidated; science in the modern sense is one of the ways of observing the world, nor is it necessary in order to study what Owen Barfield many years ago named the 'appearances' to accept the materialist standpoint. The greater knowledge does not invalidate the partial, but can include it. It is the claim of the natural sciences to be that all-inclusive knowledge that is no longer tenable.

Would such a change — will such a change — or dare I say, *is* such a change — a venture into a new and unknown experience, or is it not rather something already familiar, which in our heart of hearts we already know? There have been societies, indeed civilizations, where the unity and wholeness of being which our own has gradually lost, has been understood by the wise and the simple alike. Blake supposes it to be man's primordial condition to contain in his mighty limbs all things in heaven and earth. Have we not all read Laurens van der Post's poignant accounts of the doomed African Bushmen whose physical survival was precarious indeed, but who felt themselves, so he tells us, to be perfectly at one with their world, because nothing in that world was alien to them, nothing without meaning? I quote from his latest book *Testament to the Bushmen*:

> The essence of this being, I believe, was his sense of belonging: belonging to nature, the universe, life and his own humanity. He had committed himself utterly to nature as a fish to the sea. He had no sense whatsoever of property, owned no animals and cultivated no land. Life and nature owned all and he accepted without question that, provided he was obedient to the urge of the world within him, the world without, which was not separate in his spirit, would provide. How right he was is proved by the fact that nature was kinder to him by far than civilization ever was. This feeling of belonging set him apart from us on the far side of the deepest divide in the human spirit.

And Laurens van der Post goes on to write:

> We were rich and powerful where he was poor and vulnerable: he was rich where we were poor, and his spirit led to strange water for which we secretly longed. But, above all, he came to our estranged and

211

divided vision, confident in his belonging and clothed as brightly as Joseph's coat of dream colours in his own unique experience of life.

Above all the Bushman experienced always 'the feeling of being known'. And the author confesses that he himself experienced an overwhelming sense of nostalgia:

> for this shining sense of belonging, of being known and possessing a cosmic identity of one's own, recognized by all from insect to sun, moon and stars which kept him company, so that he felt he had the power to influence them as they influenced and helped him.

Earth was not only the Bushmen's home, source of material nourishment and shelter, but also of their spiritual food. The earth is full of meaning; tells them those marvellous stories of Mantis and the Lynx and the Morning Star, of lizard and beetle and wild freesia, living in their rich and manifold lives some one or other aspect of the world's one and indivisible being. As Blake says, earth would 'talk' with the husbandman and the shepherd. All is a subtle, profound, mirthful and delightful continuous epiphany of the great mystery in which we live and move and have our being.

With this imaginative apprehension goes always a sense of the sacred; for the sacred is an experience of a certain kind, precluded by the materialist mentality whose world is a lifeless world. But for primitive peoples of all times and places — the Australian aborigines no less than the indigenous North American peoples — Blake's words are true, that 'everything that lives is holy'. Sacred rocks, sacred trees, sacred animals and totem birds and holy mountains. But where are the holy places of the modern technological world? But do we need holy places, all those sacred springs and wells and rivers and trees and anthills and caverns and mountains where the gods live? I would reply that, since we have the capacity to experience awe and wonder and love, these are within the range of human experience without whose use we are diminished, as by blindness or deafness. Modern secular man finds no burning bush, no Presence which commands 'Take thye shoes from off thye feet for the place whereon thou standest is holy ground.' But in losing the capacity for awe, for wonder, for the sense of the numinous, the sacred, what we lose is not the object but that part of ourselves which can find in trees or churinga-stone or the dread cavern of the pythoness the correspondence of an aspect of our humanity of which these are the objective correlative, the correspondence, the mirror, the 'signature'. The Presence that spoke to Moses from the Burning Bush speaks on in every age: 'I am that I am'. A mystery insoluble!

For the secular mind, in common modern parlance, a 'mystery' is a problem to be solved, a puzzle in the manner of a Sherlock Holmes story in which something that seems frightening, inexplicable, or mysterious proves after all to be simple, explicable and trivial. Such is the reductionist spirit of our culture, that has invented Sherlock Holmes as the embodiment of the prevalent reductionist mentality. That shallow rationalism can exorcise the Hound of the Baskervilles or the Speckled Band for us. Yet they live on in the depths. The terror that they evoke is more real than the exorcisms that banish them. But to a child a pebble can speak, or a withered leaf, or the eye of a bird, or a tree or a running stream, the cosmic word 'I am that I am'. For these are Presences, not objects merely, as to the 'detached' mind of the investigator. Have we not all memories of this world of presences, fearsome and beautiful — infinitely strange and infinitely familiar?

We will never, certainly — nor should we wish to do so — return to the innocent world of the Stone Age. We can never un-know what the scientific investigation of nature has presented to us. It has described in the minutest detail and the grandest scope that image in the 'vegetable glass of nature'. But until we have experienced the unity of all things not as a natural fact but as a living presence we shall never, in the early mystic Traherne's words, know the world 'aright'.

What this learned and cultured divine has written re-echoes down the ages from the Stone Age to ourselves:

> You never enjoy the world aright, till the sea itself floweth in your veins, till you are clothed with the heavens, and crowned with the stars: and perceive yourself to be the sole heir of the whole world, and more . . . because men are in it who are every one of them sole heirs as well as you . . . Till your spirit fills the whole world, and the stars are your jewels.[15]

In our secular world it is customary to look at scientists for truth, to the arts for entertainment: I suggest that this attitude is deeply mistaken. Perhaps it should be reversed, for it is the part of the poet to present to us that total view and experience of reality which includes all aspects of our humanity in the context of every age. Or that situates every age, rather, in the context of the everlasting. Such poets have, even so, written in this century — I think of Valéry and Claudel, of Rilke and of Yeats, indeed of T.S. Eliot and of Edwin Muir and Vernon Watkins, of Robert Frost — and there are others less complete or less

illustrious. I know no poetry that goes beyond that of Rilke in stating
— suggesting rather — who we are, what our place is in the universe.
Rainer Maria Rilke, near the end of his life, in a brief period of
continuous and prophetic inspiration, completed his two greatest
poetic works, the *Duino Elegies* and the *Sonnets to Orpheus*. Rejecting
institutionalized religion he was the more free to experience those
'angels', intelligences of the universe, 'beyond the stars'. What are we,
he asks, beside these great transhuman orders? And he replies:

> Praise this world to the Angel, not the untellable; you can't impress
> him with the splendour you've felt; in the cosmos where he more
> feelingly feels you're only a novice. So show him some simple thing,
> refashioned by age after age till it lives in our hands and eyes as a part of
> ourselves. Tell him *things* . . .[16]

To the things of this earth it is mankind who gives their reality. It is
these only we can tell the Angel:

> . . . Above all, the hardness of life,
> The long experience of love, in fact purely untellable things. But
> later, under the stars, what use? the more deeply untellable stars?
> For the wanderer does not bring from mountain to valley a handful
> of earth, for all untellable earth, but only a word he has won, pure,
> the yellow and blue gentian. Are we, perhaps, *here* just for saying:
> House, Bridge, Fountain, Gate, Jug, Fruit-tree, Window — possibly:
> Pillar, Tower . . .[17]

It is we who give meaning to these things by our words, by
performing Adam's appointed task of 'naming' the creation. Thus we
bestow on the creatures not a merely natural, but a human, an
imaginative and *in*visible reality. And Rilke continues his thought that
we are here 'just for saying' the names:

> . . . but for *saying*, remember,
> oh, for such saying as never the things themselves
> hoped so intensely to be. Is not the purpose
> of this sly earth, in urging a pair of lovers,
> just to make everything leap in ecstasy in them?[18]

The world finds in us an intenser, a totally new mode of being; as if we
are here to perform an alchemical transmutation of crude base
'nature' into the gold of Imagination. And to the Angel we can show
'how happy a thing can be, how guileless and ours'; even in its
transience:

> . . . These things that live on departure understand when you praise
> them: fleeting, they look for rescue through something in us, the most

214

fleeting of all. Want us to change them entirely, within our invisible hearts into — oh, endlessly — into ourselves. Whosoever we are.[19]

Whosoever we are. That is a mystery which we cannot in our very nature hope to resolve. It has been the *hybris* of science to hope to know everything. The poet, more humble, seeks to discern who and what we are within a totality greater than ourselves, a finally unknowable order. We are nevertheless the custodians and creators of that order of values and realities that are properly human, that human kingdom of the Imagination 'ever expanding in the bosom of God'. That 'divine body', the human Imagination, is the underlying order which bounds, embraces and contains the human universe.

Within the tradition of spiritual knowledge which I have indicated the underlying order is not some system of natural laws but being itself, at once the 'person' and the 'place' of the universe. Boehme called it the 'imagination' of God, and Blake, following him, 'Jesus the Imagination'. To the Jews it is Adam Kadmon, to Swedenborg the Grand Man of the Heavens, the Self of the Upanishads. The unity of this Being — of Being itself — is not that of a mechanism but of a consciousness, 'in whom we live, and move, and have our being'. Within this whole we are, in our present state, aware only of the limited field of our own lives. We are aware of other lives, and great fields beyond us, other times and places and being and modes of being surrounding us like unexplored forests or unclimbed mountains or unsailed seas. A sort of fragrance, or music, is sometimes borne to us on an invisible wind from those far-off fields of knowledge and experience, and we wish we could experience more of that whole of which each of us is at once an infinitesimal part and an infinite center.

At the British Museum I walked from one exhibit to another at the recent exhibition of Buddhist scriptures, devotedly and minutely transcribed in languages unknown to most of those who visited that exhibition, on tablets of wood or pages of palm-leaves, by forgotten monks whose days were spent in meditating the truths of a great civilization that rose like a tide over the Eastern world, to ebb again, and whose records end in a museum as in an honoured grave. And before, the unwritten knowledge and unrecorded visions of civilizations still more remote. And again beyond the vast regions of the once known and the knowable, that given an infinite number of lifetimes — perhaps that very infinite number of which there are, or have been or will be, human lives —there may be other beings attuned not to the spectrum of our human senses but to other, ampler magnitudes. And in every hedgerow are there not minute lives of birds and bees and insects, whose worlds are to us impenetrable? And yet in us something seems to discern an underlying order, a unity of being, 'the One' of which Plato wrote, the All, the God Itself. Or, as the subtler, deeper wisdom of India in one of the Vedic hymns takes us to the extreme limit of the known and the knowable:

> But, after all, who knows, and who can say
> > whence it all came, and how creation happened?
> The gods themselves are later than creation,
> > so who knows truly whence it has arisen?
>
> Whence all creation had its origin,
> > he, whether he fashioned it or whether he did not,
> he, who surveys it all from highest heaven,
> > he knows — or maybe even he does not know.[20]

Notes

1. Geoffrey Langdon Keynes, ed., 'A Vision of the Last Judgement' from *The Complete Writings of William Blake*, Oxford University Press, London, 1966, p.617.
2. *Ibid*, p.431, 'Auguries of Innocence'.
3. *Ibid*, p.709, 'Jerusalem', plate 71, lines 46-9.
4. W.B. Yeats, 'Blood and the Moon' from *Collected Poems*, Macmillan, New York, 1956, p.268.
5. Geoffrey Langdon Keynes, ed., *op.cit.*, p.195, 'Visions of the Daughters of Albion', plate 8.
6. *Ibid*, p.315, 'Vala VI', lines 134-7.
7. *Ibid*, p.649, 'Jerusalem II', plate 27.
8. *Ibid*, pp.605-6, 'Vision of the Last Judgement'.
9. *Ibid*, p.649, 'Jerusalem II', plate 27.
10. *Ibid*, p.516, 'Milton', plate 29, lines 4-13.
11. *Ibid*, p.805, 'Letter to Thomas Butts', 2 Oct. 1800.
12. *Ibid*, p.193, 'Vision of the Daughters of Albion', plate 5, lines 33-41.
13. *Ibid*, p.502, 'Milton', plate 20, lines 28-31.
14. *Ibid*, p.355-6, 'Vala VIII, lines 561-83.
15. Thomas Traherne, *Centuries of Meditation*, London, 1950.
16. J.B. Leithman and Stephen Spender, trans., *Duino Elegies*, W.W. Norton & Co., New York, 1939, IX.
17. *Ibid*, IX, 1, pp.25-35.
18. *Ibid*, pp.35-9.
19. *Ibid*, pp.64-8.
20. A.L. Basham, *The Wonder That Was India*, Grove Press Inc., New York, 1954, p.248.

CHAPTER 16

The History of Religions and the Primordial Tradition

James Burnell Robinson

The name of Huston Smith has been particularly associated with the concept of the 'primordial tradition' in recent years.[1] In this paper I wish to do two things: first to suggest some ways in which the discipline of the history of religions can contribute to the study of the primordial tradition, and then to suggest ways in which both contribute to what has come to be called 'the dialogue of world religions'.[2]

It is particularly appropriate to explore the connections between the history of religions and the primordial tradition, since Huston Smith's scholarly career encompasses the concerns of both. The book for which he is perhaps best known, *The Religions of Man*, explores the great world religions in their diversity, a text so durable that it has been in print for thirty years and was used as reference text for home study in connection with the television series 'The Long Search'. His second book, *Forgotten Truth*, moves from religions in their historical and cultural setting to their great common underlying themes.

In his most recent article published in the *Journal of the American Academy of Religion*, Fall 1987, Professor Smith defends the concept of a primordial tradition from the criticism of Steven Katz who denies that one can find a commonality in either mystical experience in particular or religion in general. Professor Smith says that the question of the perennial philosophy (the term he uses to correspond to the language of Katz's attack) rests, not on a question of data but rather on certain metaphysical intuitions.[3]

Professor Smith goes on to expand upon that:

Let us be clear: the perennial philosophy is a philosophy, not a sociology or anthropology that would jump out of the empirical bushes if only we squinted hard enough. The perennialist arrives at the ubiquity of his/her outlook more deductively than inductively. Having encountered a view of things s/he believes to be true, s/he concludes that it must be true universally for truth has ubiquity built into its meaning . . .

Philosophy is not concerned with particulars such as what's happening in Berkeley; in the end it is concerned with the whole of things. The topic is too vast for individual minds. They need help, which help the perennialist finds in the world's enduring religious or wisdom traditions. In theistic terminology, these traditions stem from divine revelation, but if that way of speaking closes rather than opens doors, one can think of them as wisdom reservoirs. They are tanks, or in any case deposits: distillations of the cumulative wisdom of the human race.[4]

In affirming this priority of the metaphysical over the empirical, he is following the work of René Guénon, Frithjof Schuon and other great exponents of a perennial philosophy who also begin with metaphysical principles and see historical data as their particular embodiment. S.H. Nasr, in his Gifford Lectures published as *Knowledge and the Sacred* (Crossroad, 1981), refers to religions as archetypal patterns unfolding in history.

Responding to the obvious question about the manifest differences in specific doctrines among religions, Professor Smith immediately acknowledges them; the perennial philosophy or primordial tradition does not regard them as irrelevant but as providential. He uses an analogy — red and green are very different from each other, but these differences are clearly subordinate to the fact that they are both light. This is a very suggestive image; perhaps the various world religions are individual facets of a *pleroma* of divine wisdom, as red and green are distinct hues in the fullness of color and light.

Granting that the differences among religions are providential, it is certainly instructive to know the specific patterns of those providential manifestations and how they fit together. Truth is found in the concrete as well as in the abstract. If the metaphysical intuitions of the primordial tradition do not rest on specific experiences or data in religious studies, surely, since truth is one, specific experiences and data will serve to amplify and confirm the intuited principles. The archetypical patterns are embedded and embodied in culture and history; studying their manifestations as such in space and time must surely illuminate them. To take an image from *Forgotten Truth* (p.40), the archetypes are like magnets organizing iron filings; we learn about the magnet by studying the patterns of filings.

The discipline of the history of religions works in the counter-direction, using an empirical rather than a metaphysical starting point. It looks first at the data then suggests the more general principles from that data. But these two movements should not be seen as opposing each other; rather as offering each other mutual support. The history of religions provides data in support of specific claims for a primordial tradition. This is not as trivial a support as it might at first sound, since the philosophical temper of the age, for better or worse, trusts historical and cultural data more than it does metaphysical intuition. And conversely, the primordial tradition offers the history of religions a unifying perspective that can take us beyond the sifting and coordinating of data toward applying it to the world in which we live.

If there is but one reality and if religion relates to that reality (and every religion claims it does), then what we are to make of the many different forms of religion stands as a central question in religious studies. At this point, the concept of a primordial tradition must be taken very seriously in the discipline of the history of religions.

What is the History of Religions?

The term 'history of religions' was coined by one of the pioneers of religious studies in the United States, Joachim Wach, who established the study of 'the history of religions' at the University of Chicago.[5] For Wach and his successors, foremost of whom was the late Mircea Eliade, the term 'history of religions' renders the German term *Religionswissenschaft*; it connotes a critical discipline with a characteristic method and a specific body of phenomena which it studies. Hence, *Religionswissenschaft* might conceivably be translated as 'the science of religion'.

But Wach and his colleagues recognized such a translation might be misleading for the fledgling area of religious studies. The word 'science' has a different connotation in English from the word *Wissenschaft* in German; the term 'science of religion' might suggest emphasis upon quantification, statistics, an experimental method, none of which really fits what *Religionswissenschaft* was about. And in the academic atmosphere of the early part of this century, there were many who had considerable emotional investment in the dichotomy of religion and science. To such people, 'the science of religion' might seem presumptuous or even a contradiction in terms. So Wach and his associates used the term 'history of religions' as somewhat more descriptive of what this discipline was trying to do. The aim of the history of religions as Wach and his school saw it was to study religion as it occurs all over the world, and to formulate basic patterns in the phenomena of religion, eventually to interpret their meaning for the human experience.

Another term sometimes used to describe *Religionswissenschaft* is 'the phenomenology of religion'. Now the word 'phenomenology' can be used in very technical ways in modern philosophy, particularly in connection with the methodological program of the philosopher Husserl. But it is sufficient for our purpose to say that the historian of religion as phenomenologist of religion, is someone concerned first to study in a systematic fashion the phenomena that can be called 'religious', and who attempts to understand that body of data in its own terms in historical and cultural context. A particular doctrine or practice or artistic creation is seen in terms of who or what gave rise to it and what results followed from it. That item is also fitted into the network of other elements in making up that particular religion. Such a scholarly endeavor clearly calls upon a number of methodologies and results of other disciplines, such as anthropology, history, area studies, philology, geography, and many others.[6]

More than that, the understanding of any religion is measured by how closely that understanding is recognized by those within the tradition being studied. W.C. Smith, in *Toward a World Theology*, says that any explication of Buddhism or discussion of Islam should be such that a Buddhist or Moslem would say, 'Yes, you have understood us.'[7]

But what distinctive contribution does the historian of religions make over and above the specialists in particular cultures and religions? Simply analyzing specific phenomena within their own tradition, while indispensable as a beginning, can lead to an incomplete and fragmented view of the more general nature of religion. Even if we come to understand a given religion in great depth, very few religions have developed without contact and interaction with other religions. This indubitable historical fact in itself must push the study of a particular religion beyond self-defined borders. A Buddhologist, for example, with complete justification may say: 'I will limit myself to the study of Buddhism; after all, there is more than enough there for a lifetime of study.' But if that program were to be carried out rigorously and consistently, it would not only relegate the rich interaction of Buddhism with other religions throughout its history to the periphery of study, but it would deprive the Buddhologist of many insights to be derived from parallels and similarities to Buddhism found in other religions.

The historian of religions seeks as far as possible to shed light on the phenomenon of religion as a whole, that is to say, religion as it has been an integral feature of virtually every culture and society we know. Being firmly grounded in the data, the historian of religions seeks to explore meanings and implications, seeing parallels and analogies among religions that illuminate what religion may mean to the human condition. Now the historian of religion finds him or herself on territory very familiar to the perennialist.

Mythological Motifs: Sky gods and Storm gods

Those studying religion from the point of view of the primordial tradition have drawn extensively from the area of religious symbolism. René Guénon's classic study, *The Symbolism of the Cross*, is a model of what can be done in drawing parallel motifs together to form an image of the cohesive whole. Huston Smith's second chapter in *Forgotten Truth* illuminates spatial imagery in religion from a rich range of traditions. Mythological motifs are a perennial resource for those who discern archetypal patterns unifying diverse cultural outlooks. Historians of religion are also very fascinated by mythological motifs and religious symbolism.

Let us take an example. In Vedic literature, one can follow a progression: in the earliest time, there was a sky-father Dyaus Pitar who was paired with an earth-mother goddess Prthivi.[9] By the earliest Vedic hymns, Dyaus Pitar had been supplanted by Varuna, another sky god who was guardian of the over-arching cosmic-moral law.[10]

By the time the Vedic peoples had arrived in India, Varuna was growing more remote and Indra was now becoming one of the most commonly referred to gods in the Vedic hymns. He slew the dragon Vrtra with his thunderbolt (the *vajra*) and released life-giving waters.[11] He is associated with the storm among natural phenomena and with the warrior class in the old Indo-Aryan society. This storm god, the soma-drinking, chariot-riding, thunderbolt-wielding dragon-slayer and fort-shatterer is the analogue of Thor in the ancient Norse religion, and of Zeus among the ancient Greeks. This suggests that Indra reflects some god among the archaic Indo-European speaking peoples.

The Norse god, Thor, shares the hard-riding warrior image of Indra though he prefers to throw a hammer rather than the double-sided vajra of Indra. While Indra slays the serpentine Vrtra (whose name means 'the encloser') Thor is to do battle with the Midgard serpent whose body encircles the world. Both Vrtra and the Midgard serpent are reminiscent of the Gnostic image of the Ourobouros, the snake in the circle, holding its tail in its mouth.

Zeus is more complex. He holds a thunderbolt, portrayed in a double-forked form, directly analogous to the iconographic portrayals of the vajra, and he retains connections with the storm. His name, however, is directly related to Dyaus and he acquires many of the sky-god of justice functions of Varuna, though he is separated by a divine generation from Ouranos, the god of the heavens and Greek form of Varuna.

Particularly interesting is connecting the Indra-god with the Babylonian Marduk, since the Babylonians were not an Indo-European people though they did clearly have contact with I-E peoples such as the Hittites. Marduk is also a dragon slayer, in this case Tiamat the embodiment of oceanic chaos. And in at least one instance, on a wall panel in the palace of Ashur-nasiripal II (885-860 BCE), the divine weapon which Marduk uses is portrayed in a carving as a double-forked thunderbolt.[12]

Marduk is a storm-god, identified with the old Mesopotamian storm-god Enlil. The Mesopotamian mythology, like the Vedic mythology, shows significant tension between sky-god Anu and storm-god Enlil, the former being regarded as exalted but remote and unable to deal with Tiamat, the latter technically subordinate but more forceful and dynamic. [13] One might be tempted to include the conflict between the sun-goddess Amaterasu and the storm-god Susa-no-wa in ancient Japanese myths, as a further example. Clearly the human experience of the over-arching sky and the intervening storm clouds provides a naturalistic starting point for this tension, though the religious dynamic is more complex.

If the French scholar Georges Dumézil is correct, it may reflect differing conceptions of political sovereignty as much as an observation of nature. Dumézil argued, on the basis of comparative studies, that the society of the Indo-European speaking peoples had three distinct classes: priests, warriors and herdsmen/commoners. The sky-god embodies the priestly view of sovereignty based on the authority of transcendent law and sacred power, whereas the storm-god represents sovereignty based on charismatic leadership and martial force as might be found in heroic warriors.[14]

To take this further, examples from African and Australian aboriginal religion show a sky-god who becomes more and more remote, to be superseded by lesser deities who have a more direct connection to human life. Father Wilhelm Schmidt argued that this mythological pattern reflects a pattern in human development, an original naturalistic monotheism which degenerates into animism and polytheism. More recently, the Italian historian of religions, Raffaele Pettazzoni, has continued this line of research.[15] The psychologist C.G. Jung considered the sky-father as an archetype, a primordial pattern in the human psyche, which is expressed in culturally specific forms in many times and places. If this is the case, the tension of sky-god and storm-god may well be indicative of psychological forces at work in human growth.

Making these analogies and parallels establishes a dialectical relation in which Indra, Thor, Zeus and Marduk enable us to delineate a certain type of deity better and to understand certain patterns in ancient religion and ancient society. Conversely, these broader patterns enable us to understand each particular instance better. We understand Indra more completely when we recognize his parallels in Thor, Zeus and Marduk. And confronted with the recurrence of the motif in many times and places, we are caused to reflect whether it might point to something beyond merely historical or cultural occurrences or idiosyncratic environmental factors.

A further example, inspired by the third chapter of *Forgotten Truth*, is the case of devotionalism. The historian of religions might note how certain forms of Christian devotion to Jesus are similar to the devotion of certain Hindu groups to Krishna. Comparison and contrast of these two forms of devotionalism helps us to understand the general category of devotional religion: it is not something unique to a certain religious tradition but points to a more general human response to personalized forms of the sacred. If we were to broaden our nets to include the Pure Land Schools of Buddhism devoted to the Buddha Amida and his Western Paradise, we will learn even more about what devotional religion is all about. Conversely, learning about devotional religion in general, we are better able to understand the specific forms of devotionalism in Christianity, Hinduism and Buddhism.

Noting the similarities throws the profound theological differences among these religions in sharp relief. Jesus is the incarnation of the personal Creator God; the historical nature of his incarnation, teaching, death and resurrection are very important to Christianity. Krishna is the incarnation of Vishnu, a deity sharing attributes of the Judaeo-Christian God, but the historical nature of his incarnation is less significant to his believers. Unlike the unique nature of Jesus's incarnation, Krishna is only a particularly important incarnation among many others that Vishnu has made.

The Buddha Amida is technically not a god at all, but in the far distant past was a man who vowed that when he became a Buddha he would cause to be reborn in his paradise anyone who called upon him in faith. Now that individual is in fact a Buddha who has both the power and compassion to make good on his vow. That Amida actually exists and can do the things it is claimed he can do is certainly important, but, to my knowledge, few Pure Land theologians have attempted a reconstruction of the historical details of Amida's original earthly life, if indeed he ever lived on this planet.

Having pointed out differences, I shall end this example by swinging back to similarities. Characteristic of devotional religion, human effort is seen as inadequate to accomplish salvation, however defined, so salvation can only be accomplished by divine initiative, using divine here in its broadest sense. The question then arises as to what role, if any, human effort plays. All three devotional religions mentioned have felt this tension in distinctive but similar ways: Pure Land Buddhists distinguish self-power religion and other-power religion, the Vaishnavites talk of 'monkey-hold' theology where God extends his salvation irrespective of human effort, and Christians talk about the relation of faith and works. If, as perennialists say, each religious expression is an archetype, studying the particular embodiments helps to delineate the complexity of its form.

History of Religions and the Complexity of Religion

In many ways, the history of religion seeks to carry out the program of what used to be called 'comparative religion', which also

224

studied the various world faiths with an eye to showing similarities and differences. However, in the late nineteenth and early twentieth centuries, when all the scholarly studies of societies were in infancy, it is not surprising that men and women examining religion brought particular agendas that encouraged a rather selective use of the data.

Some saw comparative religion as establishing the superiority of Western Christianity over the beliefs and thought-forms of Asian and African peoples; the study of different faiths was to aid the missionary endeavor. More liberal scholars were eager to show the religious or moral unity of humanity. Those influenced by movements such as Theosophy made much of similarities that could be found in the world religions to argue for their own syncretism. Some ecumenical attempts often slighted or ignored the historical development or cultural context of the religions they studied.

Apart from agendas, a systematic weakness of the old comparative approach was that it tended to focus upon doctrine and belief; religion was understood as 'creed', and creed was understood as assent to some body of propositions about the world. A corollary to this is presuming that religious practices are derived from creeds and so are to be measured and judged by creeds. The widespread assumption that a religion is purest at the time of its formation and that later history is a fall from that purity, it might be argued, is not just a Christian but more particularly a Protestant model of religious history. It was the same reductive understanding of religions as propositions that enabled positivists to believe that with a few strokes of their logical sword they could render the word God into a meaningless syllable rhyming with 'cod'.

As scholars studied religious traditions, they came to realize that religion is much more than belief. A Christian is more than someone who subscribes to a creed; a Christian also goes to church, participates in Christian rituals, has Christian ideals as more or less an operative factor in his or her life. Furthermore, in some religions, belief is not always a primary category; often a religion is a community carrying out particular practices rather than a people who consciously assent to a shared body of doctrine. A rabbi once said that a Jew is not defined by certain beliefs about life after death; a Jew is someone who gets a Jewish funeral. And scholars of Indian religion have long known that it is often more fruitful to approach Hinduism as a common interlocking system of practices rather than attempt to construct some common belief system which all Hindus hold.

Religion is something that is lived and so shares the diversity of human life; every religion known to us has many dimensions and features. Joachim Wach posited that every religion has at least three elements: belief, practice and social expression. Ninian Smart in his recent book *Worldviews* cites six 'dimensions' of religion: the experiential, the mythic, the ritual, the ethic, the social and the doctrinal.[16] The use of the word 'dimension' is significant here; it suggests that any given element of a religion is like a point in the space of a universe of discourse in which all six dimensions can simultaneously intersect. Today, religious studies seems to be enriching the number of categories relevant to studying a religion and is more deeply appreciating the degree to which any set of categories must overlap and interpenetrate.

One more example brings these dimensions together to deal with a specific feature of a religion. A key religious term in Mahayana Buddhism is *śūnyatā*, usually translated as 'emptiness': all existent things in the world are 'empty' of any underlying substantiality or self-existent being.[17] More positively, everything around us is the product of conditions and causes; they continually change as conditions change. The deepest perception and fullest realization of emptiness is the content of the Buddha's enlightenment, and the key to releasing us from the miseries inherent in the ordinary human life and to actualizing our deepest human potential.

The historian of religions might first approach the understanding of *śūnyatā* by studying the basic texts: first the Mahayana *Perfection of Wisdom Sūtras*, in which the doctrine of emptiness plays a central role. Then one might turn to commentarial literature and philosophical treatises (*śāstras*), particularly the work of Nāgārjuna.

Nāgārjuna, one of the great philosophers of India, wrote several works in which he gave specific rational arguments for *śūnyatā*. Nāgārjuna seems to suggest that emptiness is simply an extension of that basic Buddhist doctrine of anatman, or 'no Self'. To understand anatman means further study of texts, and understanding the climate of thought in which the Buddha preached. To complicate things further, the denial of an eternal self is usually taken in the West as an anti-religious position. Such a view will not get one very far toward understanding a religion which holds that 'no atman' is essential for our salvation.

The figure of Nāgārjuna is no less complex. While it is tempting to see him as a type of skeptic, Mahayana Buddhism sees him as a saint and a holy man, a supporter and embodiment of the religious life. Stories tell of extraordinary accomplishments and a preternaturally long lifespan. While these legends may be viewed with considerable reserve by Western scholars, they are indicative of how Nāgārjuna was seen by his own tradition.[18]

And any attempt to understand *śūnyatā* as a religious phenomena must also look at the broader scope of Mahayana Buddhism. For the same tradition that says all things are empty, also gives honor and veneration to a whole range of quasi-divine figures, the great cosmic bodhisattvas such as Mañjuśrī, Avalokiteśvara and Tārā. Mahayana proliferated a richness of religious practices and liturgical usages while at the same time denying a concept of ultimate reality that supports and sustains similar religious practices in other religions.

Let us take this one step further. If one considers emptiness only in Nāgārjuna, one might consider it a philosophical construct. But Buddhists say that emptiness is something that can be directly experienced in meditation, not as a working hypothesis but as the nature of reality. The Tantric schools took Mahayana philosophy and sought new means of making it the experiential basis for life in the world, an aspiration never absent in the Buddhist religion.

The Tantras do not talk about *śūnyatā* philosophically but as it is experienced in meditation. Here emptiness is 'the Clear Light'. The use of light imagery to describe an experience in profound meditation is suggestive of connection with great mystical experiences in other religions in which light imagery is also an important feature. Do we have here a connection with the perennial philosophy? This point has been hotly argued, but whatever the result there can be no denying that the concept of emptiness is very rich indeed.

To understand a particular element of a religion, one must see it in its historical and cultural context as part of a network of beliefs and practices at any given time, and also look at the historical antecedents and results of that element. One can go further, to compare and contrast that element with similar elements in other religions, to see patterns of connection beyond any one religious tradition to enable us to understand other religions as well.

At some point, it is appropriate to subject the concept of emptiness to a rigorous and critical analysis for it intends to tell us something about the nature of the world and humanity, and this claim should be fairly weighed and assessed as philosophers have done with other religious claims. But we can only do this with emptiness or, for that matter, any other religious concept, once we have clearly established its meaning and its place in the religious system. To criticize before this explication has been done is at best premature, and at worst a wilful distortion of what a religion is about. It does little good to construct a devastating refutation of a position that no-one actually holds.

So where does the history of religions bring us? By focusing on parallels and analogies, the history of religions is trying to illuminate an important component of human life. Religion has been the repository of human values, hopes and aspirations for most of history. Only most recently have shapers of culture attempted to define what it means to be human independent of traditional religious reference points. The jury is still out as to whether that secular enterprise can be successfully accomplished. However one feels about that attempt, understanding religion is crucial to knowing what humanity has been.

At the very least, the study of religion in this broad way can shed light on human culture and the human mind. The religions of human beings have been diverse as human beings themselves are. Yet the diversity of human culture and human history points beyond itself to our common humanity which we share along with the diversity. Likewise the diversity of religions may point beyond itself to some common ground or reference point. If this is true, then it may be that the patterns discovered by the history of religions tell us not only about human history but perhaps reveal the very nature of reality itself.

The discipline of the history of religions provides several things for the study of the perennial philosophy:

1. Concrete support for a primordial tradition by studying religion from the point of view of finding parallels and similarities which may be thought of as the 'archetypes' of religion.

2. Illumination of difficult phenomena by placing them in a historical context and framework which may suggest that certain features of religion are more similar than their surface differences would suggest.

3. Clarification of the multi-dimensionality of religion. While Schuon, Smith and Nasr have all been deeply sensitive to religion as lived in traditional societies, those who hold to the perennial philosophy have

sometimes been criticized for appearing to reduce religion to doctrines and theology. But it is not simply in doctrine that convergences appear. The data of the history of religions can show convergences and analogies in practices, rituals and social outlooks as well.

Now, if the perennialists should take the history of religions seriously, the historian of religion might well ask why he or she should take seriously the concept of a perennial philosophy or a primordial tradition. The key to answering that question lies in the fact that both the primordial tradition and the history of religions must finally be concerned with the question of the truth of religions.

The primordial tradition offers the history of religions a unifying perspective that can take us beyond the mere collection of data to applying it to the world in which we live. The perennial philosophy is not merely a particular theory about the phenomenon of religion but is, at least in principle, as all-encompassing a view as Marxism or Freudianism; and perennialists would say even more encompassing since these latter two exclude the transcendent from their consideration.

It is in the nature of religion to make claims about the nature of reality and the correct way to live in relation to that reality. It is also the case that different religions say very different things that are incompatible with one another if read without any further organizing principles. It follows, then, that one of the following possibilities should hold: (a) one or a particular subset of the religions is true and the others are false; (b) all of them are false; (c) they are all true in some sense, though a body of principles is needed in order to reconcile apparent contradiction.

The first option is the one chosen by most of the world's believers who affirm the unconditioned truth of their own tradition either in ignorance of or in the face of other competing claims. One may, as a believer, wish to affirm the truth of one's own tradition, but since each of the many traditions makes the same claim, it is difficult to sort them out. And this approach ignores the similarities among religions. For example, a Christian monotheist must give some recognition that there are other monotheistic religions, and these, obviously, cannot be entirely in error.

The second option is, of course, a very widespread one, particularly in the academic world that holds that the very diversity of religions suggests that, in matters of truth claims, they cancel each other out.

None of them is true in any significant sense of the word, whatever their social and psychological value may be for human history and culture.

But this cannot be fully satisfactory either, for it fails to account for both the longevity and power of something that is considered at heart illusory. What is it that we know that the long history of religious people did not know, that renders religion false or improbable? Indeed, it might be argued that contemporary epistemology has narrowed the range of the knowable to the empirical and the scientifically verifiable, that in things beyond the world, we know (or are at least willing to affirm) less and less about the area of human life to which religion is most directly relevant. In other words, we do not know what they knew or at least we are not in a position to evaluate it.

If these considerations hold, then the third possibility — that all religions are true — must at least be a claim to be taken seriously. The question then is, what principles enable us to sort out the truth from apparent contradiction?

Conclusion

It is a cliché, but a true one, that the world is growing smaller and more interconnected. Religions that a century or two ago developed in some isolation from one another now have been thrust against one another with inevitable conflict and misunderstanding. New ideologies and worldviews have arisen to challenge traditional outlooks. It is clear we need all the tools of understanding that we can muster. We must find guideposts to help us in a religiously diverse world. The discipline of the history of religions can play an important role by bringing correct understanding of a religion to replace prejudice and misinformation.

Certainly one of the most common terms to be used to facilitate the encounter of religions is 'dialogue'.[19] Dialogue is more than just interesting interchange of opinions. If the dialogue is to be worthwhile, each participating religion seeks to understand others and seeks to help others understand it. Inevitably each religion will help clarify the others, either by suggesting similarities or by heightening and sharpening the contrast.

The history of religions has the potential of being able to help religions engage in a creative dialogue by clarifying these areas of similarity and difference. The history of religions is not in itself religious; it is a scholarly discipline which can be of use to those within specific religious traditions, just as in the same way the study of political science is non-partisan but may be used by Democrats, Republicans, Socialists, etc., to better understand what they are about.

If the dialogue is to continue to be of value, it becomes a dialectical procedure in which common ground for agreement is being ever widened even while distinctiveness is maintained. The dialogue finds these points of overlap and builds on them. Would it be implausible to suggest that the dialogue of religions, if carried out in a meaningful way, might well tend toward something like a perennialist position?

It has been suggested that religions, considered as human constructs, are fingers pointing to the moon. In one sense, no religion is completely adequate because human language is inadequate to ultimacy. Yet in another sense, every religion is completely adequate, if, performing as the finger, it redirects our gaze from the impermanent and transient world to that which is beyond it. There can be many fingers by many people in many different conditions and situations pointing at the same moon.

The Buddhist mythology says that the god Indra has a net, at each node of which is a jewel. Each of these jewels, while having its distinct place, nevertheless perfectly reflects all the other jewels. This means that one can find in any one religion the insights about the nature of reality that is to be found in any other religion. Inevitably there will be different emphases, depending upon cultural and historical variables which it is the business of the history of religions to explicate.[20]

The primordial tradition is often thought to be reminiscent of the Vedantic 'one truth under many names'. But another dimension of the religious plurality of India is sometimes overlooked. Not only in theory are there many discrete ways to the truth, but in practice there is also a vast interlocking mythology to which the worshippers of Vishnu, Shiva and the Shakti can relate. It may be a promising future that sees not just the evolution of a world theology, as Wilfred Cantwell Smith suggests, but also a world mythology, an interlocking set of images, heroes and heroines, historical and non-historic events, to which we in our common humanity can all relate as well.

I also see a negative scenario, where the dialogues of religions cancel each other out, and the world sinks into secular ennui. But the history of religions offers us hope, for it seems that the spirit, like nature, abhors a vacuum. Buddhism, Christianity and Islam arose in cultures where religious diversity had seemed to provoke in many an indifferent shrug and a 'who's to say' attitude. Perhaps now, something will emerge to address our time in the same compelling way these religions did in theirs, restating the eternal truths in a way we find meaningful.

Notes

1. Huston Smith, 'Is There a Perennial Philosophy?' from *Journal of American Academy of Religion*, Vol.LV, 3, Fall 1987, pp.553-66. While this term is virtually synonymous with what is often called 'the perennial philosophy', I shall use 'primordial tradition' in this paper. Professor Smith uses it in his book *Forgotten Truth* as a subtitle, and he has elsewhere pointed out that while the term 'perennial philosophy' stresses the recurrent and universal nature of this system of thought, the term 'primordial tradition' emphasizes a depth dimension, implying that this outlook serves as fundamental ground from which all religions spring and in which they are rooted. Thus 'primordial tradition' encompasses both temporal and spatial metaphors. 'Primordial tradition' may also be preferable since 'philosophy' has come to have a narrow sense of doctrine and belief usually in a very rationalistic mode, and I would argue we can find these perennial and primordial patterns in rituals, artistic forms and social structures as well as in belief systems.

2. Portions of this paper were given as a speech, 'What it Means to be a Historian of Religion', in December 1986 at the University of Northern Iowa, as part of a public forum series, 'What is Religion?'

3. Huston Smith, *op.cit*, p.554.

4. *Ibid*, pp.560-61.

5. This section is drawn particularly from *The History of Religions in America* by Joseph Kitagawa, Eliade & Kitagawa, 1959, pp.1-30.

6. Ninian Smart, *Worldviews*, Chas Scribner's Sons, New York, 1983, pp.17-27.

7. Wilfred Cantwell Smith, *Toward a World Theology*, Westminster Press, Philadelphia, 1981, p.84.

8. René Guénon, *The Symbolism of the Cross*, trans. Angus MacNab, Luzac & Co., London, 1958.

9. Wendy O'Flaherty, trans., *The Rig Veda: An Anthology*, Penguin Books, New York, 1981, 1.160.

10. *Ibid*, 5.85.

11. *Ibid*, 1.32.

12. John B. Noss, *Man's Religions*, Macmillan & Co., New York, 6th edn, 1980, p.37.

13. H. Frankfort, H.A.Frankfort, John Wilson & T. Jacobsen, *Before Philosophy*, Pelican Books, Middlesex UK, 1949, pp.150-7.

14. Scott Littleton, *The New Comparative Mythology: An Anthropological Assessment of the Theories of Georges Dumézil*, University of California Press, Berkeley, 1973, pp.1-19.

15. Mircea Eliade & Joseph Kitagawa, *The History of Religions*, University of Chicago Press, Chicago, 1959, pp.59-66.

16. Ninian Smart, *op.cit*, pp.7-8.

17. I held in my review of *Forgotten Truth*, in *Religious Studies Review* October 1985, that emptiness and anatman appeared to be a significant exception to the pattern found in the primordial tradition, particularly the Self-Infinite component of its metaphysics discussed in chapters 3 and 4. Certainly it appears so on the surface, and at the time I had written the review I felt the exception went deeper. I have since then given this problem further reflection and this section represents some fruits of that. While I am not yet as confident that Buddhism exemplifies the primordial tradition as fully as Professor Smith has affirmed, my own study of the complexity of the issue has moved me closer to, not further from, his position.

18. A fuller discussion of the complex figure of Nāgārjuna is to be found in Jan Hai-hua, 'Nāgārjuna, One or More: A New Interpretation of Buddhist Hagiography' from *History of Religions*, Vol.10, 2, November 1970, pp.139-55.

19. A number of individuals have been very articulate in presenting that position, prominent among them the philosopher of religion, John Hick; see, for example, his *God Has Many Names*, Crossroad, 1982.

20. John Hick also used this image of Indra's net in a public address given at the third session of the Buddhist-Christian dialogue held at Purdue University, West Lafayette, Indiana in October 1986. However, the use of it in this paper is my own and does not necessarily reflect his views.

Additional bibliography

Nasr, Seyyed Hossein. *Knowledge and the Sacred*, Crossroad, New York, 1981.

Smith, Huston. *The Religions of Man*, Harper & Row, New York, 1958.

Smith, Huston. *Forgotten Truth*, Harper & Row, New York, 1976.

CHAPTER 17

Is There a Primordial Tradition in Ethics?

Henry Rosemont, Jr.

A great deal of research that has been carried on in the social and behavioral sciences for the past half century or so may be seen to fall roughly into one of two categories. The first has focused attention on the similarities between human beings as a species, and all other forms of sentient life. There are interesting exceptions, but in general we have been consistently urged to see ourselves as almost wholly other than Huichol shamans, Renaissance Venetians, Ptolemaic astronomers, Zande witches, sixteenth-century French physicians, and the authors of the Upanishads on the one hand, and on the other to acknowledge our very close kinship with the other anthropoids (we are the naked ones), and other organisms as well, from pigeons to planaria.[1]

Many interesting insights into what it is to be human have issued from both of these overarching perspectives in the social and behavioral sciences, insights anyone concerned about the human condition would be ill-advised to ignore. But these orientations, by their nature, make it more difficult to see or appreciate what might bind all human beings together, and what distinguished them collectively from all other life forms. This latter scholarly search has been muted in recent decades, but some voices have been heard, Huston Smith's pre-eminently among them.[2] From his early *Religions of Man* to his most recent essays, Huston has studied and described what links us rather than what separates us; what is highest rather than lowest in us; and what we share with our ancestors early and late, in the West or East, North or South, despite great distances of time and space.

234

To be sure, his scholarship will strike some as not 'realistic'. Everyone aware of the horrors of World War I, the Holocaust, Hiroshima and Nagasaki, gulags, My Lai, the crack-filled streets of American inner cities, and a materialism run amok, cannot but be sceptical of the Enlightenment (or Greek, or Chinese, etc.) ideal of and for humankind. 'Realism' in this sense, however, suffers from some conceptual problems of its own. In the first place, to believe that we are all of us different, isolated individuals seeking our self-interest easily becomes a self-fulfilling prophecy: if it should become a truism — even though it is false — that 'nice guys finish last', we shall eventually see to it that they do. Second, such beliefs lead all too regularly not to scepticism, which we all need, but to cynicism or nihilism; which, if *homo sapiens* is to survive, we do not need. Third, many forms of 'realism' — people are not linked, they are greedy, selfish, inconsequential in the larger scheme of things, and so forth — generate a sense of powerlessness which the powerful and their academic propagandists have been, and continue to be, anxious to reinforce.[3]

The U.S. government, for example, aided and abetted by the standard news media, has given us images of such Muslims as Muommar Qaddafi and the Ayatollah Khomeini as evil incarnate, generating strong anti-Arab (i.e. racist) sentiments in America, coupled with an antipathy to Islam. How could any decent human being be a Muslim? Well, turn to the chapter on Islam in the *Religions of Man*; tolerance, respect and a sense of hope should accompany the reading. (And similarly it is more difficult to be anti-Semitic after reading the chapter on Judaism.)

In this light, I personally consider Huston Smith to be one of the most salutary of contemporary philosophers; he is in the very best tradition of humanistic scholarship, by seeking what is ennobling. His major thesis — that there is a 'primordial tradition' in religion — has two claims at its core: (1) that all human beings are ultimately spiritual beings; and (2) that there is an ontological 'Great Chain of Being' which it is our task to apprehend as directly and fully as our ancestors did.[4]

To rehearse the many and varied arguments that Huston advances for his thesis is beyond the scope of this paper. Rather would I like to support the thesis, albeit in a somewhat roundabout way. If Huston is correct in maintaining that all human beings have a very similar religious impulse, it would surely be odd if they did not also have a similar ethical impulse. I should thus like to maintain that the several versions of moral relativism that have been current in all scholarly circles, and dominant in some, for the past few decades, may well be false. More specifically, I want to argue: (1) that there may well be an ethical commonality among human beings, physiologically and mentally constituted as we are:[5] (2) that this commonality has been obscured by the thrust and scope of modern Western moral philosophy: and (3) that we may begin to recapture that commonality by re-examining discussions of it by thinkers of the past — from the primordial tradition.

As my concrete example I will focus on the *Lun Yu*, the brief recorded conversations between Confucius and his disciples. Some of my arguments are logical and linguistic, others somewhat phenomenological. They will probably therefore convince no one, but conviction is not my goal; I shall be pleased to add a candle to the many Huston has lit to make what we see through the glass a little less dark.

It is a commonplace — perhaps too common — that Confucius and his followers were not metaphysicians. They did not ask what was real, enquire about the origins of the universe, ground knowledge, have a theory of truth, etc. (Given that mathematics — especially geometry — was developed, by the Pythagoreans, *before* Socrates in Greece but *after* Confucianism in China, we should not be surprised at the differences between classical Greek and classical Chinese philosophy.) But it is agreed on all sides that Confucius was greatly concerned about morals, and, because he discoursed on the subject, it follows that he was a moral philosopher, and that he had a morality. I want to question this perspective: did Confucius have a morality?

In common everyday parlance we regularly lump together many of the beliefs and principles of people and refer to this collectivity as a 'morality'. There is a prevailing morality in Cedar Rapids, Iowa, to which most denizens thereof subscribe more or less. And this morality is akin to, but slightly different from, the morality that dominates Manhattan's East Village, which in turn is akin to, but different from, the prevailing morality in Carmel, California.

Specifying precisely the beliefs and principles which comprise any of these or other moralities is of course a difficult, if not impossible, task. Despite the ontological postulates of most statisticians, there may well be no average Cedar Rapidian, East Villager, or Carmelite.

Moreover, moralities seem to shade imperceptibly into other sets of beliefs and principles, such as social mores, lifestyles, political ideologies and much else that does not conduce to clarity of understanding. But these difficulties notwithstanding, we do at least roughly understand what it is to 'have a morality', usually prefixing 'good' to those moralities closely consonant with our own, and 'bad' to designate those moralities we find loathsome. For many of us Martin Luther King, Jr., had a pretty good morality, while Heinrich Himmler's was paradigmatically bad, or evil.[6]

In this common, everyday use of the term 'morality', the answer to the question asked must be obvious: of course Confucius had a morality; to deny that he did would be tantamount to denying that he had standing in the human community, an extreme position which even the most hardened sinophobe or moral relativist would be reluctant to endorse.

Moreover, when we read in the *Lun Yu* the advice Confucius gives to his disciples, we do not find that advice at all morally unusual: we should not act impulsively, selfishly, or be cowards; we should keep our word, strive for the good, help others, and so forth. Even the Golden Rule appears to find paraphrased expression in the *Lun Yu*.[7]

For these reasons, then, it would seem perfectly straightforward to say that Confucius had a morality; indeed, a morality not very far removed from our own. And because he elaborated and defended his moral views, it would seem equally straightforward to say that Confucius was a moral philosopher.

But such reasons, and a large body of excellent sinological research based on those reasons notwithstanding, I believe it is misleading at best, mistaken at worst, to describe Confucius as having a morality, as being a moral philosopher. The question 'Did Confucius have a morality?' is grammatically almost precisely similar to 'Did Confucius have a birthmark?'. They are nevertheless very different sorts of questions, for the latter pertains only to Confucius and his physicality, whereas the former pertains no less to ourselves than to the Master, and is in the realm of the conceptual.

I want first to present briefly two sets of arguments — the first logical and linguistic, the second based on some characteristics of modern moral philosophy — to suggest that 'morals' and 'morality' are not particularly helpful terms to apply when studying the *Lun Yu*. Believing as I do that despite the gulf that separates Confucius from modern moral philosophers, he has a great deal to say to us, I will then quickly sketch the beginning of a Confucian alternative to modern moral philosophies, and, as a corollary, suggest that the gulf separating Confucius from modern moral philosophers does not at all strengthen the case for moral or cultural relativism, but on the contrary goes some way toward showing why and how moral relativism may be false; and that there may indeed be a primordial tradition in ethics.

The first set of arguments centers on methodological issues of translation and interpretation, and rests on the purported distinction between concepts and terms (if any) which express those concepts. Simplistically stated, the question, first raised sharply by Wittgenstein, is whether a person may be said to have a concept X if she or he has no term for X in her/his vocabulary. For a number of philosophical reasons too complex to narrate here, some people have answered this question affirmatively.[8] But it seems to me that any scholar who works with texts very distant in time, space and culture must answer the question negatively. Again, the reasons are fairly complex for full narration, but the following points should be noted.

First, one sense of 'having the concept X' is where X is the statement of a *rule* followed by the person said to have the concept. To the extent that 'knowing a language' means 'knowing the rules of a grammar', there is nothing wrong in saying that a person 'follows the rules' of the language spoken, even though the person almost surely could not state the rules for that grammar as described by a linguist. In this sense people might indeed be said to have linguistically unexpressed concepts. But it must be noted that in *this* sense of 'having the concept X', the only evidence for the possession of such concepts would lie in *behavior*, i.e. whether the person(s) in question did or did not exhibit the linguistic (syntactic) behavior conforming to the postulated rules.

A second, although related, sense of 'having the concept X' is where X is simply a predicative expression. Here anti-Wittgensteinians claim that one can surely have concepts without having terms to express them, and to argue otherwise is to be, for example, 'unfair to babies'. But we may attribute pre-linguistic awareness to babies — it would be irrational not to — awareness of pain, heat, hunger, etc., without talking of their having concepts; to be in pain is clearly distinguishable from having the concept expressed by the open English sentence '. . . is in pain'. On the basis of this distinction it can be maintained that human beings have both sensations and concepts, and that we attribute specific sensations to them either on the basis of their overt behavior or what they say, but that we attribute concepts to them only on the basis of the latter.[9]

Now, if we have warrants for claiming that concepts and terms which express them are at least methodologically if not ontologically equivalent, the warrants are of significance for all comparativists in general, and sinologists in particular. Working with texts the authors of which have long since passed to their reward, we obviously cannot ask those authors for clarification, paraphrase, or elaboration; nor, of course, can we examine their behavior. All we have are the texts themselves, a finite corpus, and therefore the only way it can be maintained that a particular concept was held by an author is to find a term which at least roughly approximates that concept in his or her text, and also to find other terms associated with it that correspond to associated terms in our own language. Thus my conclusion, which I would generalize as a methodological principle of translation and interpretation: we should not, in the target language, say of authors that they 'had the concept X', or that they had 'a theory of X', or that they 'espouse X principles', unless a fairly proximate X — and other terms necessary for the definition of X — are contained in the lexicon of the object language in which the author(s) wrote.

Of course the absence of a term, or terms, in a language to denote certain activities does not imply that the speakers of that language did not engage in those activities; finding a language which contained no lexical item corresponding to the English 'skip' would go no way toward proving that the speakers of this language did not or could not engage in that type of bipedal locomotion. But among speakers of that language, anthropologists, linguists, or philosophers would look in vain for a theoretician of skipping, because they could not possibly discover linguistically when such a theory might be being articulated.

Against this fairly abstract background I now want to become more concrete. If we wish to say of Confucius that he 'had a morality', or that he was a 'moral philosopher', or that he had a 'theory of morals', or that he 'espoused moral principles', we must find some Chinese graph in the *Lun Yu* to assign a meaning to 'morals' or 'morality'. I think that upon reflection it will be clear that no such Chinese graph can be found. The issue is by no means 'just a matter of semantics', but is rather both more general and more exact. For example suppose we follow D.C. Lau in his often sensitive rendering of the *Lun Yu*[10] and translate *i* as 'morals'. Immediately we are faced with a difficulty, because Lau himself does not consistently render *i* as 'morals' or 'morality'; about 40 percent of the time it is rendered as 'right' or as 'duty', which can only muddy the moral waters, because 'what is right to do' is not synonymous with 'what it is morally right to do', and all of us have duties which are not moral duties, no matter what our moral allegiance.

But let us look closer. The term 'i' will immediately be associated in the *Lun Yu* with *jen, chih, li, xin, shu, xiao* and so on, just as in the *Bhagavad-Gita* 'Dharma' is associated with *moksha, karma, avidya, Brahman, maya, guna*, etc. 'Morals', on the other hand, we immediately associate with other English terms like 'freedom', 'rights', 'autonomy', 'individual', 'choice', 'rationality', 'dilemma', 'ought', 'subjective', and all the other terms which comprise the concept-cluster of contemporary Western moral theorizing.

Clearly the authors of the *Lun Yu*, and of the *Bhagavad-Gita*, and of contemporary Western moral writings, are all of them concerned with describing, analyzing and evaluating (some of) the conduct of human lives. But 'morals' is *our* blanket term (concept) for these efforts, and it is intimately associated with all of the other English terms (concepts) adumbrated above. That is to say, a full definition of 'morals' must include most, if not all of these other English terms. Consequently it cannot be that we can simply seek a term corresponding to 'morals' or 'morality' in other languages, because the sphere of modern Western moral philosophy is designated only very roughly by the term itself; a clear delimitation requires all of the English terms just given, plus some others. And if we cannot (do not) talk about moral issues without using terms like 'choice', 'freedom', 'rationality', 'subjective', 'autonomy', 'rights', 'individual' and so forth, and if none of these terms occurs in the language of the *Lun Yu*, then it follows that Confucius could not have a morality, or be a moral philosopher in our modern sense, and we will be guaranteed to miss what he might have to tell us about human conduct, and what it is to be a human being, if we insist upon imposing on the *Lun Yu* the concept-cluster constitutive of our modern moral discourse. We should not, in other words, read the *Lun Yu* asking 'to what extent does this text suggest answers to vexing moral problems?'. Rather might we ask, 'to what extent does this text suggest very different philosophical questions?'.

I should like now to turn to a second set of arguments, by

suggesting some significant commonalities among seemingly divergent Western moral philosophies, and an attendant sharp contrast with the views of Confucius.

It is not too grand a generalization, I believe, to say that ever since the time of Hobbes, Western philosophy — not alone moral philosophy — has increasingly abstracted a purely cognizing activity away from concrete persons, and insisted that this use of logical reasoning in a more or less disembodied 'mind' is the choosing, autonomous essence of individuals, which is philosophically more foundational than actual persons; the latter being only contingently who they are, and therefore of no great philosophical significance.

Nowhere is this view of human beings as purely rational agents more obvious than in modern moral philosophy, ranging from the deontological views of Kant, through Bentham's and Mill's utilitarianism to Rawls's more recent rights-oriented moral and political theory, which I will take as typical of modern moral philosophy.[11] All of these moral philosophies are, in the first instance, value-free. For Kant, Mill and Rawls, and for almost all other modern moral philosophers, the questions of what kind of life you should lead, what goals are good and which are bad, for example, do not fall within the compass of moral philosophy. On the contrary, for these philosophers moral philosophy is solely concerned with the determination of a moral theory, such that once in possession thereof, the purely rational autonomous agent will make the correct choices in matters deemed of great significance to others and to society (these choices are called 'moral choices'); with the only proviso that the purely rational agent have the 'good will' to effect the choice he or she has made.

To amplify these points, first, moral philosophy is value-free in the following way. If you address the writings of Kant asking whether you should pursue a career in politics or scholarship; if you ask how you should raise your children, be a friend, serve your community; if you should ask about aesthetic pleasures; if you should ask these or any other questions about personal goals in life, Kant is silent. All such matters have to do with hypothetical imperatives, which are not at all his concern. Rather is he concerned with the categorical imperative, that which comes into play only when a major choice affecting others or society (called a 'moral choice') comes to hand; and to make the correct choice involves only the purely rational autonomous agent, who will, after deliberation, instantiate her or his choice, i.e. the universalizable maxim, by an act of good will.

Similarly for Mill, who is explicit in denying that the good can be ascertained in general. Indeed, his construal of liberalism rests on the supposed fact that the good *cannot* be ascertained to the agreement of all, which is what we mean by the *private* sphere of life.[12] Each of us pursues our own definition of the good, and we pause in that pursuit only when a major choice affecting others or society (called a 'moral choice') comes to hand; and to make the correct choice the purely rational agent need only calculate the greatest happiness for the greatest number, instantiate the choice, and then resume the pursuit of her or his individually defined goal of the good. The major thrust of *On Liberty* rests on Mill's efforts to protect the private lives of individuals, the pursuit of autonomously chosen individual goals, from the pressures of the public society.[13]

In being value-free, John Rawls's *A Theory of Justice* is even more explicit: one of the veils of ignorance that must obscure our vision in the original position is that we *not* know what our own goals will be, that we *not* know our own conception of the good. *Only* in this way, Rawls is insistent, can we come to agree on the principles of justice and equality; only, that is, if our deliberations are those of purely rational autonomous agents.[14]

Put another way, neither the moral, nor the liberal, nor the just societies of Kant, Mill or Rawls can conceptually rest on a majority vote; unanimity is necessary. But there can be, according to these thinkers, no unanimity where values are concerned, so it should not be surprising that values cannot be entered into the deliberations about the moral, liberal, or just society. Only pure reason can show us why we must give allegiance — logical allegiance — to the kingdom of ends principle, or the greatest happiness principle, or the justice, equality and difference principles.

Now I have altogether obliterated the many and real differences that distinguish the deontological, consequentialist, and rights-based moral theories that have been developed over the past three centuries, and at least a few philosophers who might be considered moral theorists, like Kierkegaard and Nietzsche, I have not considered at all. Nor have I mentioned recent efforts to reintroduce virtue-based moral theories into contemporary ethical discourse.[15] But all of the theories I have mentioned do have the properties I have ascribed to them, and they are just the kinds of theories that come immediately to mind when discussing modern moral philosophy.

From these considerations two syllogisms suggest themselves: (1) all modern moral theories are value free, the *Lun Yu* is value-laden, therefore nothing resembling a modern moral theory will be found in the *Lun Yu*; (2) modern moral philosophers articulate theories of abstract principles grounded in pure reason, and they elaborate and defend those theories in their writings; no such theories are articulated, elaborated, or defended in the *Lun Yu*; therefore Confucius bears little, if any, resemblance to modern moral philosophers.

Now I think these arguments show how and why it is highly misleading to talk about the Master's morality, or his moral philosophy, but to strengthen the case I would like to note a further characteristic shared by modern moral philosophers that is not to be found in the *Lun Yu*; namely, the sharp distinction that is drawn between the moral and the non-moral realms of life. My words may be deceptive here, because if you read Kant, Mill or Rawls closely, you will find that none of them — or anyone else — ever provides clear criteria for distinguishing moral from non-moral choices in our lives. Rather do they simply presuppose — as we all do, most of the time — that everyone simply knows when a moral issue is at hand and when one is not. But imagine attempting to explain, in advance, to someone from a very different culture, like Confucius, which human actions are to receive moral praise or blame, and which human actions should not be evaluated in those terms.

To assist your imagination, consider the following. First, it is entirely possible on Kantian, Millian or Rawlsian grounds to be obtuse, uncaring, insensitive, clumsy, even disgusting in much of our behavior, and yet escape moral censure. If, when the appropriate moments arrive, moments which we must somehow intuit as those where a moral choice must be forthcoming, we take account of the situation, invoke our favorite theory, turn on our moral computer for a decision procedure, and then act on the decision, we will all of us be moral agents, no matter how boorish, aimless, repulsive, or empty our lives may otherwise be. How might we explain this to the shade of Confucius? Think of *i* as 'morals' again: are there any passages in the *Lun Yu* which would suggest there are realms of *i* and non-*i* human conduct? Are there any cases in which we are not required to follow the *dao*? Implement the *li*? Strive for *jen*?

These questions are not rhetorical. If our imaginations are beginning to fail us about how to explain the distinction between the moral and the non-moral realms, the problem is not with our imaginations but with our absorption in the concept-cluster of modern Western moral theory, for I would maintain that *we do not* have clear criteria for distinguishing the moral from the non-moral choices we ostensibly make.

Consider the following example. I am tired after a long week of teaching, and so is my wife. I wish to have a sandwich and go to bed early, she would like to go to a restaurant for dinner. No moral theorist can help me here, because according to them, supposedly no moral issue is at stake; it is all a private matter between consenting individuals with autonomously chosen goals. If I elect to stay at home, I may well be acting selfishly, and being insensitive to my wife's needs; but technically I will incur no *moral* blame.

Matters, however, are even worse when we come from the other side: as I deliberate about whether to go out or not, I realize, as anyone must today, that tens of thousands of my fellow Americans are homeless and hungry, and that the same may be said for many more millions of people around the world. Now I must decide whether to spend $60 or so on feeding my wife and myself an elegant meal, or give $50 to Oxfam or a similar group, to feed many more, and use the remaining $10 to buy some steaks and salad greens to eat at home. Having put the question this way, there is only one answer possible, however much Kant, Mill or Rawls might try to object. But now I must ask the question again: why spend $10 on ourselves, when we could purchase enough to get by on for $2, and give the remaining $8 to Oxfam? But if I ask these questions constantly, I will quickly become destitute, I will almost surely go mad, and, until I am hospitalized, will live a life marked by joylessness, guilt, a total lack of spontaneity, with precious little genuine human intercourse. Thus the force of the question: how distinguish the moral from the non-moral realms of life?

This, then, all too quickly, is my second line of argumentation against describing Confucius as having a morality, as being a moral philosopher, and, simultaneously, against value-free, purely rational modern moral theories to be invoked at we-know-not-when-but-appropriate times by freely-choosing, autonomous moral agents. This modern philosophical stereotype of a disembodied, logically calculating mind is, I believe, far removed from what we feel and think human beings to be. It has also generated problems that appear incapable of solution within its parameters, and it is therefore becoming increasingly difficult for moral and political philosophers embodying this stereotype to have much purchase even on ourselves, not to mention the 3½ billion people who do not live as inheritors of the modern Western moral tradition.[16]

To be sure, it may appear that I have not given this tradition its due. To take only one small example, what is civil and sensitive behavior on my part may be rude and uncaring to you, and it was surely a human step forward when tolerance for diversity of manners and behavior accompanied the rise of the bourgeoisie in late seventeenth-century Holland. I, of course, agree; but even speaking as a philosopher within the modern Western moral tradition it can be maintained that the merits of moral theories requiring great doses of tolerance can be greatly overstated. If you eschew any real judgements about how I live my life when I am not making moral choices — i.e. 98 percent of the time — you are depriving yourself of judgements of your own possibilities; when we adapt an altogether non-judgemental stance about the ostensibly private (non-moral) conduct of others, we run a serious risk of living an aimless life. If *de gustibus non disputandum* is literally true, where could we possibly look for human guidelines to establish human goals worth striving for?[17]

There is an even more basic question to ask of modern moral philosophy along these lines, namely if a person is indeed obtuse, insensitive, boorish, etc., how or why can we have any confidence that she or he will even perceive correctly those exceptional circumstances supposedly calling for moral choice when they arise? Any set of circumstances can be seen in a variety of ways; can a highly insensitive person perceive accurately what the categorical imperative requires, or what will truly bring the greatest happiness to the greatest number, or what it means to genuinely respect the rights of others?[18]

These questions, I submit, cannot be answered without explicitly considering values, seeing human beings as value carriers, and seeing them as value carriers all of the time; which brings me, finally, to Confucius.

Describing the lexicon of Confucius and his followers — their concept-cluster — is beyond the scope of the present paper, but this much should be said: the Chinese philosophical terms focus attention on qualities of human beings, as a natural species, and on the kinds of persons who exemplify (or do not exemplify) these qualities to a high degree. Where we would speak of choice, they speak of resolve; where we invoke abstract principles, they invoke concrete human relations, and attitudes towards those relations. Moreover, if the early Confucian writings are to be interpreted consistently, they must be read as insisting on the *altogether* social nature of human life, for the qualities of persons, the kinds of person they are, and the knowledge and attitudes they have are not exhibited in actions, but only in *inter*actions; human interactions. While reflection and solitude are necessary ingredients of our human lives, we are never alone. And our cognitive and affective qualities can never be wholly divorced.

Against this background, let me attempt to sketch briefly the early Confucian view of what it is to be a human being.[19] If I could ask the shade of Confucius 'who am I?', his reply, I believe, would run roughly as follows: given that you are Henry Rosemont, Jr., you are obviously the son of Henry, Sr. and Sally Rosemont. You are thus first, foremost, and most basically a *son*; you stand in a relationship to your parents that began at birth, has had a profound influence on your later development, has had a profound effect on their later lives as well, and it is a relationship that is diminished only in part at their death.

Of course, now I am many other things besides a son. I am husband to my wife, father of our children, grandfather to their children; I am a brother, my friend's friend, my neighbor's neighbor; I am teacher of my students, student of my teachers; and colleague of my colleagues.

Now, all of this is obvious, but note how different it is from focusing on me as an autonomous, freely-choosing individual. For Confucius there does not seem to be any 'me' in isolation, to be considered abstractly: I am the totality of roles I live in relation to specific others; unless there are at least two human beings, there can be no human beings. By using the term 'roles' here I do not wish to imply that the *Lun Yu* is the earliest treatise in sociology. But if we read closely and sympathetically, we can see a clear emphasis on the inter-relatedness of what I am calling 'roles'; that is to say, the text makes us cognizant of the fact that the relations in which I stand to some people affect directly the relations in which I stand with others, to the extent that it would be misleading to say that I 'play' or 'perform' these roles; on the contrary, for Confucius I *am* my roles. Taken collectively, they weave, for each of us, a unique pattern of personal identity, such that if some of my roles change, others will of necessity change also, literally making me a different person.

Marriage, in a quite literal sense, makes one a different person; so does divorce; so does parenthood. Further, my role as father is not merely one-one with my daughters. In the first place, it has a significant bearing on my role as husband, just as the role of mother bears significantly on my wife's role as wife. Second, I am 'Samantha's father' not only to Samantha, but to her friends, her teachers, someday her husband, and her husband's parents as well. And Samantha's role as sister is determined in part by my role as father.

Going beyond the family, if I should become a widower, both my male and my female friends would see me, respond to me, interact with me, somewhat differently than they do now. A bachelor friend of mine, for instance, might invite me as a widower to accompany him on a three-month summer cruise, but would not so invite me so long as I was a husband.

It is in this epistemologically and ethically extended meaning of the term 'roles' that the early Confucians would insist that I do not play or perform, but am and become the roles I live in consonance with others, so that when all the roles have been specified, and their interconnections made manifest, then I have been specified fully as a unique person, with few discernible loose threads with which to piece together a free, autonomous, choosing self which acts as a purely rational moral agent.

None of this, however, is to suggest a rigidly conformist social life, devoid of spontaneity, for obviously there are many ways to be a good parent, a good teacher, a good friend. There is a great deal of room for creative and imaginative activities within the roles that govern our lives, just as there is a great deal of room for creative and imaginative moves within the rules that govern chess.

Moreover, seen in this socially contextualized way, it should become clearer that in an important sense I do not alone achieve my own identity, am not solely responsible for becoming who I am. Of course, a great deal of personal effort is required to become a good person. But nevertheless, much of who and what I am is determined by the others with whom I interact, just as my efforts determine in part who and what they are at the same time. Personhood, identity, in this sense is basically conferred on us, just as we basically contribute to conferring it on others. Again, the point is obvious, but the Confucian perspective requires us to state it in another tone of voice: my life as a teacher can only be made significant by my students, my life as a lover by my lover, as a friend by my friends, as a scholar only by my fellow scholars.

All of the specific human relations of which we are a part, in which we interact with the dead as well as with the living, will be mediated by the *li*; i.e. the courtesy, customs and traditions we have shared and continue to share as our inextricably linked histories unfold; and by fulfilling the obligations defined by these relationships we are, for the early Confucians, following the human Way. It is a comprehensive 'Way'. Quickly sketched, by the manner in which we interact with others our lives will clearly have an ethical dimension infusing *all*, not just some, of our conduct; no distinction to be drawn here between the moral and the non-moral realms. By the ways in which this ethical interpersonal conduct is effected, with reciprocity, civility, grace, respect and affection, and governed by custom, ritual and tradition, our lives will also have a satisfying aesthetic dimension for ourselves and for others. And by specifically meeting our defining traditional obligations to our elders and ancestors on the one hand, and to our contemporaries and descendants on the other (i.e. both our benefactors and our beneficiaries), Confucius offers an uncommon, but nevertheless spiritually authentic form of transcendence, a human capacity to go beyond the specific spatio-temporal circumstances in which we exist, giving our personhood the sense of humanity shared in common, and thereby a sense of strong continuity with what has gone before and what will come later. There being no question raised in the *Lun Yu* about the meaning *of* life, we may nevertheless see that the view of what it is to be a human being which emerges from the text provides for everyone to find meaning *in* life.[20]

Of course, even if my very large claim can be sustained, a number of philosophical questions would remain. Is it possible to have an ethical and/or socio-political *theory* that did not employ the concepts of autonomous individuals, or choices, or freedom, or rights, and did not invoke abstract logical principles? Could there be such a theory, grounded in a view of human nature as *essentially* involving interpersonal relations, a theory that accorded both with our own moral sentiments, and with the views and sentiments of those 3½ billion human beings who do not live in the Western industrial democracies? If there were such a theory, could it conceivably be conflict-free?

I do not know the answers to these questions, but do know that if reading the *Lun Yu* can assist us, as scholar-sinologists, as philosophers, and as human beings, to see more clearly the presuppositions and shortcomings of the concept-cluster embedded in modern moral theories, then I will admit, be pleased to admit, that Confucius did indeed have a morality, and more than that: I would even suggest that he was one of the greatest moral philosophers of all time. If this be granted, and remembered that Confucius is separated from us by half a world and two and a half millennia, we should be willing to entertain the possibility that there is a primordial tradition in ethics; a possibility I am confident Huston Smith would entertain seriously.

Notes

1. I am delighted to have been invited by Professor Sharma to contribute to this *Festschrift* for a revered and beloved friend. Ideally, perhaps, my contribution should focus on a specific theme or issue in Huston's writings. But if there is one invitation he extends to all of us in those writings, it is to 'go beyond . . .'. Moreover, he has regularly accorded me the honor of citing my work in his writings, and I know that what follows in this paper, however imperfectly put forward, complements his own views, and deals with topics that interest him deeply. My opening paragraph is taken from my 'Against Relativism' in Gerald Larson & Eliot Deutsch, eds., *Interpreting Across Boundaries*, Princeton, 1987. Portions of this paper were read at the Association of Asian Studies Annual Meeting, San Francisco, March 1987. I am grateful to Bao Zhiming, David Nivison, David Keightley and Philip Ivanhoe for their comments and encouragement. My generalizations about Huston's scholarly range and purposes are based on the following: *The Religions of Man*, New York, 1958; *Forgotten Truth*, New York, 1976; *Beyond the Post-Modern Mind*, New York, 1982; and a number of his articles, including 'Man's Western Way: an essay on reason and the given', 'Transcendence in Traditional China', 'Tao Now: An Ecological Testament', 'Western & Comparative Perspectives on Truth', 'The Crisis in Philosophy', 'Is There a Perennial Philosophy?', his Introduction to the Folkways album on the Music of Tibet, and on many and enjoyable private conversations.
2. Equally, Noam Chomsky. For fuller discussions and references, see my 'Against Relativism', *op.cit.*
3. Well brought out by Noam Chomsky, *The Culture of Terrorism*, Boston, 1986.
4. See especially *Forgotten Truth.*

5. For fuller argumentation, see 'Against Relativism', *op.cit.*
6. For more on 'having a morality', see Jonathan Bennett, 'The Conscience of Huckleberry Finn' from *Vice & Virtue in Everyday Life*, ed. Christina Hoff Summers, San Diego, 1985.
7. *Lun Yu*, 15:23.
8. For fuller discussion and citations, see my 'Kierkegaard & Confucius: On Finding the Way' from *Philosophy East & West*, July 1985; and 'Against Relativism', *op.cit.*
9. *Ibid.*
10. *The Analects of Confucius*, Harmondsworth, 1974.
11. Immanuel Kant, *Groundwork of the Metaphysics of Morals*, New York, 1964; J.S. Mill, *Utilitarianism*, New York, 1957; John Rawls, *A Theory of Justice*, Cambridge, 1970.
12. Mill, *On Liberty*, New York, 1956, esp. pp.67ff.
13. *Ibid.*
14. *A Theory of Justice, op.cit*, esp. pp.12-17.
15. Especially Alastair MacIntyre. See his *After Virtue*, Notre Dame, 1981; and *Whose Justice? Which Rationality?*, Notre Dame, 1987.
16. See 'Kierkegaard & Confucius: On Finding the Way', *loc.cit.*
17. Joel Kupperman has argued this point well. See his 'The Place of Character in Ethics', unpublished manuscript.
18. Again, the point is Kupperman's, *op.cit.*
19. Portions of the following argument are taken from my 'Why Take Rights Seriously? A Confucian Critique' from *Human Rights and the World's Religions*, ed. Leroy Rouner, Notre Dame, 1988.
20. For a somewhat different account of the secular and the sacred in ancient China than the one adumbrated above, see Huston's 'Transcendence in Traditional China' from *Religious Studies* Vol.2, 1965.

CHAPTER 18

The Question of Buddhism's Influence on Christianity Re-opened

Delwin Byron Schneider

We all relate our thinking more or less consciously to that of teachers and predecessors. It was Bernard of Chartres in the twelfth century who is credited with first using the phrase 'shoulders of giants'. He observes that we are like dwarfs seated on the shoulders of giants; we may see more things than the ancients saw, but this is due neither to the sharpness of our intellect nor to the greatness of our learning ability, but because we are raised and borne aloft on those who have gone before us. For many years, since my return from graduate studies in Tokyo, I have been challenged by the thought of Huston Smith. His creative imagination and always eloquent statements, first in *Religions of Man* and then, for me, *Forgotten Truth — The Primordial Tradition*, opened up new possibilities of understanding and raised new questions. Seldom is there anything new under the sun, as the Book of Ecclesiastes suggests, but once in a while the human spirit brings forth a glimpse of something genuinely new. This new glimpse that Huston Smith gave to me was that of holding truth with conviction while remaining open to revision or even new truth. He challenged my understanding of human religiousness and spirituality even when these concerns were not specifically mentioned. The journey he has taken is the journey we are all compelled to take, beginning with our own deeply held tradition, not to stop there but to pass over to another perspective, and then to come back to our own to enrich it with new insights.

251

For scholars and researchers who seek dialogue and reconciliation of the world religions, the eye is always open for parallels among them. For many Westerners, Buddhism and Christianity seemed in the past like a world or even a universe apart. In spite of the fact that the religion named after Gautama Siddhārtha is one of India's and the world's most profound contributions to religious history, the terms 'Buddhist' and 'Christian' did not suggest parallels but disharmony and conflicting viewpoints, and centuries of separation due to ignorance and neglect on the part of each. Today, thanks to the scholarship of the last one-hundred years, Buddhism and Christianity are often compared, and when comparisons are made among them they appear in great number. There are parallel ideas of ethics, of life styles and disciplines, ideas that manifest striking similarities in secondary characteristics, even though in the primary ones they may not appear to be so parallel.[1] These similar traits, appearing in two different areas of the world, in time removed by 600 years, are enough to make a researcher pause and to probe more deeply.

The problem of similarities and, therefore, of derivation, as Richard Garbe saw already in the early part of this century, is a sensitive issue because it is often treated as if its solution would somehow affect the value of Christianity and Buddhism as religions.[2] The whole question of similarity and influence is without any great significance for the character or 'essential truth' of either religion. Neither Buddhism nor Christianity has anything to gain or lose from the answer to the question of their connections. No religion springs *de novo* and fully developed from a purely original source. The whole matter is without religious significance, although as we shall see (in the case of Johannine thought) it may have theological implications and be of value for the history of religious literature.

Scholars have noted that the *Dhammapada* ('Verses on Dharma'), the best loved book of the Theravada tradition, is strikingly similar to the Sermon on the Mount, a favorite text of Christians.[3] The moral teachings of both messages bear a remarkable resemblance to one another. The historian of Indian historians, K.A. Nilakanta Sastri, in *Cultural Expansion of India*, makes clear that in Indian minds at least the message of Jesus as found in the Gospels has been influenced in numerous passages by Buddhist (and therefore Indian) sources.[4] He agrees with Sarvepalli Radhakrishnan, India's most noted philosopher-historian, that the debt when comparisons are made must lie on the side of Christianity. Convinced that Jesus came under Indian influence, Radhakrishnan says that to love one's enemies, to turn the other cheek, to do good to them who hate, to give all to him who asks, which are the teachings of Jesus, 'are precepts not only taught but practised in their extreme rigour by the Buddha in his many lives, according to the *Jātakas*.'[5] Many Indologists are quite confident that the Christian message drew inspiration from India, either directly or indirectly, and the avenue of transmission by which this took place was through an oral tradition by way of Iran.

Other scholars have been fascinated by the similarities in the life-styles of both Gautama the Buddha and Jesus the Christ, and found that at approximately the same age both Gautama and Jesus left their fathers' house, both exchanged 'home for homelessness', both spent time in solitude, and both wrestled against the temptations of the devil and Māra in defense of their ministries.[6] Then, as teachers, both gathered around themselves bhikṣu and disciples who, after their death, carried on their Dharma and Gospel that eventually spread throughout the world. Furthermore, one has only to look to the second of the 'Baskets' of the Buddhist Scriptures, the Sutta-piṭaka, as J. Duncan M. Derrett suggests, to find there the many expressions and moral injunctions that are strikingly close in meaning to the sayings of Jesus and the Gospel message.[7] Committed to writing during the first century BCE in Ceylon after four centuries of oral transmission, the Sutta-piṭaka contains for the Buddhist world some of the finest literary pieces in Buddhist literature. Divided into five collections, the fifth collection contains the *Dhammapada*, 423 verses in twenty-six chapters, that embodies better than any other piece of literature the spirit of the Buddha's teachings. And when compared to the Sermon on the Mount, one cannot read the Sermon without feeling that it is an abridged version of parts of the *Dhammapada*.

A scholar of both Mahāyāna Buddhism and New Testament thought, J. Edgar Bruns, turns our attention from the message of Jesus to the Gospel of John and suggests that Johannine thought is structurally closer to that of Nāgārjuna's Mādhyamika Buddhism than it is to either the Judaic or Hellenistic categories of thought.[8] He makes the case that John's theology of God as experienced through love ('horizontal theology') is best understood if compared with the Buddhist experience of *Prajñā* (perfect wisdom) through *Śūnyatā* (emptiness). In Bruns' genuinely new approach, the incarnation of Jesus is not only the gracious entry of God in history from his abode beyond ('vertical Christology') — using the image of heavenly Father who intervenes in human history from above, the traditional or Synoptic Gospel approach — but in the non-traditional approach the incarnation is seen as the self-manifestation of God's operative presence through love in the whole of human history.

Thus it appears to Bruns that John's thought shows some structural affinity to Mahāyāna Buddhism. The influence of Indian philosophy on the intellectual milieu of the Mediterranean world in the first century of the Common Era, he suggests, was greater than anyone could have thought of even a hundred years ago. John's Gospel is the masterpiece of that world, and it was developed in relation to Gnostic and Buddhist thought. What is suggested here is that the evangelist was aware of Mahāyāna Buddhist doctrine through his disciples, and found the Buddhist way of picturing the Absolute and the human response to it most suitable for the articulation of his own religious faith and experience. As noted earlier, this derivation does not effect the essential truth of Christianity, but it does have theological implications. Gregory Baum observes that if a Buddhist understanding of God has helped to shape the Johannine proclamation of the Gospel, then modern-day Christians will be encouraged in their present effort to understand the great world religions and to seek harmony through dialogue with them.[9] Furthermore, if it can be shown that the 'pragmatic-ascetical' approach of Mahāyāna Buddhism has been used in the Fourth Gospel to set forth the mystery of God in Jesus Christ, then for the Christian the doctrine of God should be able to be expressed in a manner closer to the Asian tradition and the doctrine of the Trinity, in greater harmony with contemporary Western thought.

These similarities of passages in Buddhist works of various ages to passages in the Gospels exercised scholarly minds between 1880 (when translation of Buddhist works became more readily available)[10] and 1930 when interest in the question diminished. At the beginning of the twentieth century, early investigators like Garbe took the more positive approach on the controversy which generated so much literature that it required a bibliography of its own in 1922.[11] But around 1930 hostility to such ideas became so strong that a reaction set in. It seemed that while dozens of incidents and expressions having striking resemblances to the Gospel message appeared to be discovered, as time went on scholars lost interest, and the number of supposed parallels became fewer and fewer until interest in the project was lost altogether. The prevailing mood today is that the

Indian notion of New Testament dependence on Buddhism may be due to an error in historical judgment.[12] On the other hand, it may be that the problem lies elsewhere; it may be that thus far no scholar of New Testament literature, with few exceptions, has been at the same time a student of Indian and Buddhist textual material. As a result, very little dialogue and exchange has ensued between experts in these two fields of inquiry. Research in this field will be denied, furthermore, wherever the idea is dominant that Christianity will lose something of its essential truth if it were to owe something to Buddhism. From an Indian point of view, India and Buddhism have deeply influenced the West even though documentation is slow in establishing itself.

Thus this question of influence continues to fascinate the researcher and scholar. The case for the Gospel's dependence on Indian or Buddhist material in some form was argued in the past with such a wealth of evidence that it had to be taken seriously. This is in spite of the fact that the headwaters of each stream are so vastly different. On the one hand we have Buddhism, originating in northern India six centuries before Christ, reflecting the cultural traditions of South Asia, and, on the other, Christianity originating around the Mediterranean Sea, reflecting its cultural institutions and beliefs. From two widely different streams, two masters emerge with similar life styles, similar messages, and confronting similar events in their ministries. Garbe, for example, turns to those cases — four in number — in which after long consideration he had become convinced that Buddhist influence in the Gospel stories cannot be denied.[13] First, the Buddhist story of the aged saint Asita and his glorification of the child Buddha (found in the Sutta-nipāta, one of the oldest Pāli sources) is compared with the story of Simeon in the temple (Luke 2:25-35). Second, the story of the temptation belongs to the most striking and most generally discussed parallels between Buddhist literature (in the Samyutta-nikāya, and the Mahāparinirvāṇa) and the Gospels (Matthew 4:1-11 and Luke 4:1-13). Third, to Peter's walking on the water (Matthew 14:25-31; Mark 6:45-51; John 6:16-21) we have a parallel in the Introduction to Jātaka 190 (part of the Sutta-piṭaka), where the similarity is far greater than usual. Finally, the miracle of the loaves (Matthew 14:13-31; Mark 6:30-44; Luke 9:10-17) is strikingly parallel to the Introduction to Jātaka 78, where it is related that Buddha fed first his five-hundred disciples and then all of the inmates of a cloister with one loaf of bread that was put in his begging bowl, and that a great deal of bread besides was left over.

Thus the question we raise again is whether we can assume some kind of historical or textual connection between the practices and teachings of Gautama and Jesus. At first glance it appears to be a question of priority. Which came first? The famous stupa and sculptures at Bharhut and Sāñci in central India, already erected in the second century BCE, depict the legends of the life and teachings of the Buddha. Parts of the Buddhist Canon, the Tripiṭaka, were chanted shortly after Gautama's Parinirvāṇa and then settled in various Councils which took place many years before the Common Era. Long before the Christian era, many Dharma-envoys were sent out to place the Dharma-wheel in motion, and as a result Buddhist missions began operating at that time in western Asia.

The question, then, of priority is well established. Which came first, Buddhism or Christianity? But the dating problem is not that easily solved. The question may be turned around. Some of the Buddhist Scriptures, its stories and narratives, were not actually written down until well after the birth of Jesus. Perhaps the borrowing was on the part of the Buddhists rather than on Christian sources. For some aspects of Buddhism, this remains a possibility. The British interpreter of Buddhism for the West, Edward Conze, cautions us in our attempts to find parallels between Buddhism and Christianity.[14] He observes that this search is full of dangerous pitfalls because the dissimilarities in these two religions are as striking as their similarities. Some parallels are fruitful and of importance that may lead to further development, but others appear at best incidental and fortuitous. Since the rise of the Mahāyāna tradition (that emerged out of the Mahāsaṅghika sects, 'Great Assembly-ites') in earliest Buddhism coincides with the beginning of the Christian era, Conze believes that Buddhism may have been influenced by the Christian message. Mahāyāna gathered momentum in the first pre-Christian centuries, although it goes back in many of its basic ideas to the fourth and fifth century BCE, if not to the Buddha himself. But the literature which sets out the specific Mahāyāna doctrines is attested only for the beginning of Christianity, and this raises an interesting, and so far unresolved, historical problem. So Conze asks the question of how we can account for the fact that Buddhism, just about the time when Christianity was getting its start, had itself undergone a quite radical form of its basic tenets which made it more similar to Christianity than it had been before.

This promises to be a fruitful field for further study. At the present we cannot account for the parallels between the Mediterranean and Indian developments which occur at the beginning of the Common Era. But Buddhists themselves believe that for the interpretation of the Mahāyāna tradition, these developments are significant. And Christians have also come to believe that those close relationships that run parallel to each others' traditions cannot be ignored. But we acknowledge the fact that as we attempt to recapture the optimism of the pre-1930s, we are taken out on a scholarly limb. Thus far no real textual or historical evidence has been discovered to substantiate this issue one way or another. For the most part, the tendency is to look upon the Buddhist texts as earlier and, therefore, to look more closely at those Biblical passages which seem curiously parallel to them.

Meanwhile, Indologists are divided between those who are confident that the Christian story drew inspiration from India, directly or indirectly, perhaps through oral tradition by way of Iran, and those who say that while the possibility of Christian dependence on Buddhist literature cannot be ruled out, these sources have not been sufficiently proved. No method has been discovered so far whereby the proved similarities are to be accounted for. The scarcity of direct evidence on these important issues is a severe limitation. In the meantime, New Testament scholars have lost interest in the question as temporarily incapable of conclusive treatment. The challenging works of recent scholars in this area of inquiry remain unanswered. As Merritt suggests, if no New Testament scholar gives Indian claims on their texts any credence, it may not be because the claims are false but because the scholar's training and mind is not prepared to deal with the subject.[15] The intriguing problem remains with us. In the present state of our knowledge, not only of Buddhist literature but of the history of the relationship between India and the Mediterranean, it may not be possible to answer the question to everyone's satisfaction. If any influence is to be admitted, there is still the question of which way it works. But it merits a reconsideration and an openness to materials that may still lie hidden, awaiting discovery.

Some Aspects of India's Cultural Exchange With the West

Buddhism emerged in the sixth century BCE out of an earlier

classical synthesis of two cultures in Indian civilization. The first Indic culture was established during the Harappā and Mohenjo-Daro period in the Indus Valley in the northern area of India and Pakistan. It began around 2300BCE, when a well-planned, advanced urban life began to spread along the Indus River. This civilization was counted as among the early organized societies that arose in the third millennium BCE, along with the civilizations that developed first in the Valley of the Euphrates and then in the Nile. Contacts between India and these centers go back in a continuous, if not always unbroken line, at least to the time of their flourishing. The natural frontiers of India, the mountains and the seas that serve to emphasize her inherent unity, have seldom acted as barriers to her intercourse with foreign lands. Bruns reports that many of the 'distinctive steatite seals' from the Indus Valley have been unearthed at Sumerian excavation sites. There are also references in the 'Sumerian economic texts' to the ships from Dilmun; that is, from the East, and the only land rich enough east of Sumer from which ivory could have been exported was India.[16]

About a thousand years after the flourishing of the Indus Valley civilization, bands of semi-barbarian nomadic cattle herders, the Indo-Aryans, began moving into the Indus Valley, bringing an Indo-European culture and religious cult, and an early form of writing known as Sanskrit (a remote cousin of many Western languages). Intercultural exchange between Mesopotamia and India continued after the Aryan invasion when the early Brāhmī script first appeared around the eighth century, which was an adaptation of the Phoenician alphabet which found its way through Assyria. At this time also, certain Semitic legends were introduced into Indian literature, 'most notably that of the deluge, which is recounted in the Sattapatha Brahmana'.[17]

The Indo-Aryan people absorbed what survived of the indigenous civilization of the Indus Valley and began to move into the subcontinent to finally settle in the Ganges River Valley. Out of this double heritage, the so-called Western Aryan culture and the Eastern Indo-culture, India's major religious traditions, including Buddhism, came into being. The birth of Gautama Siddhārtha took place around 580BCE, and his enlightenment some thirty-six years later established him as the Buddha.[18] This epoch-making event which transformed the ascetic Gautama into the Buddha of this age is attested and described several times in the Pāli Canon in the Majjhima-nikāya (suttas nos. 4, 19, 26 and 36).

During this time in the sixth and fifth centuries BCE, cultural exchanges between East and West were on the increase. In this formative period of Buddhist history Cyrus the Great (558-530BCE), the founder of the Persian empire, extended his rule to the borders of India, and Darius (521-486BCE) continued the conquests, making northwest India a province called the 'twentieth satrapy' of the Persian empire. For nearly two hundred years the Iranians, who were themselves kinsmen of the Vedic Aryans, ruled the region. According to the Greek historian Herodotus, the twentieth satrapy paid more tribute to Persia than any other division of the empire, and a contingent of Indian warrior-archers served under the Persian emperor Xerxes (486-465BCE) in his invasion of Greece in 479BCE. Darius also dispatched an expedition commanded by Skylax of Karyanda, with orders to prove the feasibility of a sea passage from the mouth of the Indus to Iran. Skylax equipped his fleet and in the thirteenth month reached the sea, thus enabling Darius to control the Indus Valley and to send his fleet into the Indian Ocean.[19] Thus up to the time of Alexander's invasion of 327BCE, which occurred during the rule of the Nandas in Magadha, the Indus River was regarded as the traditional frontier of the Persian empire. The proximity of the northern part of India to territory which was a Persian province, along with the constant (although unrecorded) intercourse which must have existed between the Achaemenid dynasty and the Indian kingdoms, causes one to wonder whether Vedic (and early Buddhist?) thought and philosophy may have succeeded in becoming familiar to the people of the Persian empire.

We are also reminded that in an earlier period in the Greek city of Miletus in Asia Minor, there were philosophers who were beginning to reason about the universe in a way which was hitherto unknown in Greece, and a kind of thinking which in all probability was influenced by ideas derived from the older civilizations of Mesopotamia and the Middle East. These 'presocratic philosophers' were involved in a movement of thought which led to the separation of philosophy and science from one another and from other archaic ways of thinking. A foremost Indologist has suggested that to the traditional Western mind that looks to the discursive and rational as its guide, the theories of the presocratic philosophers like Heraclitus may come as a surprise. But as Richard Zaehner observes, it comes as a rather pleasant surprise to find that in the cradle of Western civilization — in supposedly rational Greece — the 'wisdom' of the East appears in all its 'ambiguous paradoxicality'.[20] There is indeed so striking a resemblance between the thought of Heraclitus and many of the other presocratics and that of the Vedic Upanishads, that many thoughtful people have been driven to the conclusion that somehow or other, Indian ideas must have penetrated into Greece as early as the seventh and sixth centuries BCE. What is still baffling to the scholar is how, and through what, channels.

It has long been known that Greek thought was influenced not only by its Lydian and Phoenician neighbors, but also by the civilizations of Egypt and Mesopotamia. But how is it that what would seem to be specifically Indian ideas should reappear in the Greek world at much the same time that they were being formulated in India itself? How is it that the correspondences between the two are often so disconcertingly exact? Does it mean that a direct influence was at work? Researchers today are still looking for the 'missing links'. And in most cases where the attempt is made to prove that such direct influence did exist, it is not always convincing. Zaehner suggests that there is no direct evidence that the Persian empire was a great melting pot of ideas in which a cross-fertilization between the Indian and Greek civilizations could take place. But we must allow for the possibility that interplay may have taken place, perhaps not by any exchange and translation of written documents, but by personal contact of like-minded people. Interest in cosmogony was strong throughout the Greek world at this time, and there is good evidence of an openness to Persian and Babylonian sources. Amore suggests that not only did Persian thought influence Greek thought, but that it played a part in the teachings of Judaism and in the lifestyles of some branches of Palestinian Judaism centuries before the Common Era. It is relevant, he notes, that the Essenes and also the important Pharisee party were influenced by Persian religious motifs, and that such influence 'must have been a continuing one during the centuries leading up to and including the birth of Jesus.'[21]

Zaehner reminds us, furthermore, that in the axial sixth century BCE the prophet of Persia Zarathustra, or Zoroaster (628-551 BCE), brought a message of a sovereign God (Ahura Mazda) that became incorporated in part in Judaism, Christianity and Islam. This message of Zoroaster became embodied in the national religion of the Persian empire and served as the bond that sustained the Persian people over the centuries in their confrontations with the Greeks, Romans and

Byzantines. Under the rulers of the Achaemenid monarchy, a number of strong effective kings ruled who dominated the Middle East, including Babylonia and Egypt. Through the diffusion of ideas whose transmission is still unclear to us, much of what the Persian prophet taught continues to live in the three religions of the Western world. It is from Zoroaster that the Jews derived such ideas as the immortality of the soul, the resurrection of the body, the idea of a devil as an enemy of God, and perhaps too, of an eschatological saviour who is to appear at the eschaton. The Zoroastrian idea of the dualism of soul and body appears in the works of Greek philosophers like Plato, as well as in the teachings of the Christian (and Buddhist?) Gnostics. Traces of the Zoroastrian concepts of the soul's fate after death are found in the Qu'ran of Islam. We are thus reminded that while Christianity lays claim to the prophets of Israel as its rightful heritage, it is no less heir to the prophet of ancient Iran.[22]

An investigation of these facts establishes a fairly reliable case for the influence from Iran on Judaism, Christianity and Islam, but what about the possibilities of Buddhist influence before the Christian century? It might be argued that even as the Jews were influenced by Iranian modes of thought during this time, so they may have been open to Buddhist ones as well. It can be shown that since Buddhism was rapidly spreading westward into areas formerly part of Persia, the same cultural connections that continued to bring Zoroastrian ideas into Palestine in the third and second centuries before Christ could have brought Buddhist ideas as well. We are asked to picture Jews from Parthia and other eastern fringes of the diaspora making the occasional pilgrimage to Jerusalem, filled with the latest religious teachings of their day, some of them Buddhist.[23] The weakness of this type of argument is that no evidence exists that such Buddhist ideas, as opposed to Iranian ones, filtered into Judaism, yet it seems reasonable to allow for the possibility. Two people can hardly live side by side in the same country for a long period of time without a certain amount of mutual borrowing, but the evidence is still waiting to be discovered.

The idea that Jerusalem and Galilee were exposed to Eastern influences at this early time is strengthened by two factors: the East-West trade route passed through Palestine, and as we shall see later, Buddhism was expanding westward. The land of the silk routes, that vast area of steppes and deserts between China and Iran, has been a region where peoples from almost all parts of Asia came into contact with each other. The routes connecting China with India, Iran and the Middle East served not only for the development of barter of goods, but also of ideas. Adherents of the major religions of Asia met here and lived side by side. Buddhism and Confucianism, Hinduism and Zoroastrianism, later on Nestorians and Gnostic Manichaeism (a valuable link between Buddhism and Christianity in the later centuries), and Islam were represented sooner or later by believers in the towns of this vast basin and the adjoining areas in the East and West.

The Middle East served as an ideal region for the exchange of goods and ideas. In its eastern part, it was intersected from north to east by two great rivers, the Tigris and Euphrates. To the west in Egypt the more placid and easily navigable Nile, flowing northward from the south, has always been an almost perfect carrier of goods and ideas. The Arabian desert, like the sea, not only divided but also joined, for it was a thoroughfare open to trade from every side. On the eastern side of the Arabian desert stretched the favored plateau of Iran, and to the south and east of it, beyond the Persian Gulf, the fabulous wealth of India. To the west, the Red Sea separated Arabia from, and yet at the same time connected it with, central Africa. In the north, the Isthmus of Suez linked the Arabian desert to Egypt, and a number of excellent harbours on the shores of Palestine, Phoenicia, and Syria brought it into close relationship with the Mediterranean lands of Greece, Italy and Spain. These were the trade routes that connected India and northern China to the east with Egypt to the west. Included in this route was a major branch that extended south from Afghanistan down into the northwest part of India, passing through what is now Pakistan, and from there connecting with other trade routes across India. At the same time, the first ships began to traverse the sea, putting out from Egypt and from the shores of the Persian Gulf, from southern Arabia, and from the sea coast of India. It is to this connection with India and Africa that the great cultural center of Alexandria owes its development. The attempt was made to seek to navigate a route to India without any call at Arabian ports. One daring merchant after another tried it. Two successful voyages of Eudoxus of Cnidus in the late second century BCE were made. The result was that in the first century BCE one of these merchants, Hipparchus, discovered the monsoons, rendering possible a direct trade route between India and Egypt, and thus making the wisdom of India more readily accessible to the West.[24]

Buddhism's Contact with the West

It was not the Indians who finally ended Persian rule of the 'twentieth satrapy' in India. In 331BCE, the Macedonian conqueror Alexander won a crucial victory against the Persian forces near the Tigris River. He entered India in 327BCE to take possession of the Persian territory, and for a moment in the history of northwest India it seemed that one ruler would be permanently replaced by another. But within two years his raid suddenly ended on the west bank of the river Hyphasis, where his army refused to march any further into alien territory. Alexander left India, never to return. His dream of uniting the East and the West remained unfulfilled, for his army's advance into India was still hundreds of miles from the center of Magahdan political power (and the center of growing Buddhist influence).

We are cautioned by A.K. Nilakanta Sastri that the importance of Alexander's campaign in India must not be exaggerated. Apart from the cultural intercourse with Mesopotamia and Egypt in the earliest centuries, however, Alexander's invasion started a genuinely new era in Indo-European relations.[25] Beginning with the age of the Nandas and the Mauryas (about 400-185BCE), great changes were occurring over the face of western Asia, over lands with which India had much to do from its earliest history. The great change as a result of the Macedonian episode opened an era of several centuries during which Hellenism was to become the prevailing factor of government and civilization on the western borders of the Indian world. After Alexander's withdrawal, these contacts continued when penetration of the Bactrian Greeks began in the extreme northwest and north during the decline of the Mauryan rule. According to Nalinaksha Dutt, the Bactrian Greeks adopted Indian culture and carried the tale of Indian (and Buddhist) wisdom and prosperity across the Indian frontiers to the Central Asian steppes, as well as to the Greek-Roman world in the West.[26]

Unfortunately we know less than we could wish of the interaction between these two civilizations, and what we do know is one-sided. We see what little Indians took from the Greeks, because Indian literature and artifacts attest to it — Mauryan architecture and sculpture, some court ceremonials and functions of government — but it is not easy to see what the Greeks took from the Indians because the Greek literature of this period is lost. It was lost in the history of Hellenism when the Greek accounts which once existed of their empire in Bactria and India were allowed to perish. We may speculate, however, that the West was not as isolated from Indian, and perhaps Buddhist, influence as Western historians had first thought. A busy life was throbbing on both sides of the northwest frontier and caravans were moving back and forth, trafficking in all sorts of merchandise and ideas as well.[27]

With Alexander's premature death in 323 BCE, the resulting vacuum created in India a great military and political opportunity. The small outposts and garrisons left behind by the Macedonians soon withered away, and Aśoka's grandfather, Chandragupta Maurya, was ready to fill the void. In 321 BCE, roughly when the Mahāsāṅghikas and the Sthaviras were dividing in Buddhism, Chandragupta Maurya succeeded to the throne of Magadha. By 303 BCE he controlled the lands from Bengal to eastern Afghanistan and as far south as the Narmada River. In 305 BCE he met and defeated Seleucus Nicator, a successor of Alexander's who was attempting to recover the dead emperor's Indian provinces, and as a result the two emperors came to a division of spheres of influence. Chandragupta's son, Bindusāra (297-272 BCE) acceded to the throne, conquered the Deccan and Mysore in central India, and in the far south brought the Tamil country under his sovereignty. Friendly Mauryan-Seleucid relations were established under Chandragupta and his son Bindusāra, as evidenced in the exchange of correspondence between the two courts, and in the continuing exchange of ambassadors of whom Megasthenes, the Seleucid envoy to Chandragupta, was but one. The Greek Seleucid and later Ptolemaic emissaries to the Indian courts — Megasthenes, Deimachus and Dionysius — all wrote down their impressions of India, of which we now have only fragments.[28]

When Aśoka became emperor in 272 BCE, the neighboring Greeks were quite familiar in Mauryan circles and were called *Yona*, a term derived from the Greek province Ionia. With Aśoka and his missionary zeal, the real story of contacts between Buddhism and the West begins. In 260 BCE, Aśoka conquered Kaliṅga in northeast India, an area refusing to submit to Mauryan rule, and extensive bloodshed and destruction followed. Filled with remorse, he repented of his actions, began the study of Dharma, and became a Buddhist lay disciple. He embarked upon a 'Reign of Dharma', seeking to inculcate in his subjects the moral precepts of non-violence, non-covetousness, and respect for all religious teachers. He appointed officers, called Dharma-mahāmātras, or commissioners of Dharma, to propagate his ethical values. Five years after Kaliṅga, he had a series of fourteen edicts engraved on rocks throughout his empire (the earliest surviving inscriptions of a lay Buddhist disciple), and he instructed his Dharma officers to read them to the public on festival days.[29] Thirteen years later, he began issuing another series of seven edicts which were inscribed on polished stone pillars. The Rock Edict V from Shahbazgarhi (near Peshawar in the upper Indus) described the work of the Dharma officials in this way:

> Now, in times past (officers) called Mahāmātras of morality [Dharma] did not exist before. But Mahāmātras of morality were appointed by me (when I had been) anointed thirteen years. These are occupied with all sects in establishing morality, in promoting morality, and for the welfare and happiness of those who are devoted to morality [Dharma] (even) among the Yōnas, Kambōyas, and Gandhāras, among the Raṭhikas, among the Pitinikas, and whatever (other) western borders (of mine there are).[30]

David A. Scott observes that all of these groups mentioned in Rock Edict V come from the northwestern part of India. In sending out his Dharma-envoys to these Greek communities, Buddhism was communicating its message to a people who did not share in the Indian customs and worldview with which Buddhism had previously had to deal. This was an important development in Buddhist thought as it broke away from its previous Indian restrictions.[31]

As a result of Aśoka's conversion and promotion of religion, the moral tone of his empire underwent change. More important for Buddhist historians, however, is his role in extending the sphere of Buddhism not only to the Greeks situated within the Mauryan boundaries, but to the larger Hellenic world that lay beyond the western frontiers. According to traditional accounts, Aśoka is said to have called a Council of all Buddhist communities around 250BCE. At this Council those holding views contrary to the orthodox Saṅgha of Buddhists at Pāṭaliputra were expelled, apparently an indication that Aśoka favoured the traditional Sthaviras (or Vibhajyavādins). This expelled group migrated to the northwest and is thought to be the forerunner of the Sarvāstivādin school of Buddhism that flourished in Central Asia.

One of Aśoka's edicts, Rock Edict XIII, reports that in 256 and 255BCE he sent Dharma-envoys to the old Alexandrian empire, to the Greek rulers of Syria, Egypt, Macedonia, Cyrene and Epirus. Rock Edict XIII reads:

And this (conquest) has been won repeatedly by Dēvānāṁpriya both (here) and among all (his) borderers, even as far as at (the distance of) six hundred yōjanas, where the Yōna king named Antiyoga [Antiochus II of Syria?] (is ruling) and beyond this Antiyoga (where) four — 4 — kings (are ruling), (viz. the king) named Tulamaya, (the king) named Antekina, (the king) named Makā, (and the king) named Alikyashudala, (and) likewise towards the south, (where) the Chōḍas and Pāṇḍyas (are ruling), as far as Tāmraparṇī.

Likewise here in the kings' territory, among the Yōnas and Kambōjas, among the Nābhakas and Nābhapaṅktis, among the Bhōjas and Pitinikas, among the Andhras and Pāladas — everywhere (people) are conforming to Dēvānāṁpriya's instruction in morality.

Even those to whom the envoys of Dēvānāṁpriya do not go, having heard of the duties of morality, the ordinances, (and) the instruction in morality of Dēvānāṁpriya, are conforming to morality and will conform to (it).

This conquest, which has been won by this everywhere, causes the feeling of satisfaction.

Firm becomes satisfaction, (viz.) the satisfaction at the conquest of morality.[32]

Unfortunately, unlike the missionaries that Aśoka had sent out to Ceylon and to southeast Asia, his missionaries at the Hellenic courts left no traceable impressions on the Mediterranean world. Kenneth K.S. Ch'en suggests, however, that along with the diplomatic agents that Aśoka sent to Hellenistic countries, it is very possible that Dharma-envoys were also dispatched to administer to the needs of the members of the various embassies, as well as to propagate the message of the Dharma to the local people as the occasion arose.[33]

Many questions remain unanswered because of the scarcity of the materials that are at hand. The sending of missionaries to announce the Dharma by Aśoka to the Seleucid and Ptolemaic courts was quite feasible, and as Scott suggests, by just a small geographic extension to the other Hellenic kingdoms. The thought of Buddhist envoys walking the streets of Antioch and Alexandria, Athens and Jerusalem, stirs the imagination. We are to imagine not only Megasthenes and his fellow philosophers coming to India, but Hindu and Buddhist teachers returning to Greece and to the new intellectual metropolis of Alexandria where the Gnostic and Essene movements came under their influence. We could reasonably speculate also that this influence was more than a vague influence. One would expect the same fervor of missionary activity that won Ceylon and Burma for Buddhism, or, a few centuries later, that won Greece and Egypt for Christianity. In the first century BCE, contacts between the Greek-speaking world and India increased dramatically with the establishment of Roman rule in Egypt and the discovery of the monsoons in the Indian oceans. In the present state of our knowledge, however, not only of Buddhist literature and Greek material but of the history of the relationship between India and the Mediterranean, we are unable to go any further in answering the question of influence to everyone's satisfaction. Neither the later classics of Greek and Roman thought, nor early Christianity, have left us any more important evidence.

Concluding Remarks

If it can be shown in this controversial question of possible influences from one religion to another, that the similarities are not the result of *direct* borrowing, and that furthermore they are not the result of completely independent internal processes at work within each religion, then a third possibility suggests itself. This idea is set forth by Richard H. Robinson in *Early Mādhyamika in India and China*, in regard to the transmission of a system of thought such as Buddhism from one culture to another. The study of cultural transmission, he writes, is 'the attempt to isolate factors in the result which have their parentage in the invaded culture from those whose parentage is in the invader.'[34] The several forms of cultural transmission — the organic, the stimulus-diffusion, the cultural amalgam — serve as models in understanding how ideas are passed on from one culture to another. In the present state of knowledge about the penetration of Buddhism in Chinese civilization, for example, Robinson suggests that all conclusions are valuable more as hypotheses for more detailed investigation than as factual judgements. The models that are posited to describe the interaction of Buddhism and the Chinese tradition serve as orientation to further studies but are not completely confirmed or refuted by them.

The anthropologist A.L. Kroeber more fully discusses this particular form of 'stimulus-diffusion' in the spread of cultural material by pointing out that this possibility, the possibility of 'stimulus-diffusion', is an attempt to reconcile the internal and external similarities within cultural development.[35] He suggests that in the special process of 'stimulus-diffusion', much interaction takes place *below* the surface of historical record, a process which leaves a minimum of historical evidence. In a great many cases, the evidence itself as to the process of diffusion is much more scant than of the effects. The evidence for this 'borrowing' is, therefore, indirect or inferred, although the conclusions may leave little doubt as to the effects. In this process, the specific items of cultural content upon which historians ordinarily rely in proving connections are likely to be few or even wholly absent. Positive proofs are, therefore, difficult to secure.

Kroeber used as examples a number of tantalizingly vague parallels between Greece and India that have long troubled cultural historians. He suggests also that there may be other connections which have not as yet been suspected. If, for instance, fifty years ago anyone had ventured to assert specific Greek influences in Indian and East Asian art, no-one would have taken such assertions seriously. The discovery of actual remains of Gandhāra art in northwestern India completely changed the picture. It may be difficult for the average person to see any but the most vague resemblances between, for example, a Chinese Kwan-yin and a European Madonna. The specific stylistic qualities of Asian and Western art remain very fundamentally different in two such pieces of sculpture. Nevertheless, the archaeologist and historian are able to trace specific connections. This is not to imply that Kwan-yin is a Chinese attempt at a replica of the Madonna, but that specific influences within the field of sculpture, and probably painting, were transferred from the West to the East.

Kroeber suggests another example of the monastic influence of Buddhism on the monastic communities in Palestine. Soon after the Buddha's final Nirvāṇa, the Saṅgha of dedicated men and women began in full operation in India. It was ascetics who had given up the secular life who were the dharma-envoys and who directed the historic fortunes of Buddhism. In the West there were monastic communities in Palestine at the time of Christ, the Jewish Essenes since about 150BCE, and later on definite monastic organizations becoming prominent fairly early in the history of Christianity, especially in the fourth century in Egypt. But so far as we now know, there is no proved historic link between Buddhist monasticism and Middle-Eastern Christian monasticism, but the relation of space and time, as well as of intrinsic concept, is such as to make one inevitably think of a connection. The point is, as Kroeber suggests, that independent origins are not necessarily proved because we are unable to show specific connection by specific historical documents. There is bound to be a category of cases which are indeterminate (or indeterminate at present) and that, in at least part of these, the principle of stimulus-diffusion may be operative.[36]

It appears that diffusion happens so frequently and so continuously that we know more about its results than about its operation. Stimulus-diffusion may be provable in only a minority of the cases in which it is suspected, but it does suggest the posture of open-mindedness toward other possible instances. In the case of Gandhāra art, the inference drawn is that contacts did occur and that they did have influence far beyond what we would directly infer from preserved documentary literature. In other words, the absence of direct historical records as to connections between Greece and India is no proof that there were no connections. Independent origins are not necessarily proved because scholars are unable to prove direct connections by specific historical documents. It is always impossible to predict what new evidence, or the analysis of old evidence from a new point of view, may bring to light. We shall have to be content with the scanty information we now possess. Future archaeological excavations may produce further materials. Continuing excavations at Buddhist sites in Pakistan, Soviet Central Asia, and Afghanistan may unearth new Aśokan Edicts, additional Buddhist textual materials and artifacts, which could extend our knowledge of the question of influence, and the ways in which this influence worked.

Notes

1. Chai-Shin Yu, *Early Buddhism and Christianity. A Comparative Study of the Founder's Authority, the Community, and the Discipline*, Motilal Banarsidass, New Delhi, 1981, pp.ix-xiii.

2. First published as *Indien und das Christentum* in 1914, and now as *India and Christendom: The Historical Connections Between Their Religions*, Open Court Publishing Co., La Salle, 1959, p.16. He mentions the most important authors that had written on the subject at that time.

3. For a recent and innovative account of the similarities of Buddhism and Christianity, see Roy C. Amore, *Two Masters, One Message*, Abingdon, Nashville, 1978.

4. Assam: University of Gauhati, 1959, pp.19-20.

5. *Eastern Religions and Western Thought*, Oxford University Press, New Delhi, 1st edn. 1939, 2nd edn. 1940, p.184.

6. Henri de Lubac, *Aspects of Buddhism*, Sheed & Ward, London, 1953. See especially Chapter III, 'Different Manifestations of Christ and the Buddha', pp.86-130.

7. In 'Greece and India: The Milindapañha, the Alexander-Romance and the Gospels' from *Zeitschrift für Religions und Geistesgeschichte*, Vol.19, 1967, pp.33-64.

8. J. Edgar Bruns, *The Christian Buddhism of St John*, Paulist Press, New York, 1971. See especially Chapter III, 'The Christian Buddhism of John', pp.24-59. See also his *Art and Thought of John*, Herder & Herder, New York, 1969. See also Valerie E. Viereck, *The Lotus and the Word: Key Parallels in the Saddharma-Pundarika Sutra and the Gospel of John*, Cambridge Buddhist Association Inc., Cambridge, 1973.

9. *Ibid*, in the Foreword, p.x.

10. 'How little the European public at the end of the 18th century knew of the Buddha and his teaching was underlined by Gibbon in a footnote (52) to Chapter LXIV of the *Decline and Fall*; he says that "the idol Fo" is "the Indian *Fo*, whose worship prevails among the sects of Hindostan, Siam, Thibet, China and Japan, But this mysterious subject is still lost in a cloud, which the researchers of our Asiatic society may gradually dispel." ' Quoted in Bhikku Namamoli, *The Life of the Buddha as it Appears in the Pali Canon*, Buddhist Publication Society, Kandy, Ceylon, 1972, pp.1ff. For the earliest documentary references to the 'Buddha', see Mrs Rhys Davids, *A Manual of Buddhism*, Oriental Books Reprint Corporation, New Delhi, originally published 1932, 1st Indian edn. 1978. See Chapter I, 'How and When We Came to Know', pp.1-21.

11. *Op.cit.*, p.35 in footnote 9, Hans Haas, *Bibliographie zur Frage nach den Wechselbeziehungen zwischen Buddhismus und Christentum*, Leipzig, 1922.

12. *Ibid*, p.35.

13. *Op.cit.*, pp.47-60.

14. *Thirty Years of Buddhist Studies*, University of South Carolina Press, Columbia, 1968. See especially his chapter 'Mahāyāna Buddhism', pp.48-86. Of significance also to the question of influence is his chapter on 'Buddhism and Gnosis', from Ugo Bianchi, *Le Origini dello Gnosticismo*, E.J. Brill, Leiden, 1967, pp.651-67. See also the conclusions that are assumed by J. Duncan M. Derrett, *op.cit.*

15. *Op.cit.*, p.37.

16. *Op.cit.*, p.24.

17. *Ibid*, p.25.

18. Richard H. Robinson and Willard L. Johnson, *The Buddhist Religion*, Wadsworth Publishing Co., Belmont, 1982. On Gautama's Enlightenment, see pp.5-20.

19. Vincent A. Smith, ed. Percival Spear, *The Oxford History of India*, Oxford University Press, New Delhi, 4th edn, pp.117ff.

20. *Our Savage God*, Collins, London, 1974, pp.74ff. See also Edward Hussey, *The Presocratics*, Charles Scribner's Sons, New York, 1972.

21. *Op.cit.*, p.110.

22. R.C. Zaehner, *The Concise Encyclopedia of Living Faiths*, Hawthorn Books Inc., New York, p.222.

23. Amore, *op.cit.*, p.110.

24. Mikhail I. Rostovtzeff, *Caravan Cities*, AMS Press, New York, reprinted from the edn of 1932, Oxford; 1st AMS edn 1971. See Chapter 1, 'Caravan Trade. An Historical Survey', pp.1-36.

25. K.A. Nilakanta Sastri, *Age of the Nandas and Mauryas*, Motilal Banarsidass, New Delhi, 1967, pp.1-8.

26. *Mahayana Buddhism*, Firma KLM Private Ltd, Calcutta, 1976. See especially Chapter 1, 'Political and Cultural Background of Mahāyāna Buddhism', pp.1-72.

27. K.A. Nilakanta Sastri, ed. *A Comprehensive History of India*, Orient Longmans, Bombay, 1957, Vol.2, pp.26-7.

28. W.W. Tarn, *The Greeks in Bactria and India*, Cambridge University Press, Cambridge, 1951; for the literature and social contacts between these two kingdoms, pp.34-70.

29. Robinson, *op.cit.*, p.47.

30. Eugene Hultzsch, Epigraphist to the government of Madras, *Inscriptions of Aśoka* (Corpus Inscriptionum Indicarum, Vol.1). The Clarendon Press, Oxford, 1925, p.56.

31. 'Ashokan Missionary Expansion of Buddhism Among the Greeks (In N.W. India, Bactria and the Levant)' from *Religion* 15, 1985, p.133.

32. Eugene Hultzsch, *op.cit.*, p.48.

33. *Buddhism: The Light of Asia*, Barron's Educational Series, Woodbury, 1968, p.116.

34. Richard H. Robinson, *Early Mādhyamika in India and China*, Motilal Banarsidass, New Delhi, 1967, p.6.

35. 'Stimulus Diffusion' from *American Anthropologist*, Vol.42, No.1, pp.1-20.

36. *Ibid*, p.12.

CHAPTER 19

Tam Antiqua, Tam Nova

James S. Cutsinger

This chapter is born of the author's conviction that the only good reason for a new book, even a *Festschrift*, has little to do with the new, and he is confident that the man we mean to honor would agree. Whether in fact there even is a truly new is only one part of the problem. The indictments of the Preacher should leave us dubious, especially when we hear of new ideas. But deeper yet is the question whether the new is ever true, whether the repetitions of the vain are merely redundant or centrifugal besides, and ever more mendacious. Either way it is clear that if there were ever a time when the Truth was not, it could hardly be true to itself as an adequation of the real, since Reality simply *is*, and is the measure of all change. The absurdity of this 'Arian' viewpoint should be obvious. Obvious, too, is the foolishness of attempting to write simply for the sake of novelty. However awkward we may prove ourselves in what follows, this mistake, it is hoped, will not be made. Our reason for writing is to encourage the reconsideration and fresh appreciation of certain ideas promulgated long ago, and to exhibit their application to the distinctive predicament of modern thought. The purpose is not the announcement of up-to-date thoughts, even if such exist, but the fresh cultivation of the very old.

It is not, however, with an 'ill-concealed glee in adopting an old-fashioned and unpopular position' that we propose this goal,[1] but to make clear if we can the essentially vital intentions, and the therapeutic and initiatic aims, presupposed by the Perennial Philosophy — what Huston Smith has called the Primordial Tradition. To say cultivation is to imply activity. If the old meant only the given, the fixed, a solid wall of accomplished fact, and if its

272

consideration meant for the mind merely a state of inertia or complacency, then to speak of the Perennial or the Primordial would be misleading indeed, for the very opposite is needed. To be guided by old ideas, however, is not to be sedated by them, nor to submit to the constraints of an accepted system or mental scheme as an end in itself. True ideas, as Plato knew well, unlike concepts generated by induction, are promptings for thought's beginning rather than markers of its end. Not just old ideas catalogued, counted and compared, but the living engagement of them, and with a view to a *new perception* — that is the goal of the traditional thinker, and our goal here as well.

But did we not say that the newness of things was beside the point? Have we not called the new into question? Careful discrimination would seem in order. It must be recognized, in other words, that old and new embrace multiple meanings, and that the chronologically new may be dry and brittle while the old may be filled with life. The traditional man is certain that there exists a vision that is 'new', which is to say fresh and vibrant and radiant with surprise. But he is equally sure that it is induced, at least in part, by meditating on old ideas, while 'ideas' apparently new are too often the façade for a thinking grown impotent and feeble. This point cannot be put too strongly, for intellectual currents today are such as to persuade us otherwise, to flatter and delude us into supposing that the *recently* new and the better are one and the same. Those who have accepted this view must ask themselves, however, whether they even know what newness is. It is not too much to imagine that none of us, however much he may champion advancement and innovation, has ever really seen the new in the way that the ancient master would wish, has ever really exercised the intellective faculty that such old ideas as hierarchy, participation, microcosm and illusion were meant to stimulate. Seeing has been fancied as easy to do as it is to pronounce. In this, I should add, there is not the slightest distance between the present writer and his readers. Lest they become suspicious, expecting condescension, or worse expertise, the word 'us' should be vigorously stressed: virtually none of *us* has seen. Like Jonathan Edwards, who though convinced of his wife's salvation was unsure of his own, the author readily numbers himself among the unenlightened and writes as much to remind himself of the fact as to persuade others of their own shortcomings. On the other hand, he believes that there have been those who could think the old anew, and for the sake of the new, even that there are those who can, and it is as an apprentice to their leadings that he writes.

Traditional thinkers have always taught that no concept or conceptual system, however much it might assist in our approach to the Truth, can ever replace what it is intended to describe, and that our need for Reality cannot rest content with thoughts about it. We must employ those thoughts instead, they believe, and the language that expresses them, as a means of direct confrontation. As Frithjof Schuon has said, 'Knowledge saves us only on condition that it enlists all that we are, only when it is a way and when it works and transforms and wounds our nature even as the plough wounds the soil.'[2] Hence the masters have always allowed a prominent place in their teaching to the disciplined and methodical excision of man's most cherished opinions and habitually protected conceptual safeguards. One of their principal tasks has been to break down the defenses of the hardened heart, to penetrate the carapace of its self-supporting expectations and assumptions, so that what really is so might come rushing in to fill the vacuum. And one of their principal means in pursuing this aim has been to teach the old ideas, specifically those we shall be considering later. It is extremely important that we remember this, lest the ancient principles in question become, not the instruments of penetration they were meant to be, but additional opinions and further safeguards.

Ours is an age much in need of this psychic surgery. For in a way without parallel, we seem intent, not on overcoming or excising, nor even concealing, but on excusing and even dignifying our weaknesses and deficiencies, that is, our obvious and universally admitted subjective imprisonment and relativistic self-enclosure, as if they were a strength. Ignorance has given way to agnosticism: what I do not know, I say that no one can know. Though we readily confess our limitations and doubts, we refuse to acknowledge any personal responsibility for them, claiming instead that they are essential to the human condition. This claim gives us comfort, no doubt — confirms and encourages our satisfaction with our situation — but it also results, however ironically, in a kind of smugness or pride. We are after all, we boast, the first of our race to face up to the fact of finitude. Of course we have our prejudices. But so have other men, nor is it possible — we say — to live without them.

There are several closely related, and nearly universal, assumptions that stand in back of this pride and that simply must be banished if a perception truly new should be gained. If for no other reason than the demolition of these, an old idea or two will be in order. Admitting of many labels, depending upon their several contexts and results, these assumptions are alike in bearing the imprint of the intellectual complacency or self-satisfaction that seems typical of our time. This feature more than any other marks the thinking of contemporary man. A smugness — or, to be less severe, a naiveté — seems to penetrate nearly all of his views, no matter the topic or application. For he appears convinced that the mind as it is, the mind with which he mows his lawn and does his income tax, can be the legitimate judge of the truth of all conceptions. If challenged to consider matters that call that mind into question, he takes refuge in what has been called by other such men the 'ordinary' waking consciousness, a phrase that reflects and serves to justify the claims of the mentality so described. The very word 'ordinary' implies of course that ideas of any other order than the everyday, even if not denied explicitly, are to be regarded as exceptional, unaccustomed, or simply strange. Though thinking today might be defined in many ways, and though possessed of various permutations and intraspecific disputes and disagreements, its idiosyncrasy may thus be found in a single fundamental conviction: that the full range of intelligible being, and therefore ideas of every magnitude, should be accessible to the most superficial of inspections and, as it were, at a moment's notice.

Whatever the more or less self-consciously modern — or, indeed, post-modern — intellectual movement or school of thought one might adduce, each seems marked by a stubborn adherence to this ordinary mind of the average man and to its characteristic arena of experience. By these we mean, to be precise, a mentality that is essentially abstractive and discursive, in fact desultory, and a level of experience defined exclusively by sense-perception. In the words of René Guénon, 'Modern man has become quite impermeable to any influences other than such as impinge on his senses; not only have his faculties of comprehension become more and more limited, but also the field of his perception has become correspondingly restricted.'[3] Thinking has become glued to the belief, even in the disciplines where one would normally have least expected it, that what we know (if we know at all) is ultimately derived from what our natural senses tell us, and that any idea worth serious consideration must in some way or at some level of practicality be applicable to the world disclosed by physical perception. Otherwise, we are told, the lurking beast of transcendental subreption will mislead one into making the worst of mistakes, supposing real the products of the finite fancy. All non-material phenomena that are inexplicable in material terms have been reduced in this way to the domain of the subjective and psychological, to say nothing of realities that are strictly trans-phenomenal, and which appear on no level at all. *De non apparentibus et non existentibus eadem est ratio.* Of course, as Coleridge remarked of his own age, 'Materialism, conscious and avowed materialism, is in ill repute; and a confessed Materialist therefore a rare character. But if the faith be ascertained by the fruits: if the predominant, though most often unsuspected persuasion is to be learnt from the influences, under which the thoughts and affections of the man move and take their direction; [we] must reverse the position. Only not all are Materialists.'[4]

Many no doubt have struggled to resist such reductionist tendencies and to escape the constrictions of the naturalistic standpoint. We do not dispute the existence of attempts to challenge the empiricist hegemony, nor would we be surprised to find that persons usually presume themselves innocent of positivism until proven guilty. We know, too, that many readers will therefore find these remarks too pessimistic and one-sided, and lacking sensitivity to subtle variations among the thinkers of these times. Nevertheless, we must stand by what has been said. For it is our position that by far the greater number even of those who wish to resist the domination of the 'ordinary' continue to display, in spite of their own best intentions, the after-effects and inclinations of sense-perception. What has been called a 'residue of unresolved positivism' still clings to nearly all their thinking.[5] If there appears to be dissension from the consensus in the case of some few renegades, persons dissatisfied with the over pretensions or more subtle consequences of the materialist viewpoint, closer inspection almost always reveals an internecine quarrel, apparent antagonists differing only in degree, only in their assessment of the place and range of the sensate in man's knowledge, but not of its intrinsic adequacy. To the extent that a given conception of spirit, for example, has meaning for a contemporary philosopher or theologian only in relation to the matter that it is not, and to which it is considered opposed, the conception is surely no less empirically determined than its apparent opposite, which would deny the existence of spirit altogether. The irreducibly disproportionate or asymmetrical relationship between these domains has necessarily eluded the grasp of even the most favorably post-critical extensions of the mentality in question. For this mentality finds inconceivable the fact that 'it is essentially the states of nonmanifestation which ensure the permanence and identity of a being',[6] far more that corporeal existence is itself only one, and that the lowest and most illusory, of the manifested states. However far-reaching the regions of discourse, however much their thoughts may strive toward *non*-empirical considerations, it is as the prefix implies always in clear sight of the senses that the work even of this cognitive minority has therefore largely been done. The physical world of solid objects has retained even for them its final jurisdiction. It is still a home to return to when speculative flights are ended.

Common of course to all the 'sensible' thinking of our times, running throughout like the thread of a seamless garment, is the fabled critical method, the characteristic and self-perpetuating instrument of the modern mind, whether in its scientific, textual, historical, or simply pragmatic projections, and with all that it implies in the way of deference to temporal limits, cultural conditionings, and the celebrated human finitude. What intellectual movement, what (as they say) influential scholar is there who does not pay lip service at least to the dictates of this method? What science, what style of interpretation, does not believe that ideas are to be approached only through the temporal and spatial contingencies that have colored their expression? There are a few exceptions, of course. But generally speaking, there should be no dispute. Ours is a time dominated by the belief that certain abstractive, comparative, categorizing, and computational operations of the regulative reason, now at the apparent zenith of its strength, exhaust man's mental powers and are sufficient for all occasions.

It is the corollary of this belief, as inevitable as it is pervasive, that is, however, even more remarkable. No use of the critical method is without this accompanying conviction, whether espoused or not, namely that man as he now seems to his own inspection, his powers of knowing and being defined by the notices and results of empirical perception, is essentially all he can and should be. There is no doubt a good bit of patching and polishing to be done. We do not mean to imply that no-one believes that mistakes are made. Man certainly realizes that his nature does not always lead him to do what he thinks to be best. And yet, whatever improvements he is able to make upon its function or operation will not change that basic nature itself and may be carried out, he appears to suppose, by faculties and techniques with which he is already familiar, in other words by 'old' abilities. Differences of degree so fascinate his mind that he seems incapable of recognizing that more intensive applications of the abstractive power and the increasing magnification of the senses are not alone enough.

In this can be seen what is perhaps our thinking's most distinctive feature, and the most in need of ancient therapy: not the cognitive restrictions, not the historicism, not the assumption that matter is the bedrock of all that exists, not even the critical approach that binds these beliefs together, but a spiritual laziness or torpor, an unwillingness to upset the intellectual *status quo*, an inability to imagine genuinely different possibilities, even a kind of resignation, which would call itself realistic and heroic, and which considers irreversible the effects of its own assumptions. 'When our times are spoken of,' writes Schuon, 'it is generally with a sort of fatalism which accepts them, even eagerly . . . as if the present process of decline were some blind force of nature for which man was in no way responsible, and as if this something inevitable — or this character of fatality — implied a more or less normative value or "a categorical imperative".'[7] There is, of course, nothing surprising in this. Nothing else could be expected of the ordinary sensate mind, which of necessity perceives itself as existing, not outside or above but within, and even beneath the weight of, a world of objects, a one among many things, all caught in the flow of time. But though it of necessity must so perceive, its hegemony is far from necessary. Man is without excuse.

We might call the set of assumptions and expectations that we have been sketching by any of several names, depending upon which of its many tendencies, implications, and results we wished to emphasize. It is empiricism, materialism, naturalism, and positivism — all of which terms reflect a fundamental belief, as Huston Smith has pointed out, that 'nothing that lacks a material component exists, and in what does exist the physical component has the final say.'[8] It is from another angle modernism, secularism, pragmatism, and humanism, or — to take advantage of the familiar eponyms — Cartesianism and Kantianism. Or again, it is relativism, reductionism, and scientism — these with respect to the results envisioned by those who would oppose this view. We could point, moreover, to specific consequences of this kind of thinking, mentioning for example the gradual displacement of metaphysics by epistemology, epistemology by linguistic analysis, and analysis by 'information theory' and cybernetics. Or we could turn to the history of modern theology, which exhibits a similar retreat from Being, talk about God having come to replace any attempt to penetrate directly to the Reality so named, a retreat that corresponds to a like withdrawal from the embarrassment of Truth — philology, archaeology, the search for historical influences and textual parallels being now much preferred. These initial observations could be rendered more concrete by mentioning the names of specific Protagoreans (to employ still another epithet), particular thinkers whom we regard as contributing most to the fixation of the ordinary mind upon itself and its seemingly fated limits.

There are several reasons to avoid specifications of the kind indicated, however, at least in the present context — and quite apart from the fact that our intentions are in no wise those of a historian. In the first place, the mentioning of particular names, whether of figures or movements, could not but be diverting. No name could help but provoke the most infelicitous of sympathies or antipathies in different readers. Those who felt opposed to the opinions of the schools in question might for that reason believe themselves free of the defect thus referred to, while those who supported such thinkers might consider the defect non-existent. Either response would serve only to distract attention from the real issue and to drain off into subsidiary channels the intellective effort needed for a change in mental habit.

And it is this, this change or transformation, that is the *sine qua non* for everything else. It is also important that one hold in check the inclination to express these matters in terms reflecting any one domain of thought to the apparent exclusion of others, for the problem at hand is not departmental. The difficulties that have led to our need for old ideas cannot be confined to a single field. While the primary goal of the Perennial Philosophy is the knowledge of God or the Absolute, and though its methods and vocabulary must at times be more theological and metaphysical than anything else, the effective pursuit of this goal depends upon the subversion of premises common today to all disciplines. If our remarks have been of a very general kind, it has been that they might indicate the indiscriminate distribution of self-satisfied thinking across the boundaries of many fields.

Yet another consideration is the most telling, however, and the best reason to eschew the use of labels as far as possible. It concerns once again the rarity of 'new' thinking and fresh perception. We have said before that none of us should suppose that he has ever really thought in the new way required by the old ideas. This is a theme that should be recalled again and again, for such thinking is the prerogative (because the achievement) only of the very few, and not of course without God's grace. Whatever the effect of our awkward attempts to realize this virtuality of the mind, they must never be allowed to lull us into fancying as actual what is at best potential. And yet, is this not the temptation presented the moment one indulges in a label or a category? To speak in terms of a category, to talk about empiricism or materialism, for example, is inevitably to feel in charge of it, in control, and thus to a certain extent outside the orbit of influence that the category delineates. No feeling could be more deceptive, however, no delusion more misleading. For the real antagonist is inside each one of us. It is inside our own minds that there exist positivism, reductionism and Kantianism enough to demand all our efforts at opposition and dissolution, apart from the relative historical or philosophical accuracy of those words. When we lament the beliefs of those who 'wish to impose on everybody else the limitations which are but the effect of their own incapacity',[9] we are lamenting an internal dimension of every man.

It is not upon intellectual movements or schools of thought, even 'perennialism', that the realization of the Truth depends, but upon the efforts of individual men to rid themselves of the effects of presumption. We must aim to work on ourselves. If specific tendencies and trends of thought, in particular those of recent influence, have been nonetheless alluded to, it is only to establish a certain tone and to point a direction, and because, though the problem at hand is finally deeper than intellectual or cultural fashion, a number of such fashions in the contemporary world have in fact made its solution all the more difficult. Whether the modern world as matrix of these fashions is spiritually more precarious than traditional civilizations, as Huston Smith and others have contended, or whether on the contrary it marks a necessary stage in the 'evolution' of man's mind, as others have argued, while obviously most important is not the present issue. The point here is neither to praise nor to blame certain periods, but to encourage a study of our own assumptions. Intellectual or academic developments are to be challenged only to the extent that they have appeared to authorize, and thus have increased, the propensity of the sensate mind in every man to think itself sufficient.

So what is the solution? What are the means of liquefaction or deliquescence that can soften the heart and open the ego and call into question the sensate mind? On one level, and that the deepest and most important, any attempt to answer such questions would require that one at least mention nothing less elaborate than the doctrines and methods of all the religious traditions of the world. For this is precisely the purpose of religion, to superintend — now with justice, now with mercy — the exploding of self-satisfaction. The dogmas, rites, symbols, exhortations, initiations, and mysteries are all directed toward this end, and toward the deliverance, salvation or union that is its issue. Clearly, however, we cannot undertake even to sketch a solution in these terms here, no matter if we wished to. This chapter, like its author's competence, is considerably more restricted.

On another level, apart from the complexity and detail of comparative religion, a truly adequate approach to the ego's explosion would be bound to embrace teachings and spiritual methods applying to every level of the human self. One would be obliged to attend, in other words, not only to the operations and habits of thought or reason — as we have done here — but to each of man's other dimensions: to the will, the emotions, and the body. For nothing could be clearer even to the most superficial of self-inspections, though nothing is any easier to forget, than that the orientation of our thinking is only part of a greater complex involving as much emotional dispositions, habitual choices, and physical postures as the conclusions and pronouncements of the mind. Epistemologies and ontologies are never divorced from the axiological preferences of those who espouse them, nor these preferences from specific emotional inclinations and aversions, nor these finally from the capacity of the body to provide or prevent them. It follows as a matter of course, we may note, that the disproportionate attachment of a man to his physical body and the material objects with which it comes into contact cannot but generate a certain philosophy, however much his mind might otherwise object.

Analyses and investigations of this sort are also, of course, beyond our present scope. There remains, however, another form of 'liquefaction', which, though considerably more limited in its purview and effectiveness, is no less essential to man's complete liberation, and no less closely related both to our theme of the old and the new, and to the problem of habit at the level of mind. Perhaps best known to the West by virtue of its prominent place in Socratic *elenchos*, it appears as well among the mystics of all the several traditions in the complementary ways of eminence and remotion, and in the purgation and illumination that are their issue. A brief consideration of its intentions and use will give us the opportunity to note the application of two specific 'old ideas' to the conditions of thought sketched above.

Traditional thinkers have always taught, we have said, that no concept or conceptual system, however sophisticated, can ever take the place of the Truth. And their principal task has been to break down the defenses of the hardened heart — a heart in part hardened by the categories and familiar notions to which the mind clings. Those who are aware of the real have always recognized that thoughts about it and images of it can have as much the effect of clouding as of enhancing their vision, and they have taught the importance, therefore, neither of affirmation nor of negation as it were on its own — neither *cataphasis* nor *apophasis* — but of their co-operation and intersection: to the end of exploding whatever we may think corresponds to the Truth, a 'whatever' that is always other than true. It would indeed seem that for the sake of new vision, the old ideas would have us relinquish the notion of correspondence itself — as corresponding, not to the actual nature of things, whether to God or the void, but only to our fears and desires. Huston Smith has drawn attention to this fact, and to the traditional means of overcoming the false associations and imprecision of both denial and assertion, by analogy with a lever:

> The governing law reads: the more developed the sense of the Infinite, the more distant from the finite it appears and the less literal positive designations will seem. The most effective way to underscore . . . how much attributes when predicated of the Infinite differ from the modes in which we usually encounter them is through paradox . . . The opposing forces that paradox generates cause it to function as a verbal lever. The mystic may begin, for example, by establishing as fulcrum the fact that God is light. This holds both metaphorically (light everywhere symbolizes knowledge) and literally inasmuch as God-incursion is often accompanied by light that is physically sensed . . . But in saying 'light' the mystic will be misunderstood, for neither the

literal nor the symbolic light he intends is the light the world knows . . .
Immediately, therefore, he must press against the word's usual
connotations. So: 'God is not light'; if 'light' denotes its conventional
referents, God is darkness. The countervailing forces raise the far end
of the lever toward light of a different order. If the alchemy works, our
minds are expanded and our souls as well.[10]

To call into question the accuracy of all our 'ordinary' language, and
hence the validity of correspondence when it comes to the Truth, is in
fact to dispute the adequacy of what we have been calling the sensate
mind, for the two go hand in hand. The physical world of solid
objects, which sensate thinking both projects and depends upon, is a
world of mutual exclusions, where — as Newtonian science would
have it (a science describing quite well the 'practical' life even of the
quantum theorist) — two bodies cannot occupy the same space at the
same time. It is a world that in every moment and at every
opportunity reinforces and aggravates the ego's insulation by
persuading it to think divisively, that is, always with respect to
division. Things are either in or out, here or there, up or down. For
the sensate mentality, to be is to exist in a place. It is easy to see that
the referential character of our ordinary thoughts and language
intimately shares in this sense of division. Our old and feeble minds
seem unable to escape conceiving of correspondence and even our
consciousness on the model of the spatial contiguities, parallelisms
and juxtapositions of physical objects. Thus, to put the matter almost
(but not quite) too simply, the relationship of rock to rock in a stone
wall comes to serve as a paradigm for the connection between not
only 'rock' and rock, but between every signifier and its signified, and
ultimately between 'God' and God. However much we are reminded
that the question of location is inapplicable to ideas,[11] it is virtually
impossible not to think of them as being elsewhere from the objects
they designate and of the mind that conceives them as also in a place.
The problems intrinsic to any theology or metaphysics based on such
a model are obvious, for the Divine Reality, by virtue of its
absoluteness and infinity, cannot but exceed position, nor can it fail to
subvert, therefore, all such positivistic references or conceptions.

In order to think in such a way as to know the Truth, it is
indispensable that we practise not thinking about it, indeed not
'about' *anything*, which is to say that we practise a 'new' form of
thinking running against the grain of the sensate and out of
synchronization with correspondence. By undermining the referential

character of ordinary language and the mind that employs it, the disciplined use of paradox and other dialectical methods can help to prepare us for this very rare, very difficult and utterly different kind of thought, which alone is able to respect the unplaceableness of God. Such preparation consists in the creation of a very specific kind of receptivity, suppleness, or flexibility in the human intellect, which the riveting demands and fixed configurations of sense-bound thoughts invariably oppose. If he is ever to understand, let alone to accept or embody what really is so, a man must first be trained to think in a new, uncommon, direction and in accordance with a syncopation that eludes the regularities and tempered intervals of physical perception. Something more than new thoughts is meant here, something quite other than additional contents of consciousness or cognitive objects. 'Neither is new wine put into old wineskins.' Not contents but containers are the issue, and the shattering of expectations.

It would perhaps be wise to insist as well that the receptivity we have in mind is altogether different from what is sometimes rather vaguely called an 'open' mind, the mind of which modern man is so proud, the essence of which is its preference for imprecision and indecision. Although the kind of thinking we need, like a liquid, is capable of receiving into itself objects of a sort that the rigid contours of the sensate mentality cannot possibly accommodate, this thinking must be liquid too, in conforming to the strictest principles — laws, one might say, of cognitive viscosity, pressure and displacement. For it is only by means of these laws, which we have been calling the old ideas, that thinking may be readied for Being. In case it is objected that *thinking* has little in common with the sudden insight often described in the direct encounter with Reality, we should add that in using the words 'thinking' and 'thought', not to mention 'ideas', we have throughout had in mind, among other traditional terms, the Platonic *noēsis*, which signifies an act of intuitive discernment as direct and immediate as that of the senses, though of course trans-phenomenal in its reach. Though care must obviously be taken never to confuse noetic thinking with the functions of the ordinary mind, it is of course characteristic of the Platonists to teach that the methodical cultivation and careful examination of ideas can have the effect of raising the power even of sensate thinking, such that it opens out of itself into contemplation. As Schuon insists, 'Sufficiently adequate thought, however tentative, can actualize a sudden awareness pertaining to a completely different dimension from the chain of mental operations, for when associated with Intellection, it provides a symbolism and a landmark.'[12]

But what exactly are the 'laws' of *noēsis*? And how can they prevent a form of thinking unattached to sense-perception from stumbling, losing direction, and ending up trapped in a maze of its own construction? Here at last we may glimpse the application of two ideas especially prominent in Perennial or Primordial teachings. We have said that intuitive thought runs against the grain of the sensate. This is the answer in essence to the questions just posed, for the metaphor is meant to be taken fully. If it is, then it will be seen that apart from the 'grain' of the physical world, the direction of the real could not be discerned. As those who have undertaken to approach the Truth have consistently found, the knowledge of things as they are is never wholly incompatible with things as they seem, as the sectarian 'gnostics' are said to have claimed. For what seems is what is, though always under the guise of its seeming. We have in mind among others the old ideas of *māyā* or 'illusion' from the Hindu East, and *methexis* or 'participation' from the Platonic West: the first with its emphasis on negation, because on the distortion of Truth by the form of this world; the second with an emphasis on affirmation, because on a perception of the world in the Truth, and hence as the Truth. It must be stressed, of course, that the cataphatic and apophatic are each essential elements of both these ideas and of the ways they project. For *māyā* is not without its meaning of 'measure', nor does *methexis* deny the fact of degree, and thus of distance. The illusion is *Ātmā*, even as *samsāra* is *Nirvāna*, while participation is in the energies, not the essence, of God — to allude to a Christian rescension of the Platonic principle. Each makes it clear that no denial, no demolition of appearances or apparent correspondence, can have its intended maieutic effect unless what is removed was first affirmed. 'Unless devotion is given to a thing which must prove false in the end, the thing that is true in the end cannot enter . . . The way must be made ready for heaven, and then it will come by some other; the sacrifice must be made ready, and the fire will strike on another altar.'[13]

This is one of the most important lessons to be learned, if not the most important of all, if our thinking today is to become truly new — if our calls for the novel and fresh are to do anything more than perpetuate our habits, if they are not to create an even thicker husk around ideas, a carapace of pleonasms and trivialities that cannot but stand in the way of our penetration to Reality. We must learn how to see, and we must therefore be shown how to look along but not at. We must above all be given the alchemist's sensitivity for how to approach what really is by means of what simply appears. We certainly do not wish to suggest that only the ideas considered here can prompt this sensitivity or flexibility, nor that our hasty allusions have been enough to prove their therapeutic power. It is a slow and deliberate reflection, a thorough introsusception of the ancient principles, that counts — a turning of them round and round to catch the light from many sides, while in suspense of our preconceptions: a turning for the sake of the Light, that it might draw us. The same could be said for the provocation implicit in *anamnēsis, śūnyatā*, the *coincidentia oppositorum*, and many others.

It is in each case as though our passage toward the real through the nature of things lay along a vector not unrelated to the correspondences observed by the sensate mind, but in indirect proportion to them, nor disconnected from the line of attachment between our thoughts and phenomenal things, but perpendicular to it, as one may look along a tunnel produced by images in adjacent mirrors. True enough, there is nothing to *correspond* to the Truth. Perhaps, in fact, there is nothing, no reality, to correspond directly to any of our concepts, removed as they are from what actually is by our ego's fears and pride, and carefully protected from invasion in a separate 'place'. And yet, on the very edges of these notions — in the interstices between our ordinary thoughts — something sometimes glistens, the token of a consubstantiality that correspondence could never rival. Even the hardest heart can never entirely obstruct Reality or hide it from itself, nor can all of its thoughts be completely mistaken. If in their challenge to our systems of reference, to all our ideologies and theories, the traditional principles can assist us to think our thoughts anew, and against the grain of our mental habits, not about but through them, up and into God himself, and in conformity with the dialectic of the traditional ways, then who would refuse them welcome? Who would then say that the old ideas are really old?

Notes

1. Though this will seem the reason to those like Alan Watts who can see in the

work of a C.S. Lewis no more than nostalgia and reactionism. See Watts' *Behold the Spirit: A Study in the Necessity of Mystical Religion*, Random House, New York, 1971, p.186.

2. *The Essential Writings of Frithjof Schuon*, ed. Seyyed Hossein Nasr, Amity House, New York, 1986, p.116.

3. *The Reign of Quantity and the Signs of the Times*, trans. Lord Northbourne, Luzac, London, 1953, p.125.

4. Samuel Taylor Coleridge, *Aids to Reflection*, Kennikat Press, New York, 1971, p.340.

5. A favorite phrase of Owen Barfield's. See Shirley Sugerman, ed., 'A Conversation with Owen Barfield' from *Evolution of Consciousness: Studies in Polarity*, Wesleyan University Press, Connecticut, 1976, p.13.

6. René Guénon, *The Multiple States of Being*, trans Joscelyn Godwin, Larson Publications, New York, 1984, p.51.

7. *Stations of Wisdom*, trans. G.E.H. Palmer, Perennial Books, Middlesex, 1961, p42.

8. *Beyond the Post-Modern Mind*, Crossroad, New York, 1982, p.132.

9. René Guénon, *Man and His Becoming: According to the Vedanta*, trans. Richard C. Nicholson, Luzac, London, 1945, p.33.

10. *Forgotten Truth: The Primordial Tradition*, Harper & Row, New York, 1976, p.56.

11. And it is an essential part of the masters' teaching, and of the initiation they intend to provoke, always to remind us of this. 'The realm of sense is localized; the intelligible realm is not' from Plotinus, *The Essential Plotinus*, trans. Elmer O'Brien, Hackett Publishing, Indianapolis, 1981, p.56; *Enneads*, V, p.9.

12. *Esoterism as Principle and as Way*, trans. William Stoddart, Perennial Books, Middlesex, 1981, pp.10-11. Persons interested in a good study of the 'syncopations' involved in noetic thinking, especially as it is expressed in the Platonic dialogues, should consult Borna Bebek's *The Third City: Philosophy at War with Positivism*, Routledge & Kegan Paul, London, 1982. Bebek observes:

> If the existence of real entities cannot be proved philosophically, then it might seem that all the authors of the Upanishads and the Orphic philosophers of Greece could hardly justify the time they have devoted to their tasks. The solution is that being or reality can be *insinuated* through philosophy. It is in order to use words in this insinuating manner and thus to account for the 'Beingly Being' (*Usia Ontos Usa*, or Brahman) that Plato creates the curious mental exercise referred to today as the *Parmenides* dialogue. the object of the *Parmenides* is to drive away all positivist representations of true being. Its author will outperform the atheists and the sophists, and destroy the last conceptual residue of this true being, which he refers to as the One. His intention is to construct a dialogue that will force the mind to grasp the unsaid (88).

13. Charles Williams, *He Came Down From Heaven*, Eerdmans, Grand Rapids, 1984, p.25.

Appendix: Questionnaire

Form used in a 1986 survey undertaken in Minnesota church populations (see page 112).

Throughout history there have been some people who have reported experiences of the supernatural, or happenings that other people usually considered impossible. Or they have told of times or events when God, the Devil, some other spiritual being, or good or evil was especially real or close to them. Or was communicating with them individually — in a vision, a voice, a dream, or some other unusual way.

This questionnaire is part of a study to find out if such things are happening today, and if so, what good they are for people.

Please be entirely open (honest) and report anything that happened to you that you think possibly fits the questions, no matter how strange or unusual the experience was, or how old or where you were when it happened.

Your answers will be kept strictly confidential. They will not be seen by anyone except the 2 or 3 people leading the study, and they will only be used by combining them with answers from other people. Also, your individual answers will never be reported back to anyone in your congregation or organization. So do not be afraid to answer sensitive questions.

1. (If you have not read the Introduction at the top of the page, go back and read it before answering this question.)

   I have in my lifetime: (check as many as apply)
   .... seen a vision
   .... heard a supernatural voice
   .... been communicated with through a dream
   .... had some other unusual experience that provided
           evidence of another world
   .... had no experiences of this sort to date.

2. (If you have had at least one such experience, skip to question 3.)

288

If you have had *no* such experiences to date, would you welcome
having them?

. . . . much

. . . . somewhat

. . . . little

. . . . not at all

3. (If you have had at least one such experience, answer this question.
If you have not had such experience, go to question 15.)

How many times total have you had each of these experiences:
(write in a number for each; if none, write '0'; if too many to count,
write '99'; leave no blanks)

. . . . seen a vision

. . . . heard a supernatural voice

. . . . been communicated with through a dream

. . . . had some other unusual experience that provided
evidence of another world.

4. Check each of the age periods in your life when you had any of
these experiences:

Saw a vision	*Heard a voice*	*Received communnication through a dream*	*Other unusual experience*
. . . age 1-10	. . . age 1-10	. . . age 1-10	. . . age 1-10
. . . age 11-20	. . . age 11-20	. . . age 11-20	. . . age 11-20
. . . age 21-30	. . . age 21-30	. . . age 21-30	. . . age 21-30
. . . age 31-40	. . . age 31-40	. . . age 31-40	. . . age 31-40
. . . age 41-50	. . . age 41-50	. . . age 41-50	. . . age 41-50
. . . age 51-60	. . . age 51-60	. . . age 51-60	. . . age 51-60
. . . age 61-70	. . . age 61-70	. . . age 61-70	. . . age 61-70
. . . age 71+	. . . age 71+	. . . age 71+	. . . age 71+

5. (If you have never had a vision, go to question 6.)
Answer concerning any *one* vision you have had:

I believe what I saw was: . . . .
. . . .

6. (If you never heard a supernatural voice, go to question 7.)
Answer concerning any *one* supernatural voice you have heard:

I think the source of the voice was:

. . . God . . . Satan . . . Jesus . . . A demon . . . An angel . . .
A dead or absent person . . . A saint . . . An animal . . .

Other (describe): .... The voice said: ....
....

7. (If you have never received communication through a dream, go to
question 8.)
Answer concerning any *one* time you received communication
through dream:
  I believe the source of the message was:
  ... God ... Satan ... Jesus ... A demon ... An angel
  ... A dead or absent person ... A saint ... An animal
  Other (describe: ....
  The message was: ....
  ....

8. (If you have never had another kind of supernatural experience,
go to question 9.)
Answer concerning any other supernatural experience you have had:
  Briefly describe what happened one such time: ....
  ....
  ....

9. (If you have had more than one of the experiences mentioned
above, answer questions 9-14 in terms of what *generally* or *usually*
happened.)
  I regarded the experience as: ... good ... bad ... neutral

10. When the experience happened, I was: (check as many as apply)
  ... facing a crisis in my life
  ... in worship
  ... using drugs
  ... trying to make a difficult decision
  ... in prayer
  ... drinking
  ... reading scripture
  ... taking medication
  ... listening to music
  ... fasting
  ... none of the above

11. Because of the experience I: (check as many as apply)
  ... was helped in making a decision
  ... felt I should make changes in my life

... made changes in my life
... made no changes in my life

12. I shared the experience with someone: ... yes ... no

13. If yes, their reaction was:
 ... supportive ... neutral ... questioning ... negative

14. I tried to get help understanding or interpreting the experience from:
 ... parents ... other family ... friend ... pastor ... Bible
 ... other books ... teacher ... counsellor ... spouse ... other

15. As a child, I had a companion (person, animal) that other people could not see: ... yes ... no

16. If yes, I experienced this companion to be:
 ... good ... neutral ... bad

17. One or more of my children had or has a companion (person, animal) that other people cannot see: ... yes ... no

18. I attend mass or worship:
 ... daily ... weekly ... 2-3 times a month ... monthly
 ... several times a year ... 2-3 times a year ... never

19. How often do you read the Bible?
 ... daily ... weekly ... occasionally ... never

20. I consider myself to be a charismatic: ... yes ... no ... don't know

21. It is important to me to spend periods of time in private religious thought and meditation: ... frequently true ... occasionally true ... rarely true ... never true

22. My age is: ...

23. Gender: ... male ... female

24. Highest educational level completed: ... grade school
 ... junior high school ... high school ... vocational training or some college ... college graduate ... some post-college education ... some or more graduate degrees

25. I would be willing to be interviewed concerning my experience(s):
 ... yes

... maybe (depending on who does the interviewing, when where) ... no

26. If you are, or maybe, willing to be interviewed (should the research team wish it), please list your name, address, telephone. Your identity will be kept secret.
Name: .... Phone: (   ) ....
Address: ....
....

Thank you very much. Please return your completed questionnaire immediately according to the instructions provided by the person who gave you the questionnaire.

HUSTON SMITH:
A Bibliography

Books

The Purpose of Higher Education, Harper & Bros, 1955. Republished by Greenwood Press, 1972. Danish translation, 1983. Chapter VI reprinted in Chas. Merrifield, ed., *Leadership in Voluntary Enterprise*, Oceana, 1961. Chapter III reprinted in L. Averill and W. Jellema, eds., *Colleges and Commitments*, Westminster Press, 1971.

The Religions of Man, Harper & Row, 1958; Mentor, 1959; Harper Colophon, 1964; Harper Perennial Library, 1964. Swedish edn, *Mansklighetens Religioner*, Raben & Sjogren, 1966. Korean edn, 1973. Pakistani edn, Suhail Academy, Lahore, 1984. Danish edn, *Religioner: Ost oq Vest*, 2 vols, Borgens Forlag, 1984. Chapter VIII, Section 8, reprinted in Donald Walhout, ed., *Interpreting Religion*, Prentice-Hall, 1963; Chapter V reprinted in R. Eastman, ed., *Coming of Age in Philosophy*, Canfield Press, San Francisco, 1973; Chapter IX reprinted in Titus, Hepp and Smith, *The Range of Philosophy*, Van Nostrand, New York, 1975.

The Search for America, ed. and co-authored, Prentice-Hall, 1959.

Condemned to Meaning, Harper & Row, 1965.

Forgotten Truth: The Primordial Tradition, Harper & Row, 1976; Colophon edn, 1977. Chapter One reprinted in D. Goleman & R. Davidson, *Consciousness*, Harper & Row, 1979. Pakistani edn, Suhail Academy, Lahore, 1981.

Beyond the Post-Modern Mind, Crossroad Press, New York, 1982. Chapter Three reprinted in *Philosophy Today*, Spring 1982, and *The International Philosophical Quarterly*, July 1982, Vol.22, No.2. Second revised edition: Quest Books, Theosophical Publishing House, 1989.

With David Ray Griffin, *Primordial Truth and Postmodern Theology*, Suny Press, Albany, New York, 1989.

Articles

The following is a select list of articles published by Professor Huston Smith.

'The Operational View of God: A Study in the Impact of Metaphysics on Religious Thought' from *The Journal of Religion*, XXXI, 2, 1951.

'Accents of the World's Philosophies' from *Philosophy East and West*, VII, 1 & 2, 1957.

'Values: Academic and Human', Chapter One, from M. Carpenter, ed., *The Larger Learning*, Wm. C. Brown Co., Dubuque, Iowa, 1960. Reprinted in *The Christian Scholar*, Vol.XLIII, Winter 1960.

'The Revolution in Western Thought' from *The Saturday Evening Post* Adventures in the Mind Series, 26 August 1961. Reprinted in Wm. Cozart, ed., *Dialogue on Science*, Bobbs-Merrill, Indianapolis, 1967; and in *Iqbal Review*, XXV, 1, April 1984.

'The Accents of the World's Religions' from *The Australian Bulletin of Comparative Religion*, I, 1961. Reprinted in John Bowman, ed., *Comparative Religion*, E.J. Brill, Leiden, 1972.

'Twenty Years of the Atom' from *The Nation*, Vol.195, No.20, 15 December 1962. Reprinted as 'The New Age' in Donovan Smucher, ed., *Rockefeller Chapel Sermons*, University of Chicago Press, 1967; and in *The University of Chicago Magazine*, LXI, 8, May 1967.

'Between Syncretism and the Ghetto' from *Theology Today*, XX, 1, April 1963.

'Empiricism Revisited' from Charles Bretall, ed., *The Empirical Theology of Henry Nelson Wieman*, Macmillan, 1963.

'The Death and Rebirth of Metaphysics' from Wm. Reese and E. Freeman, *Process and Divinity: The Hartshorne Festschrift*, Open Court, 1964.

'The Humanities and Man's New Condition' from *Liberal Education*, L, 2, May 1964.

'Do Drugs Have Religious Import?' from *The Journal of Philosophy*, LXI, 18, 1, October 1984. Reprinted in David Solomon, ed., *LSD: The Consciousness Expanding Drug*, G.P. Putnam, New York, 1964; Joel Feinberg, ed., *Reason and Responsibility*, Dickenson, Belmont,

California, 1965; Tillman et al, eds, *Introductory Philosophy*, Harper & Row, 1967; Charles L. Reid, *Basic Philosophical Analysis*, Dickenson, Encino, California, 1971; Robert Wolff, *Philosophy: A Modern Encounter*, Prentice-Hall, Englewood Cliffs, 1971; Hanscarl Leuner, ed., *Religiose Erfahrung und die Droge*, W. Kohlammer, Stuttgart, 1972; Joseph Faulkner, ed., *Religion's Influence in Contemporary Society*, Chas Merrill, Columbus, 1972; Row and Wainwright, *Philosophy of Religion*, Harcourt, Brace, Jovanovich, New York, 1973; F. Streng, C. Lloyd, J. Allen, *Ways of Being Religious*, Prentice-Hall, 1973; J. Rachels and F. Tillman, *Philosophical Issues*, Harper & Row, 1972; in part in John J. Heaney, ed., *Psyche and Spirit*, Paulist Press, New York, 1973; Wm. Alston and Richard Brandt, *The Problems of Philosophy*, Allyn & Bacon, Boston, 1974; W.L. Fogg and P.E. Richer, eds, *Philosophy Looks to the Future*, Holbrook Press, Boston, 1974; W. Bruening, *Self, Society and the Search for Transcendence*, National Press Books, Palo Alto, 1974.

'Valid Materialism: A Western Offering to Hocking's "Civilization in the Singular" ' from Leroy Rouner, ed., *Philosophy, Religion, and the Coming World of Civilization*, Martinus Nijhoff, The Hague, 1966.

'The Irenic Potential of Religions' from *Theology Today*, Vol.XXIII, No.3, October 1966. Reprinted in Edward Jurji, *Religious Pluralism and World Community*, E.J. Brill, Leiden, 1969.

'Transcendence in Traditional China' from *Religious Studies*, Vol.II, 1967. Reprinted in James Liu and W. Tu, eds, *Traditional China*, Prentice-Hall, Englewood Cliffs, 1970.

With K. Stevens, 'Unique Vocal Ability of Certain Tibetan Lamas' from *American Anthropologist*, Vol.69, No.2, April 1967.

With K. Stevens and R. Tomlinson, 'On an Unusual Mode of Chanting by Certain Tibetan Lamas' from *Journal of the Acoustical Society of America*, Vol.41, No.5, May 1967.

'Psychedelic Theophanies and the Religious Life' from *Christianity and Crisis*, Vol.XXVII, No.11, 26 June 1967. Reprinted in *Journal of Psychedelic Drugs*, Vol.III, No.1, September 1970.

'Technology and Human Values' from Cameron Hall, ed., *Human Values and Advancing Technology*, Friendship Press, New York, 1967.

'Human Versus Artificial Intelligence' from John Roslansky, ed., *The Human Mind*, North Holland Publishing Co., Amsterdam, 1967. Reprinted in *Anew*, Winter 1970.

'Secularization and the Sacred' from Donald Cutler, ed., *The Religious Situation*, Beacon Press, Boston, 1968.

'Empirical Metaphysics', Chapter 5, from Ralph Metzner, ed., *The Ecstatic Adventure*, Macmillan, New York, 1968.

'Like It Is: The University Today' from *The Key Reporter*, XXXIV, 2, Winter 1968/9. Reprinted in *The Wall Street Journal*, 20 March 1969.

'The Reach and the Grasp: Transcendence Today', Chapter 1, from J. Richardson and D. Cutler, eds, *Transcendence*, Beacon Press, Boston, 1969. Reprinted in Norbert Schedler, ed., *The Philosophy of Religion*, Macmillan, New York, 1974.

'Tao Now: An Ecological Testament' from Ian Barbour, ed., *Earth Might be Fair*, Prentice-Hall, Englewood Cliffs, 1972.

'Man's Western Way: An Essay on Reason and the Given' from *Philosophy East and West*, XL, 4, October 1972.

'Wasson's SOMA: A Review Article' from *Journal of the American Academy of Religion*, XL, 4, December 1972.

'The Well of Awareness: A Review Article' from *The Eastern Buddhist*, Vol.1, May 1972.

'The Jesus Prayer' from *The Christian Century*, XC, 13, 28 March 1973.

'The Relation Between Religions' from *Main Currents in Modern Thought*, XXX, 2, November/December 1973. Reprinted in Yusuf Ibish and Peter Wilson, eds., *Traditional Modes of Contemplation and Action*, Imperial Iranian Academy of Philosophy, Teheran, 1977.

With Samuel Todes, 'The Point of Death' from Stanley Troup and Wm. Greene, eds, *The Patient, Death and the Family*, Scribner's, New York, 1974.

'Two Kinds of Teaching' from Thomas Buxton and Keith Prichard, eds., *Excellence in University Teaching*, University of South Carolina Press, 1975. Reprinted in *The Key Reporter* of Phi Beta Kappa, XXXVIII, 4, Summer 1973; in *The Journal of Humanistic Psychology*, XV, 4, Fall 1975; in H. Chiang and A. Maslow, *The Healthy Personality*, Van Nostrand, New York, 1977; and in T.W. Bynum and S. Reisberg, *Teaching Philosophy Today*, Philosophy Documentation Centre, Bowling Green University, 1977.

'The Meaning of Tradition: A Conversation with Huston Smith' from *Parabola*, Vol.1, No.1, Winter 1976.

'Frithjof Schuon's The Transcendent Unity of Religions: Pro' from *Journal of the American Academy of Religion*, XLIV, 4, December 1976.

'Four Theological Negotiables' from *The Eastern Buddhist*, X, 2, October 1977.

'Excluded Knowledge: A Critique of the Modern Western Mind Set' from *Teachers College Record*, LXXX, 3, February 1979. Reprinted in Douglas Sloan, ed., *Education and Values*, Teachers College Press, New York, 1980.

'Feature Review Article: Coomaraswamy, Selected Papers and Biography' from *Philosophy East and West*, XXIX, 3, July 1979.

'Western and Comparative Perspectives on Truth' from *Philosophy East and West*, Vol.30, No.4, October 1980.

'The Sacred Unconscious' from *Re-Vision*, II, 2, Summer/Fall 1979. Reprinted in R. Walsh and D.H. Shapiro, eds., *Beyond Health and Normality*, Van Nostrand Reinhold, New York, 1983.

'Western Philosophy as a Great Religion' from Alan Olson and Leroy Rouner, *Transcendence and the Sacred*, University of Notre Dame Press, Notre Dame, 1981.

'Beyond the Modern Western Mind Set' from *Teachers College Record*, 32:3, Spring 1981.

'What Wilfred Smith's Against and For' from *Religious Studies Review*, Vol.7, No.4, October 1981.

'Science and Theology: The Unstable Detente' from *The Anglican Theological Review*, Vol.63, No.4, October 1981.

'Scientism in Sole Command' from *Christianity and Crisis*, 42:11, 21 January 1982.

'Evolution and Evolutionism' from *The Christian Century*, 99:23, 7-14 July 1982. Reprinted in *National Forum*, LXIII:2, Spring 1983.

'Spiritual Discipline in Zen and Comparative Perspective' from *The Eastern Buddhist*, XVI, 2, Autumn 1983. Revised for inclusion in James Duerlinger, ed., *Ultimate Reality and Spiritual Discipline*, Paragon House, New York, 1984.

'Two Evolutions' from Leroy Rouner, ed., *On Nature*, University of Notre Dame Press, Notre Dame, 1984.

With Daniel Goleman and Ram Das, 'Truth and Transformation in Psychological and Spiritual Paths', from *The Journal of Transpersonal Psychology*, Vol.17, No.2, 1985.

'Spiritual Personality Types', from *The Hamline Review*, Vol.X, Spring 1986.

'Can Religion Endure the Death of Metaphysics?' from *Religion and Intellectual Life*, Vol.III, No.3, Spring 1986.

'Is There a Perennial Philosophy?' from *Journal of the American Academy of Religion*, LV/3, Fall 1987.

'Another World to Live In, or How I Teach the Introductory Course', from *Religious Studies and Theology*, Vol.7, No.1, January 1987.

'Can Modernity Accommodate Transcendence?' in William Nicholls (ed.) *Modernity and Religion*, Wilfrid Laurier University Press, Waterloo, Ontario, Canada, 1988.

'This Ecumenical Moment: What Are We Seeking?' from *Japanese Religions*, 15/1, January 1988.

'The Crisis in Philosophy', from *Behaviorism*, Vol.16, No.1, Spring 1988.

'The Conceptual Crisis in the Modern West', in D.T. Singh & Ravi Gomatam (eds.), *Synthesis of Science and Religion*, The Bhaktivedanta Institute, San Francisco & Bombay, 1988.

'Philosophy, Theology and the Primordial Claim' from *Cross Currents*, XXXVIII/3, Fall 1988. Reprinted in Robert Carter (ed.), *God, the Self, and the Nothingness*, Paragon House, New York, 1990.

'Has Process Theology Dismantled Classical Theism?', The 1988 Bellarmine Lecture, St. Louis University, from *Theology Digest*, 35:4, Winter 1988.

'Remembering Aldous Huxley', from *Los Angeles Times Book Review*, 20 November 1988. Reprinted in *Journal of Humanistic Psychology*, 29:3, Summer 1989.

'The View from Everywhere: Ontotheology and the Post-Nietzschean Deconstruction of Metaphysics', in Henry Ruf, ed., *Religion, Ontotheology and Deconstruction*, Paragon House, New York, 1989.

Feature Book Review of *The Essential Writings of Frithjof Schuon* from *Philosophy East and West*, XXXIX:4, October 1989.

'Encountering God', in Benjamin Shield & Richard Carlson (eds.), *For the Love of God*, New World Library, San Rafael, CA, 1990.

'The Central Curricular Issue of Our Age', in Mary Clark & Sandra Wawrytko, *Rethinking the Curriculum*, Greenwood Press, New York, 1990.

'Chinese Religion in World Perspective' from *Dialogue and Alliance*, IV/2, Summer 1990.

Forewords, Prefaces and Introductions

1. Foreword to *The Three Pillars of Zen* by Philip Kapleau, Beacon Press, 1967.

2. Introduction to *A Buddhist Bible* ed. Dwight Goddard, Beacon Press, 1970.

3. Introduction to *Zen Mind, Beginner's Mind* by Shunryu Suzuki, Weatherhill, 1970.

4. 'The Relevance of the Great Religions for the Modern World'. Introduction to *The World Religions Speak* ed. Finley P. Dunne, Jr, W. Junk, The Hague, 1970. Reprinted in *Insight* II, 2, Winter 1977/8.

5. 'Let There Be Light' Introduction to *Great Religions of the World*, The National Geographic Society, Washington, 1971.

6. Preface to *Ideals and Realities of Islam* by Seyyed Hossein Nasr, Beacon Press, 1972.

7. Introduction to *The Transcendent Unity of Religions* by Frithjof Schuon, Harper Torchbook, 1975. Revised edn, Theosophical Publishing House, Quest Books, 1984.

8. Foreword to *Speculum Spinozanum* ed. Siegfried Hessing, Henley, London, and Routledge & Kegan Paul, Boston, 1977.

9. Introduction to *Buddha: The Quest for Serenity* by George Marshall, Beacon Press, Boston, 1978.

10. Foreword to *The Spiritual Heritage of India* by Swami Prabhavananda, Vedanta Press, Hollywood, 1979. Reprinted in *Vedanta for East and West*, Issue 171, January/February 1980.

11. Preface to *Meister Eckhart* trans. E. Colledge and B. McGinn, Paulist Press, Mahwah, New Jersey, 1981.

12. Foreword to *Buddha: A Pictorial History of His Life and Legacy* by Jeannine Auboyer, Crossroad Press, New York, 1983.

13. Foreword to *On Having No Head* by D.E. Harding, Arkana,

London, and Methuen, New York, 1986. German edn. *Zen und die Wiederentdeckung des Offensichtlichen*, Sphinx Verlag, Basel, 1986.

14. Preface to *Vedanta: Voice of Freedom* by Swami Vivekananda, ed. Swami Chetanananda, Philosophical Library, New York, 1986.

15. Preface to *An Experience of Enlightenment* by Flora Courtois, Theosophical Quest Miniature, 1986.

16. Foreword to *Mysticism and Philosophy* by W.T. Stace, Jeremy P. Tarcher, Los Angeles, 1987.

17. Preface to *A Treasury of Traditional Wisdom* by Whitall Perry, Harper & Row, San Francisco, 1986.

18. Foreword to *Death and Dying: The Tibetan Tradition* by Glenn Mullin, Routledge & Kegan Paul, Boston and London, 1986.

19. 'Does Spirit Matter? The Worldwide Impact of Religion on Contemporary Politics', Introduction to *Spirit Matters*, ed. Richard Rebenstein, Paragon House, New York, 1987.

20. Foreword to *The Wheel of Life* by John Blofeld, Shambala, Boston, 1988.

21. Introduction to *The Concise Encyclopedia of Islam* by Cyril Glassé, Harper & Row, New York, 1989.

22. Introduction to *Huxley and God*, ed. Jacqueline Bridgeman, Harper Collins, New York, 1991.

Films

Three film series, sixteen half-hour programmes in each, for National Educational Television:

'The Religions of Man', 1955.
'Science and Human Responsibility', with Arthur Holly Compton, 1956.
'The Search for America', 1958.

'A Conversation with Daisetz Suzuki', National Broadcasting Company, 1958.

'Meet the Professor: Huston Smith', American Broadcasting Company Television, 1962.

'A Conversation with Krishnamurti', Blaisdell Institute, 1968.

'Requiem for a Faith', Hartley Productions, 1968. Bronze Medal, 1968, New York International Film Festival.

'The Sufi Way', Hartley Productions, 1972. Red Ribbon, Church and Society Section, 1972 American Film Festival.

'India and the Infinite: The Soul of a People', Hartley Productions, 1980. Cine Gold Eagle Award, 1980 American Film Festival.

Phonograph Recordings

'The Music of Tibet: The Tantric Rituals', Anthology Recordings, AST 4005, 1970.

Interviews and Articles featuring Huston Smith

Philip Novak, 'Huston Smith: The Chun-tzu', *Syracuse University Magazine*, Vol.3, No.1, February 1987.

'You Mean *the* Huston Smith?' *Pacific School of Religion*, LXIV,4, Spring 1987.

'Huston Smith: A Scholar's Quest for Religion', *Spectrum Review*, No.2, Winter 1987.

'Huston Smith: Mediator of a "New" Worldview', *New Realities*, July/ August 1988.

'Beyond the Post-Modern Mind with Huston Smith', *Institute of Noetic Sciences Special Report*, June 1988.